WHERE CO

Ralahine Utopian Studies

Series editors:
Raffaella Baccolini (University of Bologna, at Forlì)
Joachim Fischer (University of Limerick)
Michael J. Griffin (University of Limerick)
Tom Moylan (University of Limerick)

Volume 9

PETER LANG
Oxford · Bern · Berlin · Bruxelles · Frankfurt am Main · New York · Wien

Henry Near

WHERE COMMUNITY HAPPENS

THE KIBBUTZ AND THE PHILOSOPHY OF COMMUNALISM

PETER LANG

Oxford · Bern · Berlin · Bruxelles · Frankfurt am Main · New York · Wien

Bibliographic information published by Die Deutsche Nationalbibliothek
Die Deutsche Nationalbibliothek lists this publication in the Deutsche
Nationalbibliografie; detailed bibliographic data is available on the
Internet at http://dnb.d-nb.de.

A catalogue record for this book is available from the British Library.

Library of Congress Cataloging-in-Publication Data:

Near, Henry.
  Where community happens : the kibbutz and the philosophy of
communalism / Henry Near.
     p. cm. – (Ralahine utopian studies ; 9)
  Includes bibliographical references and index.
  ISBN 978-3-0343-0133-6 (alk. paper)
  1. Kibbutzim–History. 2. Kibbutzim–Social conditions. 3.
Collective settlements–History. I. Title.
  HX742.2.A3N34 2011
  307.77'6–dc22
                                        2010053230

Cover image designed by David Lilburn. Top row, left to right: David Ben Gurion;
dining hall, kibbutz Ein Harod; veteran settlers, kibbutz Beit Ha'emek. Middle row,
left to right: on the way to a harvest festival; Martin Buber; kibbutz Beit Alpha.
Bottom row, left to right: kibbutz water tower and signal post; Joseph Bussel;
youth movement group; Gustav Landauer.

ISSN 1661-5875
ISBN 978-3-0343-0133-6

© Peter Lang AG, International Academic Publishers, Bern 2011
Hochfeldstrasse 32, CH-3012 Bern, Switzerland
info@peterlang.com, www.peterlang.com, www.peterlang.net

All rights reserved.
All parts of this publication are protected by copyright.
Any utilisation outside the strict limits of the copyright law, without
the permission of the publisher, is forbidden and liable to prosecution.
This applies in particular to reproductions, translations, microfilming,
and storage and processing in electronic retrieval systems.

Printed in Germany

Community [...] is the being no longer side by side but with one another of a multitude of persons. And this multitude, though it also moves towards one goal, yet experiences everywhere a turning to, a dynamic facing of, the other, a flowing from I to Thou. Community is where community happens.
— MARTIN BUBER, *Between Man and Man*

For Roberta

Contents

Acknowledgements	xi
Glossary of Hebrew Terms	xiii
Foreword	xv

PART ONE   The Collective Experience   1

CHAPTER 1
The Collective Experience: Universal and Particular   3

CHAPTER 2
Christians and Others   17

CHAPTER 3
I, Thou, We: Buber's Theory of Community and the Kibbutz   31

CHAPTER 4
Ben Gurion as Philosopher: Equality and Partnership   59

PART TWO   Utopianism and Post-Utopianism   67

CHAPTER 5
Utopian and Post-Utopian Thought: The Kibbutz Model   69

CHAPTER 6
Utopia Reconsidered: The Agrarian Ethos, Then and Now   101

CHAPTER 7
Post-Utopian Women: Changing Concepts of Gender Equality in the Kibbutz   109

PART THREE   Pioneering   119

CHAPTER 8
The Concept of Pioneering in Zionist Thought   121

CHAPTER 9
Frontiersmen and *Halutzim*: The Image of the Pioneer in Palestine/Israel and the US   141

CHAPTER 10
Youth Movements and the Kibbutz   169

PART FOUR   Looking Outwards   195

CHAPTER 11
Paths to Utopia: The Kibbutz as a Movement for Social Change   197

Afterword   219

Works Cited   223

Index of Concepts and Places   233

Index of Names   237

Acknowledgements

The chapters of the book are based on the following publications. They are all my own work, most of them previously published, but I have added to and/or altered the original text where I thought it necessary. An asterisk *, here and elsewhere in the book, indicates that the publication was originally in Hebrew; translations are by the author.

CHAPTER 1
"The Collective Experience: Universal and Particular." *Utopian Thought and Communal Experience.* Ed. D. Hardy & L. Davidson. Middlesex Polytechnic Geography and Planning Paper, No. 24 (1989): 37–43.

CHAPTER 2
Based on an unpublished lecture at the conference of the Utopian Studies Society, Plymouth, 2007.

CHAPTER 3
"I, Thou, We: Buber's Theory of Community and the Kibbutz." *Economic and Industrial Democracy* 7.3 (1986): 247–74.

CHAPTER 4
*"Ben Gurion as Philosopher: Equality and Partnership." *Ben Gurion and the Kibbutz.* Ed. A. Aharonson & A. Magen. Ef'al: Yad Tabenkin, 1995. 13–23.

CHAPTER 5
Expanded version of "Utopian and Post-Utopian Thought: The Kibbutz Model." *Communal Societies* 5 (Fall 1985): 41–58.

CHAPTER 6
Based on an unpublished lecture at the conference of the International Communal Studies Association, Damanhur, 2007.

CHAPTER 7
Hitherto unpublished.

CHAPTER 8
Based on "Pioneers and Frontiersmen: Two Semantic-Historical Versions of *Halutziut*." *Ivrit Safah Hayah*. Ed. R. Ben-Shahar & G. Touri. Vol. II. Tel Aviv: Hakibbutz Hame'uhad 1999, 175–85.

CHAPTER 9
Frontiersmen and Halutzim: The Image of the Pioneer in North America and Prestate Jewish Palestine. Published as a discussion paper by the Institute for Kibbutz Research, Haifa University, 1987. 56 pp.

CHAPTER 10
Hitherto unpublished.

CHAPTER 11
"Paths to Utopia: The Kibbutz as a Movement for Social Change." *Jewish Social Studies* 47.3–4 (1986): 169–206.

Glossary of Hebrew Terms

Ashkenazi: Jews of European origin (as opposed to Sephardi, of Middle Eastern origin)
Gedud Ha'avodah: "Work Legion", the first country-wide kibbutz movement (1920–9)
Halutz: Pioneer
Hashomer Hatza'ir: "The Young Guard", a youth movement and a central element in the Kibbutz Artzi kibbutz movement and the Mapam party
Hechalutz: "The Pioneer", European movement for education, training and helping in the immigration to Palestine of young adults
Hever Hakvutzot: "Organization of Kvutzot", kibbutz movement believing in small settlements and opposed industrialization of the kibbutz
Histadrut: "Organization", general federation of workers' groups, trade unions, settlements and economic enterprises
Ihud Hakvutzot Vehakibbutzim: "Union of *kvutzot* and kibbutzim", kibbutz movement (1951–80), politically allied to Mapai
Kibbutz Artzi: "Country-wide kibbutz movement", founded by graduates of Hashomer Hatza'ir youth movement, politically allied to Mapam
Kibbutz Me'uhad: "United kibbutz movement", kibbutz movement (1927–80), politically allied to Mapam from 1948 to 1954
Kvutza: Small kibbutz, until early 1950s based only on agriculture
Mapai: "Party of the Workers of the Land of Israel", Zionist social-democratic party 1930–68, dominant in Zionist and Israeli politics for most of this time; leader: David Ben Gurion
Mapam: "United Workers' Party", left-wing opposition party, 1948–97
Moshav: Agricultural settlement based on family holdings and cooperation in marketing, sales, etc.
Yishuv: Zionist community of Palestine until 1948

Foreword

This book contains a number of articles and lectures, some of them unpublished, which I have written over the past two decades. Its title requires some explanation. It opens with a quotation from one of the few major philosophers who have dealt in depth with questions of community, or *Gemeinschaft*, and indicates both the importance of community as such in my philosophical outlook, and my intention of discussing it not only as an abstract concept, but as it is realized in the communal societies in which it "happens" – kibbutzim, communes, and various other types of intentional community. The main area of my past research has been the history of the kibbutz: this book is an attempt to view my findings, and those of others, in a broader, sometimes even a universal, perspective. As for "philosophy", each of its classical definitions: a system of beliefs generally accepted by a particular community or group of communities, and the rational investigation of questions about communal life and thought, comes into play here. I describe various belief systems, and attempt to estimate their validity by a rigorous logical examination; I examine the changes in the meaning of various keywords in the lives of these communities; and I consider the ways in which communalists' belief systems change as a result of encounters with reality.

Although, as I have remarked, the main field of my research has been the history of the kibbutz, summed up in my *The Kibbutz Movement: a History*,[1] I have never considered the study of history to be only an end in itself; indeed, in my first book, *The Kibbutz and Society*,[2] I expressed the

---

[1] Near, Henry. *The Kibbutz Movement: A History.* Vol. 1, Oxford: Littman Library and Oxford University Press, 1992; Vol. 2, London & Portland, Oregon: Littman Library, 1997.

[2] *Near, Henry. *The Kibbutz and Society, 1923–1933.* Jerusalem: Yad Itzhak Ben Zvi Publications, 1984.

hope (largely unfulfilled) that my research would be of use in the rethinking of kibbutz ideology which, even at that early stage, I considered to be necessary. And it is significant that in this connection I mentioned the ideological aspect of kibbutz history; for the founders and leaders of the kibbutz movement – and, to a considerable degree, most of its rank-and-file members – were motivated by ideological considerations, which have influenced its development throughout the hundred years of its existence. Nor is it accidental that this book appears in a series on utopian thought and practice; for, as I claim below, the kibbutz has at various times been a pre-utopian, a utopian, and a post-utopian society, and this has been, and still is, a central factor in its development.

This book, then, is an exercise in the history of the kibbutz idea. But, in my view, although the kibbutz, its ideology, and its practice stand at its centre, this is not its only importance. Each of the main themes of the book is exemplified not only in the kibbutz itself but in many other intentional communities, and is often seen to be of universal importance. I have, therefore, used a comparative methodology to seek the idea of community not only in the kibbutz itself but "wherever community happens".

By and large, I discuss what is becoming known as "the classical kibbutz", as it existed before the far-reaching changes of the 1980s. This is partly because at the time when I wrote the articles presented here such changes had neither been executed nor, in general, even thought of. But it is also because I believe that the dust has not yet settled sufficiently on these changes for us to see and analyse the contemporary kibbutz clearly in the way in which I have dealt with the earlier period. And, in any case, that period stands as an independent example of ways and life and thought of universal import. In this respect, the achievements of the classical kibbutz may be compared with those of Athenian democracy at its height: the significance of both is most clearly seen during their period of glory; and most of the arguments presented here apply mainly, though not exclusively, to this period.

The first section of the book deals with a subject which I believe to be central to any theory of communalism: the communal experience. I discuss it in philosophical rather than historical or sociological terms, asking whether the conclusions drawn by communards from this phenomenon

Foreword

– widespread and often described, but never as often and as explicitly as in the kibbutz – are valid, and form a rational basis for a communal way of life.

The second section considers the kibbutz as a post-utopian society: the thought-processes resulting from the fact that pristine utopian ideals are never completely realized are described and analysed, and kibbutz post-utopianism compared with similar phenomena in the world at large.

The third section considers the kibbutz as a pioneering society, and analyses the development of the idea of pioneering (*halutziut*) from its biblical origins until the mid-1970s. Here again, the comparative method is used, and the Zionist concept of pioneering is compared with that of the United States. This section ends with a discussion of the pioneering Zionist youth movements. Though youth and youth organizations have been widely discussed in the research literature, there is no exact parallel to these movements, which not only recruited tens of thousands of young people for educational activities, but have played, and, indeed, still play a vital role in the development of the kibbutz movement.

Finally, under the heading "looking outwards", I have included a chapter which examines the way in which kibbutz members have attempted to influence the world around them.

I have added an afterword, both as a summing-up of the main theses of the book, and in order to make some attempt at considering the relevance of the substance of the book, most of which deals with a past which will never be repeated, to the situation of the kibbutz, and of communal societies in general, in the realities of the twenty-first century.

It would be hard to single out individuals to whom I am indebted for criticism and discussion of the ideas expressed here over the past twenty years. They include my Israeli colleagues in the academic field of the history of Palestine/Israel; fellow members of Kibbutz Beit Ha'emek, including my late wife, Aliza; my partner Roberta Levin; and the members of the (European) Utopian Studies Society, with whom I have conducted a fruitful dialogue since 1989. All of them added to my understanding and precluded errors; though, of course, the text as it stands is mine alone.

My special thanks to the Ralahine Centre for Utopian Studies, University of Limerick, and particularly to Dr Joachim Fischer, for editorial help, and to Oranim College, Israel, for financial support.

PART ONE

The Collective Experience

CHAPTER 1

The Collective Experience: Universal and Particular

Why do people join communes? And, having joined them, why do they stay in them, despite the peculiar difficulties and discouragements of everyday life in a closely-knit community? The answers are without doubt complex and manifold. I want to concentrate on one of them, an element in communal life which, in my view, has not been adequately discussed in the research literature. I shall refer to it by the deliberately neutral term, "the collective experience". Let me open my discussion with an ostensive definition. Here are two descriptive pieces which will give some idea of the nature of this phenomenon:

> How often in the brooding warmth and stillness of summer nights, when the senses are fairly oppressed with natural beauty [...] does the charm of nature grow so intense that [...] the senses are sublimed to an ecstasy [...]

Through this and a wealth of similar experiences, the author comes to realise that:

> The instinct of universal solidarity, of the identity of our lives with all life, is the centripetal force which binds together in certain orbit all orders of being [...]
>
> [The] passion for losing ourselves, which rebels against individuality as an impediment, is the expression of the greatest law of solidarity [...] It is the operation of this law in great and low things, in the love of men for women, and for each other for the race for nature [...] that has ever made up the web and warp of human passion. (Bellamy 24, 31–2)

This quotation is quite familiar to many students of communal societies. Here is another, more concrete, but less well known:

> It was a magical night; the stars blinked and smiled at me and I understood what they were saying; they saw in me an old friend, and called me to themselves. And I felt that my soul was lifted up close to the sky and the stars, and a delightful feeling of love suffused all my limbs [...] I ceased to think. I felt only one thing: I am alive, I am alive. And every moment is an eternity of beauty, delight, and eternal life [...] Suddenly I was awakened from my dream by the sound of many voices singing together [...] I hastened to the camp, and leapt into the circle [of dancers ...] and so we danced round and round, to the point of [...] surcease [...] Then were we all as one man, and one feeling beat within us. We were drunk with joy and youth. (Tsur 76; my translation)

The first quotation is from a short essay by Edward Bellamy entitled "The Religion of Solidarity". The second is from one of the classical texts of the early history of the kibbutz: the collective biography of the first group of graduates of the Zionist youth movement Hashomer Hatza'ir, written as a summing-up of their first year of communal life.

Note the common elements. There is a feeling of wonder at, and oneness with, nature, and with one's fellow human beings within their natural setting; and this oneness – "solidarity", in Bellamy's word, "love" in that of the young kibbutzniks – is felt so intensively that it leads to a state close to ecstasy, a sort of semi-mystic experience. In the words of another well-known description, also of a young kibbutz in the early 1920s:

> There was a sort of mutual yearning, a desire to sit together far into the night, and thereby to penetrate the very depth of the vision of communal life. Soul touched soul. We longed to become a sort of river of souls, whose tributaries would merge, and together create a fresh and mighty current of friendship and fraternity. (Likever 146–7)

So much for the content and quality of the collective experience. As for its provenance, let me note at this point that in both cases – and, in fact, quite typically – it happens to young people. Bellamy was, in his own words, "a boy of twenty-four" when he described these experiences, and doubtless much younger when he began to have them. The members of the Hashomer Hatza'ir group were roughly twenty years old. Both of these events were of very great importance in the lives of those who underwent them. Bellamy wrote: "This paper [...] represents the germ of what has been ever since my philosophy of life"; and, more than forty years after the publication of the collective diary, some of its authors told a visiting anthropologist that what happened to them in some nine months of intensive collective experience had been the basis of their values and actions ever since (Bellamy 48; Spiro 51–9).

This, then, is the collective experience which will be discussed in this chapter. It is, of course, not unknown to students of the kibbutz. Indeed, through the writings of Herman Schmalenbach and Yonina Talmon-Garber it has undergone a sort of process of reification: the word *Bund* (in Hebrew *edah*) is frequently used to denote the small, close-knit community which such experiences are thought to typify (Schmalenbach 64–125; Talmon-Garber 2).[1] I have no quarrel with this, in the context of sociological theorizing. Here, however, I am concerned to attempt to define the experience itself rather more closely, and to ask whether the claims made for it by many who have undergone it can be rationally justified: a philosophical discussion, rather than a sociological or psychological one.

I have used the phrase "semi-mystical experience". I shall start my analysis by asking which half is which: to what extent can this "ecstasy" or "yearning" properly be called a mystical state? But let me first settle a preliminary issue. Could it not be that our semi-mysticism is half true and half false, half real and half imitation? In other words, that we have here no more than a socialized – some might say a debased – form of one of the major mystical traditions?

It certainly looks as if Bellamy leads us in this direction; for much of what he has to say amounts to little more than the shibboleths of American nineteenth-century transcendentalism; and, indeed, the same path leads us to Brook Farm and similar experiments. Transcendentalism itself was, of course, not a purely indigenous school of thought, but a reworking of various imported ideas, including Eastern mysticism. (Frothingham

---

1   Schmalenbach himself sometimes uses *Bund* (badly translated in the English version by "communion") to denote an emotion, sometimes a social structure (contrasted with both *Gemeinschaft* and *Gesellschaft*). *Gemeinschaft* and, in Hebrew, *hevruta*, are also often used to denote the same phenomenon, or one like it.

chs. 6, 7; Christy). Moreover, to cite two parallel cases out of many: Gustav Landauer found inspiration for his theories of communitarian socialism in the pantheism of the medieval German mystic, Meister Eckhart; and the predilections of many contemporary communards for their own versions of oriental philosophy are well known.[2] So perhaps this is the best interpretation of the collective experience?

There is some backing for such a view in the intellectual history of the kibbutz. In 1961 David Ben Gurion, speaking of the concept of community as fundamental to the kibbutz, said: "Community is not only a supreme human principle [...] it is also a cosmic principle which embraces a whole universe." In words which were almost a paraphrase of Bellamy's he elaborated the view that men do not only form a community with each other but are part of a cosmic whole "in which there is no dying or withering away but constant renewal and eternal revitalization" (Ben Gurion, "Reflections").[3] Although Ben Gurion was never a kibbutz member he had a pretty good idea of what goes on in the kibbutz; and there may be some significance in the fact that in his only attempt at a philosophical treatment of this phenomenon he turned to the Eastern philosophers. Martin Buber, whose social philosophy influenced and was influenced very deeply by the kibbutz movement, was widely read in Jewish and non-Jewish mysticism. And others have looked for an ancestry of the collective experience of the kibbutz in the ideas and practices of Jewish mystics.[4] Maybe all that one

---

2   Lunn, 1973, ch. 3. In the 1960s and early 1970s "the doctrine of Eastern religions [...] blossomed like a springtime orchard in the emerging counterculture" (Zicklin 11). Of 120 communes studied by Benjamin Zablocki, twenty-two professed Eastern religions (Zablocki 209).
3   For a more detailed discussion of Ben Gurion's view see below, ch. 4.
4   One kibbutz group – among them many of the authors of *Kehiliateinu* – deliberately adopted the word "kibbutz" to describe their community because it was used by the Bratislav Hassidim, an ecstatic Jewish sect, as a name for their periodic gatherings (Near, "Language of Community" 26–123). It should be emphasized that the kibbutz members referred to in this chapter are not orthodox or, as a group, religious in any formal sense. There is clear evidence for the influence of Hassidism on one segment of the orthodox kibbutz movement; but these kibbutzim are, and always have been, a small part of the kibbutz movement as a whole.

can say about the collective experience is that it is a derivative phenomenon, drawing on one of the great mystical traditions – perhaps even on more than one.

It would, of course, be hard to prove that it is not so. If one looked hard enough, one could no doubt find proof of all sorts of hidden influences; and, failing concrete evidence, there is always the Zeitgeist. But I should like to present some considerations – though not, perhaps, proof in the strictly academic sense – which indicate that the collective experience often occurs as a result of the intrinsic situation, without reference to external ideas.

More than thirty years ago, when still a student, I myself described communal life as a semi-mystical experience, and spoke of "the moral revelation which springs from the common life and work of a close-knit group of people" (Near, "Elephants"). And I can testify that the experiences I spoke of were part of my own personal biography. They were not derived from my reading or from others' stories of kibbutz life, but from my own experiences with others and of others in the activities of the Jewish youth movement in which I was then active. When, at a later stage, I tried to put them into a universal conceptual framework I was tempted, as was Ben Gurion some years later, to find parallels in Eastern thought, and in mysticism in general. But the experience itself was autonomous, unmistakable, quite recognizable in the descriptions of my friends, and, as I shall now try to show, readily distinguishable from any form of mysticism proper. As I acquired more knowledge of the kibbutz and its history, I realized that my experience was not particularly unusual. I believe, therefore, that the collective experience is not an echo of some cultural tradition, but a widespread occurrence, arising spontaneously from the actions and interactions of people – particularly young people – in small groups. It can be the result of working together of singing or dancing together, or of the sort of discussion in which "soul touches soul". History also shows us that it can be the result of fighting or engaging in sport together – a phenomenon enshrined in the language as "esprit de corps". The great majority of those who undergo it feel it to be positive, significant, and worthy of repeating if possible.

According to William James' classic definition of mystic experiences, they are "ineffable, noetic, transient and passive" (James 299–301). Some of this seems to fit. The collective experience is ineffable, in that any verbal report is only a pale reflection of the real thing, and no description can be really meaningful to one who has not experienced it him- (or her)self. But, compared with the experience of the lone mystic, it is open to discussion, recollection, comparison and analysis; for it is of its essence that it is shared, and therefore in the public domain – even though the public may be restricted.

It is noetic, in James' definition: "Mystical states [...] seem to those who experience them to be also states of knowledge. They are states of insight into depths of truth unplumbed by the discursive intellect" (300). The collective experience grants knowledge of the existence of an entity – the group – which is in some sense greater than the sum of its parts. More than this – more, indeed, than in some individual mystic states – it is felt to have normative implications. They may be phrased in many different ways, but their general import is clear: it is better to cooperate than compete, better to love than to hate.

It is certainly transient, for nobody can live permanently with such intensity of feeling. It comes during the working day or at its end, in the heat of battle, during a songfest or dance. If the community is permanent, it may be repeated in many forms and at many times. In kibbutz life, for instance, many cultural events are arranged in such a way that "the together", in the Hebrew phrase, is facilitated and emphasized: the Jewish festivals, the Reception of the Sabbath on a Friday evening, a wide variety of local celebrations, are not only cultural events, but also a framework in which the whole kibbutz population can be, and feel itself, together. Much effort is invested in promoting such experiences, even though everyone knows that, while they may often be repeated, they are ephemeral.

As for passivity, it is true that the collective experience comes uncalled for, sometimes even unwanted. But it is doubtful whether it can properly be called passive in James' sense; for much can be done and is done to bring it about and repeat it. It is true of collective experiences, as of mystical states, that they can come about spontaneously, and often do in the early stages of a group's existence. But such activities as singing and dancing are often deliberate and active ways of bringing them to life again.

The Collective Experience: Universal and Particular

The few examples I have adduced, which are of course a tiny selection from the mass of evidence, show that there is such a thing as a collective experience; and I have gone some way towards defining, or at least describing, it. From the point of view of social psychology there can be no doubt that such occurrences are of great value in maintaining any small community; and it would not be difficult to bring examples from the history of the kibbutz or other communal societies to show that this is so. The question I want to ask, however, is in the range of what James calls the noetic – not whether the collective experience is socially useful, but whether it can be rationally justified; in other words, are the insights which it affords valid? My starting-point will be similar to that of the earlier part of this chapter: a comparison between the collective experience and its distant relative, mysticism.

I have said that the noetic aspect of both of these phenomena can be divided into two parts: factual, and normative. In each of these respects, the collective experience is demonstrably a more reliable guide than mystic revelations.

The problem of the truth or falsity of mystic experiences is notoriously difficult. How can there be any certainty that it was actually God who spoke to the saint, rather than the devil? Did an act of levitation take place, or was it an illusion produced by lack of food and sleep, or a process of autosuggestion? An analysis of various strategies for removing one's doubts as to the veracity of such an experience shows that there is only one unquestionable form of confirmation: the quality of the experience itself; it is, in the words of St Teresa of Avila, "so deeply graven upon the understanding that one can no more doubt it than one can doubt the evidence of one's own eyes". But the conviction that it is so is part of the experience itself, and cannot reasonably be conveyed to another with the same degree of absolute certainty: my doubts about whether Teresa saw what she thinks she saw can only be allayed by my having the same experience (or an equally convincing one). Any argument other than that of direct experience, whoever uses it (including the mystic herself) is fallible, in view of the possibility of systematic error. George Mavrodes concludes his discussion of real and deceptive mystical experiences thus:

> It may be that what happened to Teresa engraved on her soul that which her description will not engrave on our souls [...] As [...] she said: "If anyone thinks I am lying I beseech God in His goodness to give him the same experience." When Teresa prayed that prayer she may have done us her best service. (Mavrodes 257)

If I may translate this into my own terminology: mystic visions are essentially in the private domain. And, by contrast, the collective experience is in the public domain. Here is another quotation from the collective diary of the Hashomer Hatza'ir graduates:

> I love you all only at certain moments, moments of happiness without end; then I love the whole world within my kibbutz. Then I express my love by holding out my hand, by a heart-felt glance, by a sudden clasp of the hand – and it has happened that the other person has looked at me as if I were mad. (*Kehiliateinu* 59)

A person in such a situation is not in the same state as the solitary mystic. He does not have to offer up St Teresa's prayer, for it has been answered in advance. He can talk to his friends about what has happened, even though in the last resort his questions may well amount to no more than "Didn't you feel it, too?" In the concrete situation of the kibbutz, the collective experience is not only deliberately fostered. When it happens, people usually know of it. In principle, it is subject to verification of a logical order quite different from that of the mystic vision.

The analysis of the normative aspect is somewhat different. It makes sense to say that the simultaneous experiences of a group of individuals are compelling empirical evidence for the existence of a special sort of social entity. But the same does not necessarily apply to the question of whether they approve or disapprove of this entity. In 1921, when Degania, the first kibbutz, had been in existence for a decade, two opposing value judgements were made about communal life by the very people who had created and lived it. At the very same time the relations between the members were described by some as "ideal", and by others as "small minded and constricting" (Katznelson, *The Kvutza* 27; Lavi, "On Our Work" 57). This should not surprise us; nor does it involve a logical contradiction. But it does raise a number of questions, not the least of which is a terminological one: do we want to say that they all lived through the same experiences, and reached different normative conclusions? Or that people living at the same place and time, doing the same things, and interacting in a most intensive fashion, had different experiences? It may help to see the issue from a more general perspective.

One of the ways in which people make up and change their minds about moral and political issues is by conversion. Saul had a vision on the road to Damascus; lesser personages see – or are shown – the light. A view of war or riots on the television changes a person's way of voting, sometimes his whole way of life. In each case, a change of moral values is derived from an experience: Jesus is seen as the saviour, war is seen as hideous.

These experiences are but extreme and well-defined examples of a process which is basic to the formation of our moral judgements. Each of us acquires his/her values by a series of experiences which are themselves acts of evaluation. This is not the only way of making moral judgements; nor does it preclude the use of reason in ethics. But it does provide a series of what may be called moral sense-data, which can be ordered, clarified and (one hopes) made consistent by rational means.

In this area it is not appropriate to talk about truth or falsehood. Normative statements are not subject to public verification, and two people's experiential moral judgements can differ without involving a logical contradiction. One man takes part in a battle, and becomes a confirmed pacifist; another decides that warfare is the ideal life; and in the last resort, their only argument is: "That's the way I see it". On the other hand, it does seem that there are common, perhaps even identical, experiences in this sense. After all, there are churches and religious sects and pacifist movements and militantly patriotic groups; and many of their members have formed their views in just the way I have described.

So, on the terminological issue, I would say that the experience is not only seeing, but seeing as. A convinced kibbutznik can be defined as one who has, in the words of one of the founders of Degania "tasted the special taste" of kibbutz life and declared: "behold it is good" (*Tanhum* 88). Those who found the taste repulsive can be said to have undergone a quite different experience.

Is the collective experience, in its normative aspect, only a rather small species of this genus? In one sense this is certainly so. But I would add that in this respect, too, it would seem to have a special logical status. In the other cases I have discussed, there is what may be called a normative partnership between people whose experience, while apparently similar and equally compelling, is nonetheless the fruit of individual reactions to a public event. In the case of the collective experience, the partnership is the public event. Thus, the normative aspect of the collective experience is also public and verifiable, though in a different sense from that of its factual aspect.

To sum up this section: I have tried to show that the status of a collective experience is different from that of mystical experiences, individual conversions, or a series of like reactions to events in the public domain. Unlike these latter it is both sufficient evidence for the existence of a closely-knit community and a rationale for a positive appraisal of such a group. So it bears a special logical compulsion, within the general class of what I would like to call social and ethical sense-data.

I may add in parenthesis that the social genesis of the collective experience also makes it particularly powerful in psychological terms. I remarked earlier that it is typically a product of youth, and particularly – though far from only – of the youth movement; but also that it can be a crucial influence on the formation of a world outlook which still informs people's thoughts and actions many years later. Kibbutz educators are well aware of this fact, and much of kibbutz education is an attempt to create the conditions for such experiences. And, to no small extent, moral education consists in requiring young people to undergo experiences – actual or vicarious – through which they acquire a system of moral values. So in this sphere, too, the collective experience is a very powerful species of a widely spread genus (Near, "Could There Be a Torah?").

And now to close the circle, and return to Bellamy, Ben Gurion, and Landauer. Perhaps there is a basic flaw in my argument up to now. Just as there is not one, universal mystical experience, there is also no single collective experience. In the examples I have adduced, I started out by assuming that the concrete, face-to-face experience of the small group where "soul touches soul" is essentially the same as that of Bellamy when he felt his solidarity with the universe, including all mankind. But this is not so. For the arguments I have used about the validity of the small group experience do not apply to the Religion of Solidarity and kindred doctrines. I have knowledge of the social solidarity in my kibbutz in a way that Bellamy simply cannot have had knowledge of his solidarity with the rest of mankind – not to speak of past and future generations, and the whole of animate nature. My friends can talk to me, work with me, know of my existence. Bellamy and like-minded people may think that the stars smile at them; but there is no evidence that the stars know of it. So their experience of the cosmos is mystical in a sense that my experience of the kibbutz is not; my social knowledge is based on mutuality, theirs on personal conviction alone.

There is, then, a great gulf fixed between the collective experience and the concept of universal solidarity in its many forms; and the varieties of socialism which stem from them cannot be equated. Communal socialism, while severely limited in numbers, can be justified on purely experiential grounds. There are many arguments for universalistic socialism: but it seems to me that the attempt to justify it experientially – to speak of a universal experience parallel to that which takes place in the small commune – is philosophically very questionable indeed.

Why try to do it at all? The reasons seem fairly obvious. The collective experience is, as we have seen, a valid and keenly felt element in the life and thought of a specific community – a recipe for the here and now. For those who are compelled to argue with world-embracing philosophies, a creed which can be effective for a few hundred people at the most must seem paltry. Thus, it seems probable that Landauer reached his form of mystical socialism by analogy from things which he had known and felt in his own attempts to create a small community.[5] His adaptation of Eckhart's panthe-

---

5 Although Landauer began his study of Eckhart in 1899, he only reached his more mature concept of community (elaborated in *Skepsis und Mystik*, 1903) after his experience in the experimental community known as the *Neue Gemeinschaft* in 1900–1 (Lunn). Landauer's lecture, "Through Isolation to Community", and that

ism to his own purposes enlarged the collective experience to national and even cosmic proportions, and gave him a powerful weapon in his struggle against the universalistic Marxist creed.

In my view this analogy derives ultimately from the belief that all mystical experiences are fundamentally identical – a belief which a rigorous analysis of mystic writings and their implications has shown to be mistaken (Katz 22–74). Similarly, many contemporary communards believe that their own small-scale experiences are intimations of cosmic reality, and use them as proof of some mystical doctrine – sometimes of many. If my arguments are valid, they are wrong. To *oom* is human; it is not divine.

I have concentrated here on what I know best – the kibbutz movement. But I have no doubt that most of the things I have said are relevant to other communal societies no less. In particular, forms of expression parallel to those I have quoted can often be found in historical and contemporary communes.

To sum up: my arguments bring both good news and bad news for kibbutzniks and other communards. They show that the insights given by the collective experience can be philosophically justified, as well as being psychologically helpful. That is good. But the attempt to universalize these insights seems to me to be fundamentally unsound. Thus, the collective experience may be very deep, but it is doomed to be narrow; and that is bad news for anyone who wants to improve the world beyond his/her own restricted community.

Yet, in another respect, what I have said is good. I remarked that the collective experience often arises spontaneously when men and women of good will live, work and think together. In this sense, it is universal – or,

---

of his close friend, Martin Buber "Old and New *Gemeinschaft*" are both products of this period; and in both of them are many passages which may well refer to a collective experience of the sort described here (Lunn 143–71; Flohr and Susser 41–9). In 1913 Landauer wrote: "The idea that man bears the entire world in his inner spirit [...] is only a new form of an eternal teaching of philosophers and mystics, Indian, medieval, Renaissance" (Quoted by Lunn 134). For an analysis and refutation of the concept of the identity of all mystic experiences, see Steven T. Katz, "Language, Epistemology, and Mysticism" (Katz 22–74).

perhaps more accurately, eternal, as fire is eternal: not that it never dies, but that it will always break out afresh, in places ever new and often unexpected. So, whatever may be the fate of any individual community or movement or doctrine, the collective experience is here to stay.[6]

---

6   The whole of this chapter can, of course, be considered a special case of communitarian philosophy, of which a great deal has been written over the past two decades; see, e.g., Avineri and de-Shalit. My own views are close to those of Ronald Dworkin, as expressed in his essay "Liberal Community" in Avineri and de-Shalit's volume (205–23).

CHAPTER 2

Christians and Others

Monasteries

Is the collective experience indeed a universal, as I have hinted in the previous chapter? Does it exist in societies other than kibbutzim, communes and the like? The comparison between kibbutzim and monasteries, though scarcely discussed by scholars up to now, seems to be a pretty good starting-point. In many respects the structure of the monastery is similar to that of the classical kibbutz. The monks (or nuns) have no personal property; they eat in a common refectory; the monastery's property is communally owned and administered; work, allotted by the community's management, is compulsory; and the community, while not democratically administered like the kibbutz, is a dominant factor in the life of the individual. On the face of it, it would seem that here are two very similar types of community.

As was maintained in the previous chapter, the phenomenon of the collective experience is well known in kibbutz life and thought, where it has been given a special name – *hevruta*, a small or intimate community. There are also many parallels from the experience of other communes, from socialist thinkers, and elsewhere. Judging from the basic pattern of monastery life, one would have guessed that such experiences are also felt in the monastic community, and are expressed in the ways in which exponents of monasticism justify its existence. To find out whether this is so, let us begin by examining the body of writings that corresponds to the ideology of the kibbutz: monastic theology.

Essentially, monastic theology (though not necessarily monastic practice, which has a complex history of its own) derives from two biblical passages: first and foremost, from the description in the Book of Acts (iv,

32–5): "As many as were possessed of lands or houses sold them, and laid [the proceeds] at the apostles' feet; and distribution was made unto every man according as he had need." This passage is often quoted as a model for an exemplary Christian life, imitated in its essentials by the monastic community. And it is backed by a passage from the Psalms: "Behold how goodly and pleasant it is for brethren to dwell together." (Ps. 132,1)

There is a considerable literature about the monastic life, and even more written by monks about theological matters. In one of the most celebrated passages of this literature, St Aelred of Rievaulx, an English monk of the early twelfth century, writes of his feelings when entering the monastery after a journey:

> The day before yesterday, walking round the cloisters where the brethren were sitting, as it were a very garland of love, I was gazing on them as one might admire in paradise the leaves and flowers and fruit of every individual tree; and finding none there whom I did not love and by whom I did not believe myself loved, I was filled with a joy that soared above all the pleasures of the world. I felt my spirit pass out into all, and their affection flow back into me, until I found myself saying with the psalmist: Behold, how good and how pleasant it is when brothers dwell together in unity. (Matarasso 184–5)

No less deeply felt is a long Latin poem by Baldwin of Ford, an English bishop of the late twelfth century, devoted to the subject of communal life (Baldwin, lines 204, 516–62). After detailing the provenance of the monastery from the communal life of the apostles, Baldwin praises communal life as such: "Community life is, as it were, the splendour of eternal life, a radiance of unending life, a rivulet springing from the unfailing fountain whence flow the healing waters of life everlasting."[1] Baldwin draws a parallel between three different Christian communities: the community of the Holy Trinity, the community of the angels, and the community of "those who live in community" as did the disciples mentioned in the Book of Acts. Between these communards (the monks) "the deeper the love, the stronger the bond, and the fuller the communion; and, in turn, the closer the communion the stronger is the bond, and the more complete the love […].

---

1   The Latin word translated here by "community life" is *communa*.

After a very long gap in time there appeared in 2004 an article by Martha E. Driscoll, the Mother Superior of a South American nunnery, emphasizing the need for *Gemeinschaft* in the monastic community:

> Living in empty cells, using desks in a common room, eating together at a common table makes it possible for us as a coenobitic community to live a perpetual pilgrimage with nothing in our hands to weigh us down, a pilgrimage to another land and another life, symbolised by our daily pilgrimages together from the church to the chapter room or the refectory. (Driscoll 200)

These extracts, together with a few remarks by pseudo-Macarius, a rather obscure bishop of the fourth or fifth century, seem to confirm my original guess, that the social structure of the monastery, so similar to that of the kibbutz, would be a fertile ground for the communal experience. But, in fact, I have virtually drawn "a blink" in my search – "a blink" rather than a blank, for there are a few indications of its existence, exemplified by the above quotations; but the most significant thing about them is that they stand virtually alone in the monastic literature, ranging from the third century until the present day.

To understand how deep are the reservations from the concept of the communal experience, let us look at two fundamental documents in the history of monastic thought: first, a much-quoted article by St Basil of Caesarea (329–79), known as "the founder of oriental monasticism", who seems to have invented the coenobitic monastery after having visited, and rejected, the way of life of a whole cluster of eremitic congregations. This historical moment is of great importance to the present study, for it creates a possible version of Christian life and action based on a close-knit community, rather than an individual saint or hermit with, in the case of the eremitic monasteries, logistic support from a large number of disciples. It also initiated a model of what may be called active monasticism: the community as a whole does good works, lives in a town where it deliberately comes into contact with moral and economic distress, establishes a hospital and orphanage, and so forth. It is to this – the social involvement of the coenobitic monastery, as against the deliberate isolation of the eremite – that one of Basil's most frequently quoted passages is thought to refer:

> For, behold, the Lord for the greatness of his love of men was not content with teaching the word only, but that accurately and clearly He might give us a pattern of humility in the perfection of love He girded Himself and washed the feet of the disciples in person.

And, addressing the eremitic monks:

> Whose feet then wilt thou wash? Whom wilt thou care for? In comparison with whom wilt thou last if thou livest by thyself? How will that good and pleasant thing, the dwelling of brethren together, which the Holy Spirit likens to unguent flowing down from the High Priest's head, be accomplished by dwelling solitary? (Clarke 166)

At first sight this seems to be simply a defence of the coenobitic, involved, way of monastic life as against the deliberate isolation of the hermit. But it is more than that. It is also part of an apologia for community life as such. The whole passage concludes with a mention of the communal life of the apostles, as described in the Book of Acts (iv, 32–6). And it opens with a series of reasons for living together: mutual aid as the expression of Christian love; greater ability to do good works; the benefits of mutual criticism; mutual enrichment, "when a number live together a man enjoys his own gift, multiplying it by imparting it to others"; and self-evaluation in the context of the community:

> For wherewith shall a man show humility, if he has no one in comparison with whom to show himself humble? Wherewith shall he show compassion, when he is cut off from the community of the many? How can he practise himself in long-suffering, when there is none to withstand his wishes? (Clarke 163–5)

All these are no doubt cogent arguments for communal living. But they sound more like utilitarian considerations, suited to a *Gesellschaft* type of society, than an advocacy of *Gemeinschaft*. Apart from the biblical references, there is no reference to the communal experience of the sort described in the extracts quoted above.

So, at the very beginning of monastic theology, the basic motivation for communal living is not to achieve a communal experience, and to find a way to God through that experience, but to create a substructure for the elevation of the individual, and his (or her) perfection through the doing of good deeds.

As it begins, so it goes on. The *Rule of St Benedict*, which Western monks still have read to them three times in an annual cycle at mealtimes, speaks of the monastery as a school, whose purpose is to educate the monks in the ways of righteousness, and train them to lead the good life, under the guidance of the abbot (Fry 45–50). Most of this fundamental document of monasticism is devoted to technical details of monastic life, interlarded with pious exhortations intended to raise the spiritual level of the monks: all on the level of the individual, to whom the educational message of the "school" is addressed. True, the technical arrangements of the monastery include the prohibition of private ownership, and distribution of goods according to need, in formulations reminiscent of the ideals of communes and kibbutzim (Ibid. 56–7). But this is not said to be for the greater glory of the community, or any of the many reasons advanced by advocates of *Gemeinschaft*, except that "in this way, all the members will be at peace" (Ibid. 57). The final chapters of the *Rule* deal with relationships between the brethren, and an exhortation to observe the monastic rule in order to reach "the loftier summits of the teaching and virtues we mentioned above" – all of them individual virtues such as humility, chastity and obedience – but with no real mention of the community as such (Ibid. 92–5, 96).

Perhaps this can best be illustrated by a look at the structure of life in a monastery – a structure which, with very few exceptions, has remained unchanged over the past six hundred years, if not more.

There are, of course, various types of monastery. At one end of a wide range is what may be called the outer-directed community. The monks (or nuns) live together in a communal framework, but much of their time is spent in doing good works: charitable work among the poor, educational activities ranging from work with delinquent youths to the management of and teaching in a boarding-school, and many more variants. At the other end of this spectrum is the contemplative monastery. The monks or nuns are "enclosed" – that is to say, their contacts with the outside world are very limited; indeed, in the not very distant past they were completely cut off from their families and, for instance, forbidden to take part in their parents' funerals. The communal society of the monastery is their world.

Here, one would have thought, is fertile ground for the development of *Gemeinschaft*: a community focussed on its own needs and development, and based on the communal principles central to the kibbutz and other forms of communal societies. Let us see how this works out in practice.

In a typical contemporary contemplative monastery, the day is built round the Liturgy of the Hours – the seven services sung and recited in the chapel by the whole monastic community. The day will usually begin at 5.30, with Vigils, and end after Compline, at about 9 p.m.; then begins the "great silence", during which speech is forbidden until the following morning. In all, of his 16 waking hours, the monk spends some six or seven in chapel; the three meals take up about two hours, and work about four. In addition, some three to four hours are devoted to *Lectio Divina* – guided reading of sacred texts. Two periods of about forty-five minutes (one after lunch and one after supper) are devoted to "recreation": free intercourse between the monks, during which they converse freely about matters secular or divine.

Thus, by far the major part of the day is devoted to what may be seen as communal activity – prayer. Of the rest, the second greatest parts are work, which may be in the kitchen, the guest-house, or the living quarters, in the monastery's farm or in one of its workshops. Since, under modern conditions, the number of workers in each branch is small, this part of the day does not contribute greatly to *Gemeinschaft*-like experience. The same applies to *Lectio Divina*, which is, in effect, individual study and/ or meditation, under the supervision of the abbot or prior, or one of the priests. And meals are indeed eaten in common, but the monks do not talk to each other at mealtimes. They listen to readings from sacred writings and the Rule of St Benedict, read by each of them in turn according to a weekly rota.

In many respects, therefore, it seems as if the structure of the monastic day is designed almost to prevent the creation of *Gemeinschaft*. The only times in which the monks are engaged together in activities parallel to those which contribute to the communal experience in kibbutz or commune are the short periods of "recreation"; although in many contemporary monasteries opportunities are occasionally made for informal "get-togethers", celebrations of special events, and the like.

But does not the main monastic activity – choral prayer – create a form of *Gemeinschaft*? I shall deal with this question at greater length below. But preliminary consideration would seem to lead to the answer "No". True, the sight and sound of a monastic congregation, however small, singing and intoning the traditional prayers, whether in Latin or the vernacular, has a quality all its own, which makes a deep impression even on the unbeliever – and, of course, even more on the devout participant. But there are few references, if any, in the literature I am familiar with to the value of collective prayer as such. Prayer, of course, is much discussed. But prayer is the means whereby the individual finds his way to God; and the collective background is explicitly seen as a tool for the elevation of the individual.

It is no accident, therefore, that in the considerable literature about monasteries written by travellers, writers and others who set out to discover the nature of the monastery by visiting, conversing with monks, and the like, as well as by apologists for the monastic life – writers who explain the monastery to the general public, rather than to those who are themselves committed to one – the theme of *Gemeinschaft* is virtually ignored. Here are a few examples:

Peter Levi, who gives a very sympathetic account of monastic life, emphasizing its function as a framework for relief from the troubles of the world, and opportunities for solitary contemplation, writes: "The deep desire of monasteries is personal; it is the desire for God and the need for study and meditation [...] Monasticism [...] is a kind of love. The sense that such a quest can be communal has often been disappointed." And, somewhat surprisingly: "The worst of all religious penances is community life: it is not the penances of religion, which are private, but its communal pleasures which are hard to tolerate" (Levi 62, 182). This is a very far cry from the kibbutz, where the "communal pleasures" are a prime factor in the way of life and aspirations of the members.

There is little sociological research on the monastic community; mainly, no doubt, because the monks are not interested in admitting outsiders to their inner sanctuary in the physical sense, and even less to secrets of their hearts and minds, and their mutual interactions. One sociologist who has attempted such research, primarily in an American Trappist community, is George A. Hillery, Jr. He, too, speaks little of *Gemeinschaft*. One of his most revealing remarks, about an incident which occurred in the 1960s, is: "Two experimental houses were begun, composed of only four monks each. Neither house proved successful. In each case, the monks were 'searching for community'. The monastic search is, of course, for God." (Hillery 152) And an exhaustive reading of one of the most prominent apologists for the monastic life, Thomas Merton, shows no tendency whatsoever to see communal life as a religious or moral value; on the contrary, even within the religious order his tendency is to praise the life of the hermit – and, indeed, in his own life he did for a period live the life of a hermit within the monastery.

Esther de Waal's *Seeking God: The Benedictine Way* is a popular and widely-read introduction to monastic life and thought. Though herself neither a Catholic nor a monastic, she has a deep understanding of the monastic community. If we are looking for an appraisal of *Gemeinschaft*, we would expect to find it here. Yet there is no more than a cursory reference to it in either of the chapters which would seem to be relevant: on "people" and on "prayer". The first concentrates on face-to-face relationships between the monks, and between them and people from outside the monastery; while in the second, prayer is presented as a "full-time occupation" for the individual. The only reference to its communal aspect reads:

> [Prayer] is of course a corporate activity, and [...] it is important that I do not lose sight of the role that St. Benedict assigns to praying together and to sharing worship. Just because prayer is so personal and arises from the centre of my being it might develop into some individualistic self-indulgence unless anchored in the local community to which I belong. My praying must not become so hidden and so secret that it becomes an entirely private affair, no longer supported by others and by the mutual learning which contact with other people brings. (de Waal 110–11)

In other words, communal prayer, the experience which can be overwhelming in more than one sense – quantitatively, as filling the major part of the day, aesthetically, as a result of the beauty of the singing, and socially, as an expression of the "togetherness" of the whole community – is primarily an aid to the proper performance of individual prayer, rather than an end in itself in any of these respects.

A similar attitude can be seen in a recent work on monastic theology which, untypically, devotes a long chapter – almost a quarter of the whole book to the question of community. *Consider Your Call: A Theology of Monastic Life Today* (Rees et al.) is a reconsideration of monastic theology in response to the call of Vatican II to re-evaluate ways of monastic thought and life and adapt them, where necessary, to contemporary practices and thought-patterns. It is, perhaps, not surprising that on this background much of this chapter is devoted to such questions as the freedom of the individual within the monastic community, vocation and growth, and obedience, mainly in an attempt to soften the traditionally severe patterns of life in the monastery; for the attempt to modernize monastic thinking has inevitably to incorporate a favourable view of such matters as democracy, the freedom of the individual, and the like. But here, as in so many former formulations, community is seen entirely as an infrastructure for the development of the individual and the deepening of his religious experience. The communal experience as such – even the exalted experience of sung and chanted prayer, apart from the statement that it may legitimately be subject to variation – is scarcely mentioned. The matter is aptly summed up in a section on "community life and growth in love": "Love is the driving force in a monk's life, and the community is there to sustain him in his love for God and to give him the chance to realize it effectively in loving and being loved by his brethren" (Rees et al. 126). In the rest of this paragraph, this mutual love is exemplified by "real monastic friendships", which are clearly (many) friendships between pairs of monks. Though I have no doubt that in a well-run monastery there are many occurrences of the collective experience, it finds no more place in this exposition of monastic theology than in the others I have discussed above.

Why is this? Even though most kibbutzim are not religiously observant communities, we are clearly comparing two types of society based on different religious traditions and ways of thinking; and, as a result, on deeply divergent cultural and psychological patterns. In both of them the concept of salvation is very important. But Jewish salvation is essentially the salvation of the nation, the society – or, on the microcosmic level, the group (as evidenced, for instance in the writings of the Dead Sea sects). For the Christian salvation is individual: personal belief in God and in Jesus, and personal redemption in the world to come. All Jewish synagogue prayers are couched in the plural: on Yom Kippur, the holiest day of the year, Jews confess their sins in the first person plural: we have sinned, we have gone astray, we have slandered, etc. The central event of the Christian prayer is the mass, culminating with Holy Communion, which is a preliminary stage to the salvation of the individual. These differences reverberate throughout Jewish and Christian religious history, though there are, of course, variations and mutual borrowings.

It is not surprising, then, that despite the structural similarities between these two types of community the differences between them are so great. The general conclusion, if one is required, is that a simple structuralist analysis is not sufficient: societies whose institutions and methods of organization are very similar can be deeply influenced by cultural and historical factors, with very dissimilar results. My knowledge of the monastery is, on the whole, quite superficial, and I would hesitate to draw far-reaching conclusions from this minor piece of research. But, as far as the kibbutz is concerned, my conclusion is that cultural factors often not consciously appreciated by the members themselves – in this case, the Jewish religion and ethos – can have a deep and lasting effect on the life of a profoundly non-religious, and often even anti-religious, community.

Hutterites and Others

Following my investigation of the monasteries, I looked at some of the writings of the most communal of Christian sects (and, incidentally, today the biggest communal movement in the world apart from the kibbutz movement) – the Hutterites. And there I found something more like the collective experience:

> We make our fellow citizens in His Kingdom fellow heirs of all our goods, we accept one another as members of the Household of God, and we close neither our hearts nor our purses to any need of a brother ... That, and that alone, is genuine love

[...] Genuine love prompts us to give all our goods – and even our bodies – with an undivided heart [...] That is community. Where there is no genuine love, there is no faith ... Our love for our fellow men must be so great that it compels us to share all our possessions [...] the only true charity consists of acts of fervent love. (Ehrenpreis 27–9)

In monastic theology there are plenty of references to love, but it is primarily the love of God or of Christ for man. The emphasis on mutual love within the community as one of the mainsprings of belief and action is characteristic of the Hutterites; and there are clear parallels in the literature of the kibbutz, some of which have been quoted in the previous chapter.

The extract quoted above is from one of the standard Hutterite texts, a sermon of Andreas Ehrenpreis dated 1650, and frequently reprinted and retranslated since then; and the notion of love between the members often recurs in this work. Here again there is a question of balance: this viewpoint, while expressed forcefully and reasonably often, is only one of a whole battery of arguments for the communal life in Hutterite theology. But it certainly seems to be a more important – and more explicit – expression of the collective experience than is to be found in the mainstream of Christian monastic thought.

I may add that I have found similar expressions in the Bruderhof, the small but very active communal movement which has carried on a sort of love-hate relationship with the Hutterites over many years. To give one striking incidence, Heini Arnold, for many years the leader of the movement, summed up "the Bruderhof way" in his will: even before his exposition of the movement's Christian sources, he spoke of the aspiration of its founders to find what they sought in togetherness, and, as a result, in communal settlement. (Quoted by Oved, *Witness of the Brothers* 257).

Where does my research go from here? My original intention was to go further – perhaps to Buddhist monasteries, Sufi groups, and their derivatives in the Transcendentalist and New Age movements. But even a superficial study of these groups leads to a similar conclusion: the group as such is not a source of value; at the most, it serves as an infrastructure for the central process in their spiritual life: the striving of the individual soul for unity with God, harmony with the universe, Nirvana, and other variants.

So I returned to the Hutterites. One of the most powerful similes in their basic writings, and one which recurs frequently, is that of the bread and the wine:

> The grain had to die for the sake of the unity of the loaf [...] The harvested grain had to be crushed and milled if it was to become bread. Our own will undergoes the same for the sake of community [...] Not one grain could preserve itself as it was or keep what it had. No kernel could remain isolated. Every grain had given itself and its whole strength into the bread. In the same way, the grapes have to be pressed for the wine. (Ehrenpreis 23–4)

This is what Buber calls the collective, as distinct from the community, and what we would call a totalitarian society.[2] And, indeed, there is a version of the collective experience which leads directly to totalitarianism *tout court*.

One of the characteristics of the collective experience is that it is at its strongest during the period of adolescence. As a result, there arose one of the most important elements in the development of the kibbutz – the youth movement. From the beginning of the twentieth century there grew up in Europe movements which, though they differed widely in their aims and ideologies, used similar educational methods – joint physical activity, camping, hikes in natural surroundings, folk-song and dance, ideological discussions on the background of shared experiences. And prominent among their aims and educational methods was the promotion of the collective experience. In the early 1920s it became clear that, despite the similarity in educational methods, the ideological differences between these movements were too great for them to live together. From them grew the Zionist youth movements, which over the years provided the great majority of recruits to the growing kibbutz movement; and, as will be seen in a separate chapter, the educational methods of the youth movement, with their emphasis on the promotion of the collective experience,

---

2 On Buber, see ch. 3, below.

played – and still play – an important part in the educational system of the kibbutzim.³

However, there were other varieties of youth movement: among them, the nationalist movements of Germany and other European countries, which eventually evolved into the Hitler Youth and similar organizations. They, too, promoted the collective experience; but they replaced the educational message of the Socialist, Zionist, and religious movements, with its emphasis on the autonomy of the individual, and democratic and dialogic relationships between the members, with the totalitarian codes of iron discipline and idolization of the leader.

In the light of this historical sequence, it appears that the collective experience does not only appear during constructive activities such as working together, singing and dancing, nature rambles, or all the day-to-day activities of the kibbutz and its youth movements. It can also be the result of fighting, or training to fight, together – *esprit de corps*. In the kibbutz tradition internal cohesion and good relationships are seen to lead necessarily to a will to promote such relationships in the outside world. But this is not necessarily so for all versions of the communal life. There have been – and still are – enough examples of authoritarian communities for us to know that without a strong admixture of democracy communalism may become dictatorship.

One chilling reminder of this is to be found in Sebastian Haffner's posthumously published book, *Defying Hitler*. This is an account of Haffner's own experiences up to 1939, when he left Germany because of his anti-Nazi principles. In order to take his law degree he was compelled to take part in a camp specially organized for student lawyers by the Nazis. Anybody familiar with the approach and methods of the youth movement will easily recognize the system on which the camp was run: apart from ideological lectures, there were hikes, singsongs, and a variety of methods of creating, if not a genuine collective experience, something which would, similarly, serve as an important element in education (or indoctrination). The ease with which youth movement practice merged into totalitarian method

---

3   For a more detailed discussion of the youth movements see ch. 10, below.

should be a warning against the simplistic belief that the collective experience in itself is necessarily a force for good (Haffner 36).

Throughout the earliest period of kibbutz history, there was an ongoing controversy centred on the question: is the kibbutz an end in itself, or a means to an end. Eventually a compromise was reached: it is both. In my search for a rationale of communalism, I have come to a similar conclusion. And, I believe, our assessment of the moral worth of the commune will depend, not simply on the relationships between the members or the predominance of the collective experience in their lives; it will be a function of our assessment of the ends which the community sets itself.

In general, the ends the early kibbutzniks set themselves were not unity with the cosmos, as in Bellamy's philosophy, or attachment to God, as in the different religious communities. They were much more down to earth: the building and defence of the Jewish community in Palestine and Israel, political objectives, and the like. But it may be said that there was – and, indeed, still is – an immanent tension between these two aspects of kibbutz life and thought, which often expresses itself in very concrete terms: how much of the limited resources of money and manpower the kibbutz should devote to improving its internal life, and how much to activities for the sake of Israeli society. Similarly, there is an immanent tension between two aspects of the internal dynamics of kibbutz life: the individual as against the collective, I-Thou relationships as against the collective experience, democracy as against authoritarianism. The kibbutz movement has not always preserved a balance between these extremes; indeed, many would say that its present situation comprises a victory of the democratic element over that of the collective experience. But that is another part of the story.

CHAPTER 3

I, Thou, We:
Buber's Theory of Community and the Kibbutz

The kibbutz has been subjected to research from many aspects and in many disciplines: history, sociology, psychology, literary criticism and many more. It has, however, rarely been discussed from a philosophical point of view. The only major philosopher who has attempted this task is Martin Buber. In his principal work on the subject, *Paths in Utopia*, he presented the kibbutz as a possible model from which could be constituted the "organic commonwealth" which alone could solve the crisis of modern man (Buber, *Paths in Utopia* chs. 11, 12); and this book is the culmination of an advocacy, which lasted for much of Buber's adult life, of *Gemeinschaft* as a solution to the problems of modern society. His presentation of the kibbutz as an example of "an experiment which has not failed" has had no small influence within the kibbutz and outside it. So his description and analysis can serve as a good starting-point for an examination of kibbutz thought, as it has developed and crystallized over almost a hundred years.

In this chapter, I compare Buber's concept of the kibbutz with the social philosophy of the kibbutz members themselves. There is no single thinker or writer who has presented a generally accepted account of kibbutz thought. It will be necessary, therefore, to rely on the writings and sayings of a number of kibbutz members, from different sections of the kibbutz movement. Most of the material quoted will be taken from the formative period of the kibbutz, from 1911 until the early 1930s. Much of it is well known, and all representative of mainstream currents in kibbutz thought; so that it is no exaggeration to call the belief-system presented here "the philosophy of the kibbutz".

Various aspects of kibbutz life and thought will be described and analysed in terms derived from Buber, and compared with the parallel strands of thought in Buber's own writings. In this way, we shall be able to see to what degree the two versions of kibbutz thought are, in fact, similar.

I – Thou: Mutuality

The first extract precedes Buber's invention of the I-Thou terminology, though not his preoccupation with *Gemeinschaft* and the inter-personal (Flohr and Susser ch. 3). This fact is, however, irrelevant to the genesis of the idea in the place, time and form quoted here. Zvi Shatz, one of the early theorists of the kibbutz, did not attempt to derive a rationale of kibbutz life from more generalized theories, but to create an ideology (and a literature) out of his own experience of kibbutz life. The following is an extract from his first Hebrew article, written in 1917. Although it seems to have had little influence at the time, it later became part of the standard ideological literature of the kibbutz.

> We do not always know how to bring to life that which is hidden in the depths of the soul. But it can happen that one touch of the magic wand can tap the timid, hidden spring […] and there are moments when we are able simply to approach, to look in silence, to touch quietly, and to bring out to the light of the sun what is most precious: before it withers, before it passes beyond our reach.
> Life in the kibbutz is, of necessity, full of such moments. And if such moments are given to us – moments when the heart smiles, when the eyes see, and understand all, and pardon all – then we must fill our lives with them. Only the few are able to create life with the brush, the pen, or the bow. In us, too, the burning force of creation wells forth; and we can pour it out – only into a glance: a silent, luminous glance from heart to heart, sincere and direct. And it will pass like a refreshing and renovating current, joining hearts together, with ties of purity and mutual understanding. (Shatz 94–5)[1]

---

[1] As Avraham Yassour has shown (Yassour 66) Buber was well acquainted with Katznelson's anthology *Hakvutza*. It is, therefore, virtually certain that he knew this passage. It is also not impossible that he read the original version, first published

Although this view was rarely expressed with such poetic intensity and urgency, there is no doubt that it was an important part of the concept of "ideal relationships" between kibbutz members which were frequently spoken of as one of the aims of the kibbutz. The "glance from heart to heart" seems to be identical with the I-Thou relationship, as described and adumbrated by Buber in many versions, but perhaps most concretely at the conclusion of his essay "What is Man?"

> If one and another come up against one another, "happen" to one another [...] the sum does not exactly divide, there is a remainder, somewhere, where the souls end and the world has not yet begun, and this remainder is what is essential. This fact can be found even in the tiniest and most transient events which scarcely enter the consciousness. In the deadly crush of an air-raid shelter the glances of two strangers suddenly meet for a second in astonishing and unrelated mutuality; when the All Clear sounds it is forgotten; and yet it did happen, in a realm which existed only for that moment. In the darkened opera-house there can be established between two of the audience, who do not know one another, and who are listening in the same purity and with the same intensity to the music of Mozart, a relation which is scarcely perceptible and yet is one of elemental dialogue, and which has long vanished when the lights blaze up again. In the understanding of such fleeting and yet consistent happenings one must guard against introducing motives of feeling: what happens here cannot be reached by psychological concepts, it is something ontic. (Buber, *Between Man and Man* 204)

It should be noted that the I Thou relationship is purely dyadic. Both Shatz and Buber seem to see society (for Shatz, the commune or kibbutz; for Buber, the *Gemeinschaft*) as, ideally, a series of face-to-face relationships. Shatz believes that the major task of the commune is to increase the possibility of these "moments of joy". It does this by creating a background which does not divert men's attention by the distractions of materialism, competition and hatred. "In the incessant, raucous, stormy chaos of life,

---

in 1919, at a much earlier stage. It is most improbable that Shatz, who was killed in 1921, knew of Buber. Therefore, this passage, and others like it, represent parallel, rather than derivative strands of thought. It is, of course, feasible that Buber was influenced by the existence of the kibbutz (and even directly by Shatz's writings) while developing his dialogic philosophy.

the perpetual light of harmonious relationships cannot glow [...] The music of life, therefore, can only be heard in the kibbutz, in the quiet stillness that reigns there" (Shatz 94). The social structure of the kibbutz affords the possibility of direct "heart-to-heart" relationships between each pair of its members.

In Buber, too, these "ontic moments" seem to be a sort of paradigm of the I-Thou relationship: when "in one instant eye meets eye", this is the beginning of redemption; the "creative glance" can introduce the dialogic element into the I-It relationships of the workplace; and so forth (Buber, *I and Thou* 108; *Between Man and Man* 37). I believe that these moments are the central *motif* in Buber's I-Thou teaching. But, even if it is better understood in the light of the wealth of exegesis written by Buber and his interpreters, there is no doubt that the dialogic element is an essential part of his concept of the ideal community: "Only men who are capable of truly saying *Thou* to one another can truly say *We* with one another" (*Between Man and Man* 176). In *Paths in Utopia*, the most developed and explicit statement of his mature views on this subject, the emphasis on "the spirit" has the same significance; for, for Buber, "spirit", in interpersonal terms, is the spirit of dialogue (*Paths in Utopia* (1st Hebrew edn) ch. 6; *I and Thou* 97–100). The passage quoted at length above continues:

> This reality, whose disclosure has begun in our time, shows the way, leading beyond individualism and collectivism, for the life decision of future generations. Here the genuine third alternative is indicated, the knowledge of which will help to bring about the genuine person again and to establish genuine community. (*Between Man and Man* 204)

How does Buber make the leap from this series of dyadic relationships to the polytropic structure which must surely be part of any concept of community? In the bulk of his work, it looks as if the We is created by increasing the number and intensity of I-Thou relationships. Here are two quotations, from among many, which put in a concise form Buber's most characteristic viewpoint on this question.

In *I and Thou* he says: "The structures of communal human life derive their life from the fullness of relational force that permeates their members" (98). The "relational force" is, of course, the I-Thou relationship, and it appears again in a later passage of the same work:

> The genuine guarantee of duration [of the community, H.N.] is that pure relation can be fulfilled as the beings become Thou, as they are elevated to the Thou, so that the holy basic word sounds through all others ... Thus the time of human life is formed into an abundance of actuality ... it becomes so permeated by relation that this gains a radiant and penetrating constancy in it. The moments of supreme encounter are no mere flashes of lightning in the dark, but like a rising moon in a clear starry night. (163)

And in *Between Man and Man*:

> Community [...] is the being no longer side by side but *with* one another of a multitude of persons. And this multitude, though it also moves towards one goal, yet experiences everywhere a turning to, a dynamic facing of, the other, a flowing from *I* to *Thou*. Community is where community happens. (31)

In short, for Buber as for Shatz, the ideal society is that in which each possible pair of members maintains, to the greatest possible degree, a dialogic relationship: a society replete with "heart-to-heart glances".

There are, however, other elements in the concept of *Gemeinschaft*, both in Buber's thought and in the kibbutz tradition.

Between Man and Man: Mutual Responsibility

The dyadic relationships which are so important to Shatz and Buber alike take place on the background of a social structure which cannot be defined exhaustively in terms of I-Thou. One essential aspect of kibbutz life is a principle to which I have given the minimalist definition of "mutual responsibility": the responsibility of the community as a whole for the welfare of all its members, and the individual concern of each for each and each for all. In this sense, the kibbutz has been described as "the ultimate welfare state". The following quotation shows the way in which this principle was reflected in kibbutz thought, when it was at the point of transformation from an expression of "ideal relationships" (involving constant individual efforts at dyadic mutual aid) to the more institutionalized relationships of the developed kibbutz. Joseph Bussel, the central figure in the first kibbutz, Degania, wrote in 1919:

> I have never believed that kibbutz life should blur anybody's personality. I have always believed, and still do, that we have to bring all the different voices in the kibbutz choir into harmony [...] I persevere in kibbutz life, even though the relations of intimacy between me and the people who are now in Degania are weaker than they were. On the contrary, I think that the fact that I can live in the kibbutz with these people, and that we have never had any serious conflicts of the sort that occur whenever strangers live together, is a victory for the kibbutz idea. I am very happy to see that the children of a group of women who are not intimate friends are being cared for by one of those women; and, on the other hand, work and communal life create new ties of which we had not dreamed previously. At any rate, the relationships which they create are purer than in any other place. (Bussel 240)

It is not easy to find this view clearly stated in Buber's writings on social philosophy. On the contrary: in his condemnation of collectivism (as opposed to community), he remarks, somewhat scornfully, that the collective takes on itself the full responsibility for its members' welfare, but in exchange deprives them of their freedom (*Between Man and Man* 201).

Nonetheless, it does seem that the whole of Buber's treatment of the development of the socialist movement – many of whose aims he clearly approves of – implies the collective responsibility of society for the welfare of the individual; otherwise there would be no point in his (albeit limited) approval of the "experiments" in socialist life of which he speaks in *Paths in Utopia* (ch. 7); nor, indeed, in his virtual identification with Landauer; for Landauer's special contribution to socialist thought was not only the spiritual element which Buber emphasizes so heavily, but also his concern with very down-to-earth attempts to build cooperative communities which would ensure their members' social welfare (Lunn 190–200, 213–23, 229–31). It is hard to imagine, therefore, that Buber's concept of the ideal socialist society would not include the element of complete mutual responsibility, even though his main preoccupations (positive and negative) are with other elements of such communities. In fact, a crude statement of the minimum which Buber demands of a socialist society would be something like "complete mutual responsibility and maximum I-Thou relationships".

It could, perhaps, be said that, in Buberian terms, this principle has no independent validity, but is purely an extension of the I-Thou relationship. And, indeed, as I have pointed out in my comments on the extract from Bussel, in the early days of the kibbutz it was so: the concern of the community for the individual was seen as the organizational expression of each individual's concern for his fellows. But the very process of institutionalization which has been seen in progress at that point makes inevitable the distinction between the individual and society, and the shifting of responsibility to the community as a whole. It is precisely this element which distinguishes socialism, in all its forms, from liberalism with its dependence on charity for the modification of social injustices. On this issue, there is no doubt where Buber's sympathies lie.

We have seen that the above two principles are found in very similar, if not identical, form, both in kibbutz life and thought and in Buber's social philosophy. I shall now turn to a number of different elements in the kibbutz idea, and suggest that it is far from clear that Buber grasped them in the same way.

I with Us: Work

One of the central *motifs* in kibbutz society is that of work. Shlomo Lavi, one of the earliest ideologists of the kibbutz, expressed this succinctly in 1925:

> Behold! All that is true in life, all logic, all absolute justice (insofar as it exists), all that is beautiful and exalted – all this makes for the equality of every man, for the joint use of the powers of man for the sake of creation; and this is the result not of hunger and slavery, but of the free will, of a deep inner yearning and a song in the soul. (Lavi, "Four Years" 336)

The essence of kibbutz society is cooperation in work and, indeed, in all forms of creativity. The communal is not an end in itself, but an epiphenomenon, a by-product of the effort to achieve the common aim, and a means of achieving it in the most effective manner.

In later years, one of the points of controversy between the three major kibbutz movements was the question: Is the kibbutz an end in itself, or a means to ends external to kibbutz society? Among these ends are economic development and settlement, higher productivity, etc. – the results of the very creativity which Lavi exalts in this passage. Lavi himself was one of the leaders of the Kibbutz Me'uhad movement, which tended to emphasize the function of the kibbutz as a means to a variety of ends outside itself. It should be added, therefore, that, despite differences of emphasis, the idea of work – in particular, physical work of all kinds – appears as a key element in every variety of kibbutz ideology. At the very time when the members of Degania, the first kibbutz, were emphasizing the quality of their communal relationships as the key to social "redemption":

> The discussions about economic affairs were particularly difficult: on this there were differences of opinion not only about the planning of the farm, but about everyday questions of work: for the members saw these matters as the centre of their life, and their spiritual expression. We invested our souls in these matters, just as an author or artist invests his soul in his creation. For we had no other life and wanted none. (Dayan 100)

In the light of such attitudes, it is not surprising that the "ends or means" discussion was resolved by declaring that the kibbutz community was both an end in itself and a means to achievements outside the sphere of the *Gemeinschaft*.

In short: in all parts of the kibbutz movement there is agreement on the fundamental importance of cooperation in the sphere of creativity, and particularly of work, not only in order to ensure the continued material existence of the kibbutz, but as an expression of a common value. Insofar as this activity is conceived as a means to an end, this end is intrinsic in the act of creation: better crops, higher cultural standards, etc. It is only incidentally (although often quite importantly) a means to social solidarity, or the improvement of interpersonal relations.

To what extent did Buber share this view? In my view, scarcely at all. It is true that creativity plays a part in his philosophy. But the central model of a creative act is the I-Thou relationship – the artist working alone with his material, or the "originator instinct" of the child (*I and Thou* 60–1, 65–6; *Between Man and Man* 84–8). In the modern world, work is part of the world of It. It can be made tolerable by a "creative glance", or by dialogic rather than formal relations between managers and men (*Between Man and Man* 36–9). But the act of communal creativity is not in itself a thing of value, as it is in kibbutz life and thought.

There are a number of passages which seem at first sight to contradict this contention. In *Paths in Utopia*, the book which was most directly influenced by the kibbutz, Buber wrote: "A community of faith truly exists only when it is a community of work" (135). But the emphasis, here as elsewhere, is on the faith rather than the work; the act – and, even more, the concrete results – of communal creativity are viewed not as ends in themselves, but as means of enhancing social solidarity, and thus reaching true *Gemeinschaft*. The central message of Buber's 1929 lecture on education to creativity (in *Between Man and Man*) is not dissimilar. There is a short and moving passage on the importance of "sharing in an undertaking, and entering into mutuality", as opposed to the essentially solitary character of the "originative instinct". But the very terminology removes the creative act from the educational sphere, and relegates it to the realm of instinct, which may be "released", but is, apparently, not subject to the educational process. There is here little of the "song in the heart" felt in the actual process of cooperative work. Moreover, there is in Buber's concept of the kibbutz very little, if any, of the outlook common to all the Labour Zionist Movement until the establishment of the State of Israel, widely known as the "religion of labour". Work – and particularly physical work, preferably in agriculture – was considered to be both a social imperative and a morally exalting activity. In the words of A.D. Gordon, the major proponent of this viewpoint:

> We must do with our own hands all the things that make up the sum total of life. We must ourselves do all the work, from the least strenuous, cleanest, and most sophisticated, to the dirtiest and most difficult [...] From now on our principal ideal must be Labour [...] Labour is a great human ideal [...] We must all work with our hands. (Gordon 372–4)

Even though Buber more than once paid tribute to Gordon, and printed the article from which the above extract is taken in his journal, *Der Jude*, the idea of physical work (as opposed to the more general idea of "creativity") scarcely appears in his writings on social philosophy, even in his account of the kibbutz. Moreover, when work is presented as one of the essential activities of the *halutz* (pioneer), the results of his creativity are not viewed as ends in themselves, but as means to the improvement of interpersonal relationships, or to the creation of a new type of Jew. Thus, there is a fundamental difference between Buber's attitude to work and that which was shared by Gordon and the kibbutz.[2] In his comprehensive analysis of Buber's philosophy, Avraham Shapira writes:

> Buber, as opposed to Gordon, presents a conception of creativity in which the private I is not only the beginning of the object (*tachlit*) but also its end [...] in fact, he does not go beyond the dimension of the inclinations and aspirations of the individual who seeks his own "way". He does not attribute any content or substance with its own status in reality to objective or non – personal creation. (Shapira 130)[3]

---

2   Five articles by Buber in praise of Gordon are reprinted in the new Hebrew edition of *Paths in Utopia* (1983, 164–253). At the only meeting between Gordon and Buber, at the Hapoel Hatza'ir conference in Prague (1920), Buber's admiration was not reciprocated. (Verbal communication from Professor Nathan Rotenstreich.) For an extended discussion of Buber's conception of *halutziut* (pioneering), see section 6, below. He deals with this subject in "The *Halutz* and His World" (*Selected writings* 255–7) and in *Paths in Utopia* (143–7); but the clearest and most extended exposition of his views is in "The Regeneration of a People's Life" (*Selected writings* 175–91).

3   Eliezer Schweid reaches a similar conclusion in his comparative essay, "Between Martin Buber and A.D. Gordon" (Schweid).

I – We: Communion

> There was a sort of mutual yearning, a desire to sit together far into the night, and thereby to penetrate the very depths of the vision of communal life. Soul touched soul. We longed to become a sort of river of souls, whose tributaries would merge, and together create the fresh and mighty current of friendship and fraternity. (Likever 36–7)

This element in communal life, described by one of the members of Degania in its early days as a "blurring of the boundaries of personality",[4] is a polytropic relationship, in sharp contrast to the dyadic nature of the I-Thou element. This is collective experience at its most intense. The group is felt as a tangible thing, and the individual, while not losing his identity, has a strong sense of unity with and affection for his fellows – not only as individuals, but as part of a shared entity. In contrast to the I-Thou experience, the whole is felt to be greater than the individuals of whom it is composed.

In the literary sources of the kibbutz, this experience has several names ("love", "the collective experience", "together", etc.) and recurs in many situations; but it is recognizably identical in many descriptions. I have discussed it at some length, under the name of "the communal experience", in a previous chapter. Following Schmalenbach and others, in this chapter I generally call it "communion", to denote its polytropic and semi-mystical character (Schmalenbach 83–93; Rosner; Barzel 155–6). One of the classical situations for the creation of communion is the youth movement; and one of the classical sources for its appearance in the kibbutz is the diary of the first graduates of the Hashomer Hatza'ir youth movement, who saw in their communal life a continuation of their youth movement principles and experience. The collective diary recording their changing relationships and experiences was published under the name *Kehiliateinu* (Our Congregation). These young men and women had been influenced by Buber and his teachings, and *Kehiliateinu* contains a tribute to him. But

---

4   Unnamed speaker at the annual general meeting of kibbutz Degania, 1918; in the archives of Degania Aleph; documents unnumbered.

there are in the pages of this strange and moving document few traces of the I-Thou relationship in Buber's sense, and many more of the communal experience, as discussed at length in chapter 1, above.

The not uncommon mystical (and Zionist) theme of union with nature seems to lead on naturally to ecstatic communion with one's fellow-men. Like many mystic visions, it carries its own imperatives, the first of which is to return to similar states; but, like all such experiences, it is fleeting, and can leave behind it a feeling of flatness and disappointment. Here is an extract from *Kehiliateinu*:

> It seems to me that I must feel a great distance between myself and anyone who speaks of disappointments, especially when I sit among you, enveloped in a fever of direct encounter. And I know that that is when the feeling of construction, the collective strength that is in me, dominates me entirely, and this moment is not the realisation of my own dreams alone.
>
> Therefore, when it happens that the collective act does not grip us, we disperse again as if we were strangers one to another (*Kehiliateinu* 51).

Such experiences are not confined to youth movement members or graduates. Here is part of Miriam Baratz's description of her wedding day: the first wedding in the first kibbutz:

> After the ceremony, a quick meal together with the many guests – and again, a tumultuous dance, inspired and inspiring, until dawn. I milked and fed the cows, and went upstairs to sleep a little. The dawn had broken, but the sky was not yet light, when I heard in my sleep a gentle beautiful melody. It was Dvorkin's violin. He was no musical genius, and the song was one of the simplest – but it entered into and elevated one's innermost soul. I opened my door, put out my head, and saw four more heads, each of them looking out into the hall – all of them members of the Hadera commune.[5] Hand on shoulder, clasped tight to each other we started dancing – quietly at first, and then more enthusiastically. Again, I don't know how long the dance lasted. The sun rose high before we, the members of the commune, had finished our dance. This dance was one of those decisive moments in life which make a deep and indelible impression. It expressed life-long fellow-

---

5   "The Hadera commune" refers to the founding members of kibbutz Degania: a closely knit group of some ten members (including Miriam Baratz and her husband).

ship, unlimited community, loyalty to our comrades and faith in the idea which is our destiny (Baratz 2).

Here, the collective experience is felt to be an essential complement to one of the archetypal forms of dyadic relationship: marriage. On the other hand, there were certainly cases when communion appears to have taken place without a concomitant I-Thou relationship:

> I love you all only at certain moments, moments of happiness without end: then I love the whole world within my kibbutz. Then I express my love by holding out my hand, by a heart-felt glance, by a sudden clasp of the hand – and it has happened that the other person looked at me as if I were out of my mind. (*Kehiliateinu* 43)

Even if the occurrences of the communal experience are rare, their very intensity clearly makes them of the greatest importance to those who experience them. It could, therefore, be one of the objects of kibbutz society to provide the structural conditions for their maximum occurrence – just as, in the approach of Shatz and Buber analysed above, it is the object of the kibbutz to achieve the greatest number of I-Thou relationships between its members.

We – I: Solidarity

In the ecstasy of communion, the individual feels himself at once autonomous and part of the community. But there is a whole range of relationships within the kibbutz experience in which the strength of this autonomy may vary greatly.

Perhaps the best known example of one such variation is the description by the poet Avraham Shlonsky of his experiences in a kibbutz in the early 1920s. In the rough-and-ready pioneering society of the period, he had achieved some social status both by his efficiency at physical work and by his cultural achievement in organizing the kibbutz football team. He had concealed the fact that he was a poet, and thus a member of the scorned class of intellectuals. So, when his first poem was published under his own name, his status in the kibbutz declined sharply, and was redeemed again only on the football field (Shlonsky 892–4).

Though the story is told with humour, and with understanding of the social and ideological circumstances which led to the incident, it points to an important facet of kibbutz life – that, within the range of relationships subsumed here under the general description "solidarity", it is possible for the group to dominate the individual, and to lead to a *Gleichschaltung* which restricts his possibilities of self-expression and satisfaction no less than other aspects of kibbutz life can expand them.

This state of affairs is not necessarily rejected by the kibbutz members, for whom the extreme degree of solidarity may be both personally comforting and socially effective. When, in 1933, one of the leaders of the kibbutz declared that in the face of the threat of world war, "we must live today with the feeling that the individual has no value" except as a member of the collective, he was expressing a not uncommon reaction to the world crisis (Marshak 75). It was exactly this reaction, and its social consequences, which Buber rejected as "collectivism". In his terminology, We-I, if not checked by other means, can become They-I.

There is, then, a continuum of I-We relationships, ranging from communion at one end to oppressive solidarity at the other. Between them may be a number of states in which communion is attempted, but not achieved, or in which the balance between individual and community is equal, or wavering. Such nuances are described and analysed very many times in the literature of the kibbutz. For these groups of young people found in community, in its infinite variety, a source of inspiration and a vital element in their social philosophy. Buber takes no account of such subtle variations as those described and implied in these passages. For him, the community, in which man lives and creates *with* man, is totally opposed to the collective, which is "not a binding but a bundling together", where "man's isolation is not overcome, but over-powered and numbed", and "the person surrenders himself when he renounces the directness of personal decision and responsibility". In his revulsion from totalitarianism of all sorts, he imposes polarity on a reality which is often complex and ambivalent (Buber, *Between Man and Man* 31 and 201–2).

The emphasis on solidarity in certain parts of the kibbutz movement in the 1930s led to a situation bordering on what was later called totalitarian democracy, and in some cases even crossed the border. Today, such attitudes are widely rejected by the vast majority of kibbutz members, even though it has been plausibly maintained that traces of them still exist (Near, "Actress's Wisdom"). But it could well be argued even now that the historical circumstances of the time justified actions and attitudes which today would be condemned as inappropriate and even immoral. The physical struggle of the Jewish people in the Diaspora and in Palestine for survival, the Second World War, and the War of Liberation demanded a very high degree of discipline and self-sacrifice, which was expressed in all parts of the kibbutz movement by the emphasis on the value which I have called solidarity at the expense of that which I have called mutuality. Although Buber's strictures on collectivism met with a favourable response in many parts of the kibbutz movement in 1945, this reaction was by no means universal; and it is virtually certain that they would have been as widely rejected eight or ten years earlier.

Buber's "We"

The concepts of communion and solidarity are attempts to express and interpret one central fact of kibbutz life: that the community is considered to be an entity which cannot be defined simply in terms of the dyadic relationships between its members. In a sense, the main thrust of Buber's social thought is to deny this proposition. Although the community is needed as an organizational framework for the flowering of the I-Thou relationship, its functions are essentially in the It-world: morally neutral, and even negative if not shot through with dialogic relationships.

This can be shown to be true even in purely quantitative terms. Buber does use such terms as "the essential We", and "the centre", but their precise meaning is vague and controversial. They appear rarely, and far less frequently, even in the context of Buber's advocacy of *Gemeinschaft*, than the dyadic relationships which are the core of his social philosophy.

One striking example appears in his 1926 lecture on education. He uses the example of a children's choir to show how "a community of achievement" can be created by educational means. But when he continues to explain that "What teaches us the saying of *Thou* is [...] the instinct for communion", he speaks of the mother-child relationship as an instance of this communion. And in his account of the educational process, the teacher is seen dealing with the pupil, not with the class (Buber, "Dialogue" in *Between Man and Man*). There is here none of the concept of the "children's society", with its deliberate attempt to foster relations of solidarity and community, which is so central to education in the real kibbutz (Near, "Kibbutz Education" 3–4). It seems, then, that Buber's concern with the dangers of collectivity frequently leads to a semantic slide from the concept of community to that of dyadic interpersonal relationships. "Community [...] is the being *with* one another of a multitude of persons [...] [who] experience everywhere [...] a flowing from I to Thou" (Buber, *Between Man and Man* 31). There is one passage where Buber seems to refer to the relationships which I have called "solidarity" and "communion". The circumstances of the growth of the "essential" are described in terms which confirm the historical experience of the kibbutz: the community of revolutionary or religious groups, and the feeling of communion which arises in times of bereavement, suffering or persecution. But here again, the We-relationship is linked inseparably to the one-to-one dialogic Thou:

> As there is a *Thou* so is there a *We* [...] *We* includes the *Thou* potentially. The special character of the *We* is shown [...] in the holding sway within the *We* of an ontic directness which is the decisive presupposition of the *I-Thou* relationship. (*Between Man and Man* 176–7)

In many cases, too, the same applies to Buber's references to the "living centre", which is a prerequisite for any form of *Gemeinschaft*. In his classical statements of this concept, Buber emphasises that true community requires "a living, reciprocal relationship" both to a living centre and between the members of the community (Buber, *I and Thou* 94).

The notion of the "centre" is notoriously vague. In many cases, it seems to be no more than a statement of the minimal condition for the existence of any group: "When individuals really have something to do with one another, when they share an experience and together existentially respond to that experience." (*Between Man and Man* 244) But this in itself tells us nothing about the nature of the experience; and, as we have seen, Buber's tendency is to emphasize the dyadic relationships within such a group. In other cases, however, the concept of the centre – or, as Paul Mendes-Flohr (182–9) rightly points out in this context, the Centre – is clearly connected with the view that "only in the true *Gemeinschaft* can Divinity be elevated from the level of an inner experience to the level of actual living". Buber's socialism was always religious, and he returned again and again to the theme that:

> *socialitas*, that is, the union of mankind, the link between man and man, cannot develop except through a common relationship to the divine centre, even if it is still without a name. Attachment to God and communion with man belong one to another. (Buber, *Paths in Utopia* [1983] 225).

These words were uttered during the discussion on the 1945 lecture which was published later as the final chapter of *Paths in Utopia*. Referring to Jewish tradition, and the way in which the festivals were (and still are) celebrated in the kibbutz, he said:

> The major part of Jewish tradition is based on its relation to the Absolute [...] it is impossible to renew part of that tradition without taking this relation into account [...] Perhaps there is not at present a suitable name for this relationship [...] but the renaissance of (cultural) forms will certainly not come about by replacing religious beliefs with national or kibbutz beliefs. Forms of expression will only be renewed by renewing the relationship to the Absolute. (ibid.)

Here, in the specific context of the kibbutz movement, Buber returns to his contention that the social and cultural forms developed in the "living *Gemeinschaft*" lack validity without the extra dimension of the Absolute – or, in terms which he was reluctant to use at that time and place, the Divine. The secular kibbutzim which formed, and still form, the bulk of the kibbutz movement, reject this view. The festivals, and other communal events, are seen not only as cultural events, but as ways of increasing social solidarity and communion. And these in themselves are seen as autonomous sources of value, which do not require divine sanction or religious experience to legitimize them.

Thus, even though under certain circumstances the notion of the Centre can be interpreted to embrace the concept of communion, Buber's attitude again emphasizes the dyadic as against the polytropic. We could summarize this section in a manner almost identical with that on the I-Thou element, above: the ideal society is that which contains the greatest possible degree of dialogic relationships. But in this case the dialogue is between man and God. As I said at the conclusion of the previous section, Buber's anti-collectivism has in great measure been assimilated into present-day kibbutz ideology. The same could certainly not be said of his attitude to communion. There is no doubt that the effort to ensure that communion takes place is an important part of kibbutz life and practice: in the educational sphere, in the celebration of festivals and times of sorrow, and in many other circumstances. Very few, if any, members of non-orthodox kibbutzim see these moments of exaltation and fellowship as leading to, or being incomplete without, communion with a supernatural power.

Dialogue: Democracy and Equality

The only social institution which existed in the first ten years of the kibbutz's existence was the members' discussion, or, more exactly, "the table".

> The "table" discussed and decided, one could bring to it matters of personal or public concern, it could give the individual encouragement and consolation. Sitting round the table, we considered from all aspects the different economic problems of the kibbutz, how to organise the work, housing problems, how to help members' parents in distress, education, the problems which occupied the labour movement, the kibbutz movement, etc. The "table" was all-powerful. Its power stemmed from our belief in the group as a family-type *Gemeinschaft*. Between twelve and seventeen young men and women, sitting each evening after work – before or after supper – exchanging views

and impressions. In this discussion, in the most direct fashion and with the participation of all the members of the group, all the problems of our life were decided. And, if you wanted to, together with another 16 pairs of arms you could embrace problems of eternity, of the salvation of the world and of the Jewish people. (Likever 137)

This passage, a description of the early days of Kibbutz Ginegar, gives an insight into one of the most important values of kibbutz society: democracy, in the quite specific sense of public discussion and decision of all social issues. The same process, translated to the conditions of a community of more than a thousand people, was described at a much later date by a sophisticated observer of the kibbutz, the English scholar Dorothea Krook, as "the triumph of rationalism". The degree to which every aspect of life in the kibbutz was open to overt discussion and democratic decision made it, in her eyes, a rational society *par excellence*. Anybody with intimate knowledge of kibbutz democracy knows that its decisions can be irrational in many senses: marred by the clash of interests, indifference, ignorance, or stupidity. But the principle of democratic decision after public discussion on rational grounds is built into the fabric of kibbutz society (Krook).

Buber defines human relationships within the community in terms of spiritual attitudes and situations. The specifically rational aspect of these relationships is scarcely mentioned, if at all. Indeed, in some passages it looks as if the discourse, which is the literal meaning of "dialogue", is relegated to the world of It. Institutions are what is "out there", where for all kinds of purposes one spends time, where one works, negotiates, influences, undertakes, competes, organises, administers, officiates, preaches. All of these functions, most of which are performed by the democratic institutions of the kibbutz, are placed by Buber in the It–District, necessary to the ordered conduct of life, but essentially irrelevant to the interpersonal relationships without which that life is meaningless. "The statesman or businessman who serves the spirit [...] serves the truth which, though supra-rational, does not disown reason but holds it in her lap" (Buber, *I and Thou* 92–3, 98). Rationalism should be not triumphant, but subservient.

It can, of course, be argued that the I-Thou relationship subsumes (or assumes) a number of values which are normally thought to be part of the democratic way of life: consideration for others, mutual understanding, and so forth. But all of these can exist in a variety of institutions. As Buber says: "Whether it is the state that regulates the economy or the economy that regulates the state is unimportant" (99). As far as I know, Buber nowhere speaks of the rational dialogue which must surely be an element in any concept of democracy, and is certainly a vital part of the fabric of kibbutz life. It is, it seems, no accident that the term "democracy" does not appear in the index of any of the three books devoted to Buber's social and political thought (Susser; Yassour; Murphy).

What has been said of democracy can be said no less of equality. Since the earliest period of the kibbutz's existence, the idea of equality – whether in its conventional meanings, or in the widely accepted formulation "from each according to his ability: to each according to his needs" – has been a key concept in kibbutz ideology (Shur, "Equality in the Kibbutz Movement"). Again, it could be said that equality is a necessary component of the I-Thou relationship; but, apart from this rather tangential assumption, Buber does not discuss the concept of equality, either in interpersonal relationships or in the distribution of material goods.

Buber's contention that the kibbutz is "an exemplary non-failure" (*Paths in Utopia* [1949] 141) has been very widely noted and quoted. Less attention has been paid to the criteria by which, in his view, its success or failure could be assessed. On this, Buber says:

> I would apply the word "failure" [...] to those [communes] that maintained themselves in isolation. For the real, the truly structural task of the new Village Communes begins with their *federation*, that is, their union under the same principle that operates in their internal structure [...] The socialistic task can only be accomplished to the degree that the new Village Commune [...] exerts a structural influence on the amorphous urban society (140–1).

The success or failure of the kibbutz must, on this view, be judged by its relationships with the outside world: with other kibbutzim, and with the Palestinian Jewish community. But, a few pages later, Buber defines the central problem of the kibbutzim as a decline in their internal standards:

> The point where the problem emerges, where people are apt to slip, is in their relationship to their fellows [...] A real community is one which in every point of its

being possesses, potentially at least, the whole character of community. The internal questions of a community are thus in reality questions relating to its own genuineness, hence to its inner strength and ability. The men who created the Jewish Communes in Palestine instinctively knew this; but the instinct no longer seems to be as common and alert as it was (114–15).

In one sense, this contention jibes well with the view of the relationship between the kibbutz and the outside world which is hinted at in the phrase "an exemplary non-failure"; for the members of the very earliest kibbutzim believed that the kibbutz would influence the society around it by example. But even they would not have maintained, as Buber seems to be doing in this passage, that the actual work of the *halutz* – the physical redemption of the Land of Israel, which was for them (as for A.D. Gordon) the quintessence of Zionism – was of less account than the internal relationships within the kibbutz community.

Buber speaks more than once of the *halutz* – the pioneer who goes before the host – as an essential element in the regeneration of the Jewish people which is the aim of Zionism. But in his conception of the *halutz*, as in his conception of the function of labour in the rebuilding of Israel, he seems to be at odds with the accepted view in the labour movement at large, and the kibbutz in particular. The most succinct expression of this difference is, perhaps, in a passage first written in 1929, and reprinted with no change throughout Buber's lifetime. Here, the idea that the *Gemeinschaft* can be a means to an end is rejected, in terms perfectly intelligible to the men and women of the kibbutz – and no doubt intentionally so.

> In the view customary today, which is defined by politics, the only important thing in groups, in the present as in history, is what they aim at and what they accomplish. Significance is ascribed to what goes on within them only in so far as it influences the group's action with regard to its aim. Thus it is conceded to a band conspiring to conquer the state power that the comradeship which fills it is of value, just because it strengthens the band's reliable assault power [...]
>
> By this simplified mode of valuation the real and individual worth of a group remains as uncomprehended as when we judge a person by his effect alone and not by his qualities. The perversion of thought grows when chatter is added about sacrifice of being, about renunciation of self-realization, where possible with a reference to the favourite metaphor of the dung. (*Between Man and Man* 30–1)

The metaphor of the dung occurs frequently in the literature of the kibbutz, and of the Labour Zionist movement in general. The first written reference known to me is in a diary written in 1920: "All of our generation are nothing more than dung for the fields of the Land of Israel" (Tabenkin, E. 71). Similar references occur throughout the 1920s and 1930s. This attitude was certainly not foreign to the ways of thought and action of the kibbutz movement as a whole. And it is precisely this viewpoint which Buber explicitly rejects.

Buber does not deny the value of the actual activities of the *halutz* in rebuilding Jewish agriculture, reclaiming the soil, defending the country and so forth. But for him these activities are primarily instrumental; their value is in the creation of a new type of Jew, "a new type [of man], healthier in his nature, freer, more moderate, a 'regenerative' type". Such people, living in *Gemeinschaften*, will form the elite of Jewish society in Palestine. In this way they can "exert on the amorphous urban society [...] the structural influence" which will turn the kibbutz from a non-failure to a success (*Selected Writings* 80–1; *Paths in Utopia* [1949] 141).

The contrast between this view and another widely accepted in the kibbutz movement can be seen in the words of Yitzhak Tabenkin, the leader of the biggest, and in many respects the most influential, of the kibbutz movements during most of Buber's life:

> The *halutzic* value of the kibbutz is not only in its final ideal, but also in the ways in which it realises [its ideals] day by day [...] its *halutzic* value consists in the creation of an independent economy, the conquest of the soil, the creation of an economy controlled by the workers. Among its achievements: the creation of a workers' culture and social life, communal education, economic cooperation. (Tabenkin "On the Place of the Kibbutz" 7)

Like Buber, Tabenkin believes that one of the achievements of the kibbutz is the creation of a new *halutzic* type of Jew. But the *halutz*'s achievements are not in what he is, but in what he does. In the matter of the relations between kibbutzim, there was a measure of historical truth in Buber's views. By 1929, virtually every kibbutz had joined one or another of the kibbutz movements. But they did so with varying degrees of enthusiasm, ranging from those who dreamt of creating a "general commune of Jewish workers" to those who insisted on the federative nature of the kibbutz movement, and resisted any attempt at centralization. And what are we to make of Buber's contention that "even in its first undifferentiated form a tendency towards federation was innate in the *kvutza*", in view of the fact that it was precisely the members of the *kvutzot*[6] who most strongly resisted the pressure to create an overall kibbutz movement? The whole question of inter-kibbutz relationships is complex, and requires detailed treatment beyond the scope of this chapter. Here, it should merely be said that it is far from clear in what sense the kibbutzim are united, even today, "under the same principle that operates in their internal structure" (*Paths in Utopia* [1949] 141; Near, *Kibbutz and Society* chs. 2, 6).

Realization and Self-Realization

Although Buber had considerable influence on different parts of the kibbutz movement at various periods of its history, during most of his life he was estranged from most of its leaders – even though many of them had seen him as a guide in adopting the kibbutz way of life. In some cases, this estrangement was the result of a change in doctrine or attitude on the part of the kibbutz movement: Hashomer Hatza'ir's infatuation with communism, which for Buber was the embodiment of the dangers of collectivist socialism, or the Kibbutz Me'uhad's uncompromising attitude to the Arab problem. But the major bone of contention between them was in the interpretation of a concept which, in the view of at least one commentator, was one of the central themes in Buber's philosophy: the concept of realization (Hebrew: *Hagshama*; German: *Verwirklichung*) (Susser 34–7).

---

6   *Kvutza* (pl. *kvutzot*), veteran kibbutzim, such as Degania, which resisted the aspiration of the majority of kibbutzim to expansion, federation, and (later) industrialization.

The Zionist youth movements which had been influenced by Buber in their early days brought with them to Palestine a concept, derived ultimately from Hegel, which became central to their way of thought: the idea of self-realization.[7] Self-realization, in a sense common to many Hegelians, is achieved by "founding our function as an organ in the social organism." This leads to a life "spent in self-devoted service to mankind", which promotes "the common good" (Bradley 163; Green 274, 283, 323).

Clearly, this interpretation jibes well with the concept of *halutziut* expressed in the "metaphor of the dung". But a very easy semantic slide soon led to another interpretation: self-realization is not realization *of* oneself, but *by* oneself. In the practical historical circumstances of the inter-war period, it may seem that this difference was minor. But, in fact, it incorporates and emphasizes the differences of view which we have seen above, in the matters of work and *halutziut*. He who realizes himself plays his part in the redemption of the Zionist effort, and may devote all his life to a cause; but his motivation is in himself. The notion of "realizing by oneself" contains the moral imperative of practising what one preaches – or, at the least, what one believes in. Thus, the Zionist youth movements adopted the principle of *hovat hagshama* – literally "the duty of realization" – whose practical meaning was the demand that every graduate of the movement must immigrate to Palestine and join a kibbutz. Buber's view, on the other hand, is epitomized in the "Seer of Lublin's" remark, which he quotes approvingly: "It is impossible to tell men what way they should take [...] Everyone should carefully observe what way his heart draws him to, and then choose this way with all his strength" (Buber, *The Way of Man* 15). Unlike other philosophical doctrines, the notion of realizing by oneself permits – indeed, compels – an *argumentum ad hominem*. The *halutzim* who heard Buber's lectures on Zionism in Vienna during the First World War drew the conclusion that they themselves should put their Zionism into practice by emigrating to Palestine. Similarly, to be a Socialist implied personal participation in a society based on socialist principles. Buber stayed in Germany almost until the last possible minute; and, apart from a very

---

7   Hebrew: *Hagshama Atzmit*.

short period in the early years of the century, he never attempted to practise the communal life which he preached. Thus, in the eyes of his former disciples, he failed to practise not only the ideals of Socialist Zionism, but also his own principle of self-realization.[8]

Conclusions

Our first conclusion must be that Buber's portrait of the kibbutz is not faithful to the actions or intentions of the leaders and thinkers of the kibbutz itself. At the most, he has described one possible version of the kibbutz among many; perhaps even a version which has never actually existed. In his own words:

> I do not maintain that this type of communal life actually takes place in the settlements. Indeed, it is most likely that it does not take place in any one of them. But it is certainly there *in potentia*, and is actually developed, more or less, to a greater degree, in every one of them. (Buber, *Selected Writings* 181)

In other words, Buber is presenting an ideal version of the kibbutz, extrapolated from the actual kibbutz, but not necessarily representing the ideals and aspirations of the kibbutz members themselves.

Is this legitimate? If so, its justification must begin with Buber's own description of the kibbutz movement:

---

8   On Buber's connection with the kibbutz movement, see Gerson 80–3. Yassour (48–50, 60–7) emphasizes Buber's connections with certain leaders of the kibbutz movement, and his knowledge of some of the literature of the kibbutz. But both the testimony of Gerson, himself one of the main figures through whom Buber maintained his connection with the kibbutz, and Yassour's own criticism of Buber's selective interpretation of his reading (49–50), support my view, as does the oral testimony of many kibbutz members who met with Buber in his latter years: see A. Shapira 45–54.

> New forms and new intermediate forms were constantly branching off – in complete freedom. Each one grew out of the particular social and spiritual needs as these came to light [...] [thus, the kibbutz has become] an experimental station where, on common soil, different colonies or "cultures" are tested out according to different methods for a common purpose. (*Paths in Utopia* (1949), 145–6)

The kibbutz movement is a pluralist society which Buber's description fits to a very large extent. So could his ideal kibbutz not be one of the many "cultures" of which he speaks? There are two reasons why this will not do. The first is, of course, that Buber himself was never a part of the kibbutz movement. He did not work in the experimental station, but observed and reported on it from the outside. His "kibbutz" may be an acceptable human ideal. But we have given reasons for thinking that it is not the ideal of the kibbutz members themselves. And, unless it can be shown that it exists in the kibbutz movement itself – either in fact or as an ideal accepted by all or part of that movement – it is no more than an intellectual construction which cannot properly be called a kibbutz.

The second reason is connected with the nature of Buber's ideal. I have analysed the philosophy of the kibbutz into a number of elements, some approximating to Buber's ideal, other deviating from it. All of the elements I have enumerated – mutuality, mutual responsibility, work, communion, solidarity, democracy, equality, *halutziut* – exist in every real kibbutz. Kibbutz pluralism is the expression of different "mixes", variations in emphasis between these ever-present elements. Buber, on the other hand, underemphasizes elements (such as the concrete results of labour) which are a central part of all versions of kibbutz ideology; and in some cases he sees such elements as fundamentally opposed to his conception of the ideal kibbutz.

To conclude, it may be said that Buber's treatment of the kibbutz idea is similar to his method of dealing with the ideas of the many thinkers of whom he writes. In Susser's words,

> Buber consistently refrained from utopian constructions and detailed blueprints [...] [His] frame of intellectual history is highly schematic, subjective and at times impressionistic. His account of Utopian thought is an attempt to relive the birth, growth and maturation of the *essential* Utopian ideal [rather than] a history of Utopian activity or an account of the patterns of Utopian thought. (Susser 56, 70)

Precisely the same words could be applied to his account of kibbutz thought.

The experience of the past hundred years has led to a wide variety of attitudes, ideologies and value-systems within the kibbutz movement. But it appears that none of them coincide either with the actual kibbutz as supposedly described by Buber, or with the ideal kibbutz which he constructed. Specifically, both of these versions fail to emphasize the place of work, *halutziut*, and their results in kibbutz thought; give a superficial account of the varieties of solidarity; fail to recognize the value of non-religious communion; and ignore the elements of democracy, equality and self-realization. Thus, Buber does not provide a model for "the emergence of [...] a structurally new society". For, by his own argument, such a model must emerge from the "new forms and new intermediate forms" which arise in the attempt of each of these societal types "to propagate itself and spread and establish its proper sphere" (*Paths in Utopia* 145, 147–8). It must be not a Platonic – or a Buberian – idea of the kibbutz, but the kibbutz itself, with all its imperfections and in all its variety; in short, the place where community happens.

CHAPTER 4

Ben Gurion as Philosopher: Equality and Partnership

Towards the end of 1960 David Ben Gurion, then prime minister of Israel since his return from two years out of office at kibbutz Sdeh Boker, took part in a festive meeting of the governing body of his party, Mapai, to celebrate the fiftieth anniversary of the foundation of Degania, the first kibbutz. His lecture on this occasion met with much criticism from the leaders of the kibbutz movement, and he expanded his arguments in an article which appeared in March 1961. In a further set of articles he expounded his attitude to the nature and functions of the kibbutz, after a lifetime of acquaintance with kibbutzim and their leaders and thinkers, and two years of personal experience in Sdeh Boker.[1]

In the first article he claims that Degania came into existence, not as a result of its members' belief in their historical mission or any other ideological conviction, but "as a result of the inner logic of the fundamental value of labour". Only at a later stage

> The success of the farm managed by the workers paved the way to a second stage, revolutionary and creative: in the words of Joseph Bussel, "Not passive but active, not working according to the dictates of others, but the workers' creation and the workers' economy."

He remarked that a member of a *moshav* [smallholders' cooperative settlement] was also "not passive but active". In that case, he asked, what was special about the kibbutz? Most kibbutz members, he said, would say "Equality". But, although he did not deny that equality was a universal

---

[1] These articles, together with reactions culled from the Hebrew press, were collected and edited by Israel Bitman, and reprinted in *Hakibbutz* 9–10 (1984): 12–51. All the quotations in this chapter, unless marked otherwise, are from this source.

value, the equality envisioned by those who made the French Revolution was the equality of the citizen before the law. He supported this contention with some biblical quotations, and then turned to the kibbutz:

> The supreme social ideal is not isism,[2] but communism – not equality, but partnership. The highest and greatest embodiment of partnership is in the Israeli kibbutz. [...] the communist ideal, which does not exist in any [other] part of the world, undertakes to supply to each person according to his needs, and take from him according to his ability. This ideal is superior to equality; it is the most just of principles. There is no equality in nature. Men are not equal either in their physical powers or in their intellectual capacities [...] We should not lay all men down in a bed of Procrustes [...] And the kibbutz is based on partnership, maximum partnership in economic and social life.

Ben Gurion continues by elaborating on these two claims: that there is no equality in nature or in human society, and that the principle of partnership is of vital importance to the kibbutz and to all of mankind. He does not confine his remarks to the kibbutz.

> Partnership is not only a supreme pan-human principle – economic, social, national and international. It is a cosmic principle which embraces the whole world. [...] in infinite cosmic partnership there is no destruction and passing away, only continuous renewal and eternal joy [...] Man is part of his environment, and it exists within him. He absorbs his environment and is absorbed into it, and the environment includes nature and humankind, and not only the human beings who live at any given time, but those who have lived in the past and whose thoughts and actions still influence human society, as well as nature which is beyond humanity [...] Man is not alone, separated and differentiated from other men and the whole of nature. [He exists] within the great whole with its many manifestations, full of secrets and mysteries, and man seeks solutions, makes a tiny discovery and wonders at the dozens and dozens of secrets still unrevealed. For man is merged and interwoven into the cosmic web, which is also the divine web.

At this point, Ben Gurion returns to the subject of the people of Israel, who revealed cosmic partnership "when they believed in the unity of the Creator of All". Therefore, the people of Israel can be – potentially, if not

---

2   Isism: apparently an invention of Ben Gurion's, from the Greek ἴσος "equal".

actually at this time – a light to the gentiles. The people of Israel will reach its historic goal by reinforcing cooperation between past and future, between the people of Israel and the Jews of the Diaspora, between the State of Israel and every peace- and freedom-loving nation, between all workers, whether by hand or brain.

I am not primarily discussing the historical aspects of these articles, important though they may be, but the philosophy of equality and partnership. But one historical question is in order: why did he raise this question at this time, and at no other period in his life? Apart from matters connected with the two major political struggles he was waging at the time – against Mapam, the neo-Communist opposition party, and against Pinhas Lavon, who had been deposed from the leadership of the Labour Party and was seeking rehabilitation – it seems to have been the result of ways of thought typical not only of Ben Gurion but of wide sections of opinion in Israel at the time.

Many commentators have described the way in which the focal point of Ben Gurion's activities changed at different periods of his life: from Galilee to the central bodies of his party, from there to the Histadrut, thence to the Jewish Agency and, finally, to the State of Israel. It seems to me that at this period of his life there was a further movement: from Israel to the world. In these articles he presents the "theory of partnership" as a result of the aspiration to universality which characterizes the partnership between all parts of the cosmos, from the components of the atom to the furthest extent of the heavens, and comprises the human race with all its subdivisions and beliefs; and in this complex the State of Israel, and particularly the kibbutz and the *moshav*, have special significance, as "a light unto the Gentiles". In the specifically political field, too, he emphasized international activities, including those of the United Nations.

From the philosophical point of view, this universalistic tendency was most clearly expressed in these articles, with their link between Israeli and Jewish nationhood and the concept of social, religious and philosophical partnership. The theory of partnership bears clear indications of the influence of Far Eastern – Hindu and Buddhist – cosmology. Hence, I would venture another conjecture as to why this theory appeared at this specific time. In the years which preceded the appearance of the theory of partnership the diplomatic ties between Israel and Burma were strengthened, and a personal friendship between Ben Gurion and U Nu, the Prime Minister of Burma, was formed. A year later Ben Gurion travelled to Burma, with the object, among other things, of deepening his knowledge of Buddhism by a stay in a Buddhist monastery, and also in the hope of using the Burmese connection to forward the objective of peace with the Arab states. Thus, it may be that the "theory of partnership" was part of a two-edged political and intellectual strategy typical of Ben Gurion's way of acting.

It is also possible that he adopted these ideas as a result of intellectual curiosity, and his desire to apply different fields of thought – the Bible, Greek philosophy and more – to the practices of everyday life. Preoccupation with oriental thought was not unusual in the Israel of the 1950s, and a good many articles dealing with it appeared in the Hebrew press of the time. It could, in fact, be argued that all of Ben Gurion's "theory of partnership" was no more than a rhetorical elaboration of a few sentences written by one of his supporters in 1956:

> [We should aspire to] the transfer of the individual to levels of calm spirituality, less imbued with the delusion of individuality. [...] [not] to ignore personal desire, or repress it, but to reach the level of a different experience, less personal, more cooperative and collaborative. (Livneh 89–90)

All this is very largely speculative thinking. But I shall permit myself to add another speculation concerned with the application of Ben Gurion's thinking to kibbutz life. In December 1953 Ben Gurion had never been a member of a kibbutz or any other communal society. When he lived in Sdeh Boker, too, although he was formally a member of the kibbutz, he was certainly not an equal among equals. It is not unreasonable to suppose that this state of affairs influenced his views on kibbutz life. The claim that the kibbutz was based on partnership rather than on equality chimed well with his anomalous position. There is no proof of this, for he never referred to this subject again either in his published writings or in his diaries. But it seems to me that this is a not unlikely hypothesis.

The main question to be asked in this chapter, however, is whether Ben Gurion's theories were justified. Was (or is) "partnership" the central, perhaps the only, principle on which kibbutz life is, or should be, based? And what is the place of equality in the kibbutz?

First, it may be noted that on the question of equality Ben Gurion's views were much closer to mainstream kibbutz thought than appears at first sight, and undoubtedly than his critics considered them to be in 1960. In his words: "The ideal is [...] to give each person according to his needs [...] and to take from him according to his ability [...] we should not fit the whole of mankind into a Procrustean bed." In other words, he rejects the concept of "mechanical equality" as most kibbutz thinkers called it – mathematical equality – in favour of what was known as "organic equality", and is defined in these sentences. But his arguments in favour of this view did not seem particularly strong to his contemporaries, and seem even weaker today. For instance, he maintained: "There is no equality in nature [...] why should we all have black or blue eyes, be red-headed or blond, short or tall, stupid or orators?"

The argument from natural phenomena to moral principles is a serious philosophical mistake: ethical judgments do not deal with what exists, but with what should be, and to ignore the difference between them is a fundamental categorical error. His critics in the kibbutz movement did not fail to point this out.

In my view, however, despite his deficient logic, his basic claim was correct: what is often called kibbutz equality is not equality. In the life of the kibbutz – even of the privatized kibbutz – we apply both types of equality at the same time; and, despite the many questions concerning the place of each of them in our lives, it is not difficult to distinguish one from the other. Therefore, perhaps the difference between Ben Gurion's view and that accepted by most kibbutz thinkers is entirely semantic, and all that is required in order to settle the differences between them is careful formulation: whenever we speak of equality as defined in the *Concise Oxford Dictionary* – "the same in quantity, quality, size, degree, rank, level, etc." – we need to add the word "mechanical"; and when we mean "from each according to his ability, to each according to his needs" we should say "kibbutz equality". In that case, the controversy is, as many would say, purely semantic, and therefore unimportant.

I do not think so. In my view, the difference is both semantic and important, for the choice of a particular expression embodies tendencies and concepts not confined to the expression itself. If I say "The kibbutz is an egalitarian society", in ordinary speech this means that it practices, or aims to practice, equality in the dictionary sense. Any other usage alters the meaning of the word, creates a different language. But the average kibbutz member uses the Hebrew language in its accepted form: in his eyes, equality is similarity or identity between quantifiable things. Therefore, the use of this word encourages him to believe that kibbutz equality is mechanical equality; and anybody who has taken part in or been witness to a discussion of equality in the kibbutz knows that this is so. In other words, the use of the term "equality" as equivalent to "from each according to his ability [...]" obscures semantic distinctions which should, if anything, be more clearly defined.

In my view, if we want to call this principle by a single word, I would prefer "justice", or, perhaps more appropriately, "fairness". Ben Gurion chose a different word: "partnership". Two questions arise in this connection: first, Ben Gurion makes no attempt to prove that there is a necessary connection – philosophical or empirical – between "partnership" with its very broad connotations and "from each according [...]". And, judging from this particular text, it is hard to see what such a connection would be. Secondly, and of no less importance, if the whole universe, from the parts of the atom to the galaxies, partakes of cosmic partnership, what is special about kibbutz partnership? It adds nothing, and has no special moral value. The kibbutz is, indeed, part of a vast chain of being, but this does not distinguish it from any other link or collection of links in this chain.

None the less, despite the logical weakness of his arguments, I believe that Ben Gurion grasped one aspect of kibbutz life: that which I have described in chapter 1 of this book, and designated "the collective experience". I have there given reasons for scepticism with regard to the "worldsoul" to which, it seems, Ben Gurion believed that the collective experience was a portal. But most of my arguments there are of a philosophical sophistication which Ben Gurion never attained, and were first adduced long after his death. His views were far from uncommon in Israel and the world; and it seems that his acquaintance with the kibbutz, which was external even when he was living in Sdeh Boker, led him to see a truth about kibbutz life which, though lived and felt by the kibbutz members themselves, was not always emphasized in their ideological writings.

To sum up: in certain respects Ben Gurion's views cast light on aspects of kibbutz life and thought which are emphasized less by other kibbutz thinkers and leaders; but his philosophical conclusions are not always convincing after fifty years of consideration and research. His contention that "from each according to his ability, to each according to his needs" is not equality in the usual sense of that term is certainly acceptable; but the link between this view and "cosmic cooperation" is dubious, and in my view quite incorrect. As for the collective experience, Ben Gurion alludes to it – in general, obliquely – in these articles, but it is neither emphasized nor analysed sufficiently to be considered a significant contribution to kibbutz thought.

In short, as a philosopher Ben Gurion displayed originality of thought, but did not argue his thesis systematically or critically. As my teachers used to say of my schoolwork, he did not realize his full potential.

PART TWO

Utopianism and Post-Utopianism

CHAPTER 5

Utopian and Post-Utopian Thought: The Kibbutz Model

The Utopian Moment

Since the publication of Buber's *Paths in Utopia* in 1948 it has become almost a clichā to talk of the kibbutz as a utopian society. It has been described as a venture and an experiment in utopia, as an illustration of the utopian dilemma, as a utopia in crisis and at bay; and these are just a few examples among dozens (Spiro; Diamond; Kallen; Blasi).

I intend to ask whether, and under what circumstances, this terminology is appropriate, both in terms of certain classical definitions of Utopia, and, more especially, in terms of the beliefs and aspirations of kibbutz members – in particular, of the leaders and thinkers of the kibbutz movement. In my view, the kibbutz is best described not as a utopia, but as a post-utopian society. For while the original utopian visions of its founders have been altered and adapted, its members have adopted various conceptual strategies in order to retain the utopian element in their thought. In this chapter these changes and strategies will be described and analysed; and, in conclusion, it will be argued that they are examples, *in parvo*, of post-utopian thought in general. Thus, the experience and philosophy of the kibbutz, an outstanding example of "applied utopistics" (Manuel & Manuel 12) may serve as a guide to the understanding and critique of utopianism as a mode of social thought.

Although examples will be adduced from most periods of the history of the kibbutz, most will be drawn from the formative period of the kibbutz movement, from its earliest days until the mid-1930s. This period is particularly important both because of its influence on the crystallisation of kibbutz life and thought and because of the variety, scope, and originality of the ideas about the nature of the kibbutz and its place in society which were discussed during this time.

The use of utopian terminology with respect to the kibbutz clearly stems in very large part from Buber. Buber's own work on the subject was done in a very specific context, and for a clearly defined purpose: his defence of "utopian" socialism against the then dominant Marxist social philosophy. But both Marx's and Buber's use of the word "utopian" form part of a long and varied intellectual development, starting, of course, with More himself.

More's Utopia had three basic characteristics, from each of which stemmed a separate ideological and semantic tradition. It was imaginary: it was thought to be a perfect society, free from the flaws which existed in the real world, as More and his readers knew it: and its social organisation was clearly defined, and described in considerable detail. The first of these characteristics led to the equation of "utopian" and "imaginary, fantastic, impracticable" – usually in a negative sense. The second – the perfection of utopian society – generated the semantic tradition which applies the word to any attempt to create a conceptual model of the perfect society. Mannheim is, of course, in the centre of this tradition; and Kateb carried it to an extreme in defining as utopian any attempt to make far-reaching improvements on the social system (Mannheim; Kateb). Since the utopian vision, in this version, is applied to society as a whole – sometimes, indeed to a whole world or even a universe – I shall call it a "macro-utopia". It differs radically from the various "micro-utopias" which derive directly from More in that their systems of social organisation are described clearly and in detail, and the utopian society is small, and has relatively few inhabitants. Thus, a utopia of this sort can serve as a model for other forms of society, on the basis not only of the values and ideals which motivate its citizens or their leaders, but of the structure of its institutions, and the way of life of its inhabitants. Buber and others adduce the kibbutz as a central example of a "micro-utopia" in this sense.

Although there may be borderline cases between these two categories, it seems almost self-evident that the distinction between micro- and macro-utopias is of fundamental importance, particularly from the point of view of "practical utopistics". Nonetheless, virtually all analysts of utopian thought have ignored it; and when Kateb did draw attention to it, it was mainly in order to dismiss summarily the relevance of micro-utopian communities to what he saw as the prime concern of utopian thought in general – the remaking of the whole world in a new image (Kateb 12–13, 201–2). Moreover, virtually, all the anti-utopian arguments in his chapter on "attaining utopia" apply to macro-utopian theories. The legitimation of micro-utopianism would have made his counter-arguments very much more plausible.

The kibbutz was a utopia in all these three senses before it even existed. Many of the founding fathers of the kibbutz movement arrived in Palestine determined to build a society based on what one of them, Joseph Trumpeldor, called "communist settlement – a stretch of solid ground in the morass, an oasis in the desert" (Gadon 119). He and his friends drew up a blue-print for such settlements, and in 1913 founded a short-lived commune at Migdal, by the Sea of Galilee, based on these principles. The four central members of the group which in 1911 became Degania, the first kibbutz, belonged to a movement which believed in Zionist settlement "by communal means" (Gadon 27), and declared themselves a commune when they left Russian soil on their way to Palestine.

Thus, the founders of the kibbutz had a dual utopian vision: a Zionist vision of Jewish independence and creativity, and a communalist vision, of a society composed of small working communities based on equality and cooperation. And, even before the establishment of the first kibbutz, there existed a conceptual utopia – utopian in all three of the senses defined above – which was the model for the establishment of the real kibbutz.

Nor was this phenomenon confined to the earliest years of the century alone. At the very time when the kibbutz itself was in the first, hesitant stages of its existence, there were springing up in Europe groups of young Jews who created for themselves a conceptual Zionist and Socialist utopia not unlike that of the earliest kibbutz members. Although many of these groups had no broad organizational affiliations, perhaps the prime example is in the Hashomer Hatza'ir youth movement. The first group of graduates of this movement, who arrived in Palestine in 1919, had created, long before they set sail, a very special, even idiosyncratic, world outlook, designed to resolve the problems of the young, semi-assimilated, intellectual Jew rejected by non-Jewish society and repelled by what he saw as the false values of bourgeois Jewry – including his own family and his immediate social milieu.

The youth movement provided an opportunity to build an alternative value-system; and, immigrating to Palestine as a group, its members were able to attempt to put these values – cooperation, equality, love of nature, independence, and simplicity – into practice. When they developed their social ideology they had very little exact knowledge of what was actually going on in Palestine; and when they arrived, they reacted with suspicion, and even hostility, to the attempts of other groups to build a kibbutz movement founded on ideas not very far removed from their own vision of an ideal society.

No wonder, then, that in this early period they evolved a way of life and utopian thought which were in large measure isolated from the realities of life in the Jewish community of Palestine at the time. Their thought and writing at this time were clearly a continuation of the utopian ideology of the youth movement. They saw the realities of life in Palestine in the light of the vision which they brought with them from the Diaspora (Margalit 79–103).

Nor did the translation of the kibbutz from the sphere of the imaginary to that of the actual put an end to this sort of utopian thought. From the earliest years of its existence, the kibbutz became a focus for utopian longings, and utopian social constructs, which bore only a minimal resemblance to the kibbutz itself. The classical breeding-ground for this form of utopianism was and is the Zionist youth movement. Here is an extract from a description of this process at its most typical, as seen by one of the educators of the Zionist youth movement in Galicia, Poland, at the end of the 1920s:

> Instinctively, we grasped a way out of our difficulties: the kibbutz. I do not know to what extent the kibbutz in Palestine influenced us. In point of fact, we had scarcely heard of it, and its image appeared to us mistily, from afar, separated from us by the barrier of distance. We knew virtually nothing of the different types of kibbutzim. We were motivated by the desire to create new forms of life, to foster better relationships between man and man. Our ideology was very shallow, and we made no real

attempt to give it a deeper and more solid basis. Our ideas were founded more on longing than on logic. We knew of the existence of different kibbutzim and kibbutz movements, but there was no feeling of continuity, or that we should draw concrete conclusions from this fact and join these kibbutzim. (Shtok 156)

This passage exemplifies the way in which the utopian imagination used the existence of the kibbutz as a starting-point for independent utopian thought, whose results could be very different from the beliefs or situation of those who created the real kibbutz, and continued to live in it.

This phenomenon was not confined to the early years of the kibbutz movement, when very little was known outside Palestine of the reality of kibbutz life. The experience of Hashomer Hatza'ir between 1917 and 1920, and of Hechalutz in the early 1920s, was repeated almost a decade later in the Gordonia youth movement in Eastern Europe. Between 1927 and 1930, the founders of this movement built an ideal concept of communal utopia which expressed their own national and social aspirations. They derived their knowledge of the realities of Palestine from the Zionist press, meetings with youth movement emissaries, and other sources – limited and tendentious, but far more detailed than those available to the other movements discussed above. They called their ideal social construct "the *kvutza*".[1] When they came into contact with the real *kvutza*, in the early 1930s they suddenly realized that there was a very wide gap between their idealized concept and the real *kvutza* – including the current utopian ideas of its actual members. It appears, in fact, that the use of the existence of the kibbutz as a starting-point for independent utopian thought (and even fantasy) is not the result of particular historical or geographical circumstances, such as the lack of knowledge of kibbutz life at a particular time, or physical separation from the reality of kibbutz society. It appears again and again in youth movements in Israel (or Palestine) and in the Diaspora,

---

1 *Kvutza*, the original name for what came to be called the kibbutz, was used at this period to mean a small, "intimate" kibbutz, which limited its membership and was opposed to industrialization, on ideological grounds. In this chapter the words are transliterated from the original; but only in a few instances – as here – is the difference between *kvutza* and *kibbutz* significant for our present purpose.

even among young people who have spent some time on the kibbutz. It seems to be a function of age and socio-psychological development rather than of any objective historical or physical factor.

This phenomenon is well known among those who work, or have worked, with youth movements in Israel and in the Jewish communities of the Diaspora; but, as far as I know, it has not been documented, or even reliably reported in journalistic form, as a contemporary phenomenon. Perhaps I may adduce as uncorroborated evidence my own experience, and that of several members of my own kibbutz who have worked with Zionist youth movements in the UK and the US, and with the Israeli Scout Movement, and have seen many generations of young people build their own concept of kibbutz life, which is often significantly different from the real kibbutz as described to them, or even experienced by them.

The kibbutz becomes a micro-utopia. therefore, in two different cases: the first, before the foundation and crystallisation of the kibbutz in reality; and the second, at a distance from the real kibbutz, when the connection with it is comparatively weak and sporadic, and the dominant aim of utopian thought is not the desire to copy a specific existing, supposedly perfect society, but to build an alternative society in place of that surrounding the young utopians – a reality which rejects them and which they reject.

Post-utopianism begins when these ideas and ideals are translated into reality. But not immediately. If, in the circumstances I have described, the kibbutz is a conceptual utopia, they lead, in the historical process, to the attempt to build a utopia in the real world. At least for a while, the kibbutz is utopia.

The Utopian Moment – and After

There is ample evidence of the feeling of liberation and satisfaction felt by the founders of the early kibbutzim in their foundation period. It had been proved that the creation of a "new society" was possible and desirable: the utopia was being realized. Here is one example among many. One of the founders of Degania, the first kibbutz, describes a conversation with Joseph Bussel, the leader and ideologue of the *kvutza* in its earliest days:

> Listen, Tanhum, do you realize where we're sitting now? We're sitting on a heap of sheaves which we sowed with our own hands, reaped with our own hands, and brought to the threshing-floor by ourselves. It's not only that we're here on the banks of the Jordan, by the Sea of Galilee, part of a group of people bound close to each other in heart and soul. Not only that this pile of wheat which we're sitting on, the fruit of our own labours, will be divided up equally between us, all the workers, no one will get any more than his fellows. Do you understand? This work is bound up with great and elevated ideals for the whole of the world, and in particular for the Jewish people. These ideals are bringing us to the realization of Socialism. Work is the only way of salvation for the nation and for mankind. Here, on this threshing floor, are the seeds of the vision of justice and righteousness. (Tanpilov 2)

There is, of course, no certainty that Bussel's words were quoted exactly. But there can equally be no doubt of the authenticity of the experience, the feeling of a new and successful beginning. The vision had become reality — and a desirable reality. These young men and women saw the fruit of their labour, and said, "Behold, it is good". In another description of the same period, the kibbutz in its early days is referred to explicitly as "a sort of utopia, a [...] sublime portrait of the society of the future, and of socialist man". Despite the physical and mental suffering endured by early settlers, "how very special were those days, how precious and luminous" (Smetterling 8–9).

In short: at the utopian moment it was good to be alive. And, bearing in mind the age of these founding fathers, and of succeeding generations who underwent the same experience of utopia realized – virtually all of them below the age of twenty-one – cannot forebear to add "to be young was very heaven".

Utopia, then, was realized. But not for long. In some cases the equation kibbutz = utopia seemed to hold good for several years: in others the dream began to change or dissolve after a few months. And at this point, the kibbutz stops being utopia, and becomes a post-utopian society.

What went wrong? There are four major ways in which the utopian reality becomes, or is seen to be, less perfect than in the first flush of its realisation.

a) Faulty execution. The kibbutz members are unable to put their preconceived ideals into practice. Despite earlier appearances, the utopia is perceived to be unrealized – perhaps unrealizable. In Trumpeldor's group in Migdal "quarrels broke out between the women. It was our first disillusionment with human nature" (Tsirkin 366). The degrees of disillusion and the conclusions drawn from it can vary greatly. But the first phase is over. The kibbutz is no longer seen as a utopia in the naive sense of the pristine utopian moment.

b) Change in the kibbutz itself (for instance, with the birth of the first children), in the surrounding world, or in both – as in the case of technological innovations which destroyed the idyllic rural existence of the first decade of the kibbutz.

> The tractor's clamour in the fields is enough to banish any "superfluous" thoughts from one's mind. The same applies to the noise in the dining-room, the radio and so forth. Things were different in the beginning, when we followed the plough, and turned the soil, and the horses trod a straight furrow – then all kinds of thoughts would come to mind, then there was room for emotion. (*Tanhum* 88)

c) Conflicts and tensions between different aspects of the utopian model, which only become apparent in the course of time: for instance, between economic progress and the original naive conceptions of complete equality and job rotation.

d) Differences of approach between members which existed only in latent form in the period of utopian harmony. Some of these even led to the break-up of kibbutzim and kibbutz movements. In less extreme cases there was constant tension, as a result both of personality clashes and of different concepts of what the kibbutz should be and do.

Cognitive Dissonance

In each of these cases, the members underwent a process of cognitive dissonance, the social and psychological consequences of which are very similar to those described by Leon Festinger in his classic work *When Prophecy Fails*.

Festinger describes the adventures of a small cult who called themselves The Seekers. These people believed that they were receiving messages from outer space, and that on a certain day they would be visited by a space-ship, which would rescue them from the flood about to cover the whole of America. This was, therefore, not a utopian, but a "UFOpian", community.

Like the early kibbutzniks, the Seekers went through a period of utopia – in their case, prophecy – achieved, when they succeeded in deciphering extra-terrestrial messages, and began to receive orders to prepare for the great day. But, even after the fiasco of 20 December, when they waited in vain on a cold hill-top for the space-ship to arrive, the failure of prophecy led not to a loss of faith, but to its strengthening: the calculations were wrong, the code was misinterpreted, and so forth. And even after it had become clear that they had been gravely mistaken, the two central figures in the Seekers group continued to believe that they had achieved the gift of prophecy: one carried on spreading the news of a future engulfment and rescue, and "seemed to be expecting some future action or orders from outer space", while the other became an itinerant preacher, and "spread the teachings of the Guardians across the land". They believed firmly in the utopia of the past.

Some of them adopted the stratagem of utopia deferred. A series of disappointed predictions led to constant postponements of the promised day; and when this was finally decided on, and the saucers failed to materialize, the central figures in the group continued to proselytize, firm in their belief in the utopia of the future. In Festinger's words, "floundering, increasingly disoriented as prediction after prediction failed, they cast about for clues [...] in a desperate attempt to discover a clearly defined next step on the path to salvation by saucer" (Festinger 215).

They also propounded a concept close to that of present utopia. Though beset with doubts – not about the belief that they were receiving messages from outer space, but about their interpretations of these messages – the Seekers engaged in constant controversy with other UFOpians, seeking to show that they were nearer to the truth than any other group or prophet.

And finally, utopia – or prophecy – revised. The leading group of the Seekers did not take this path; for them, their specific belief-system was so deeply rooted that it survived the most cruel of disappointments. But some of the less prominent members do seem to have remodelled their beliefs, and looked forward to a new, revised utopia: one, for instance, reinterpreted her UFOpian beliefs in terms of a second coming of Jesus. And this stage is of great importance in other cases of cognitive dissonance discussed by Festinger – for instance, the Sabbataean movement.

There are striking parallels to these modes of thought in post-utopian kibbutz thinking.

a) The most frequent result of the perception of flaws in the supposed utopia was disillusionment with the kibbutz idea as such. The member, or candidate member, simply left the kibbutz. Although people have left the kibbutz throughout its history, this phenomenon was particularly severe in the period from about 1919 to 1924 – a time when many of the early kibbutzim were passing through a transitional phase from the pristine utopia to their post-utopian period. Smetterling, in referring to this change, linked the "idealization [of the kibbutz] which was once common" with "the large numbers who left" at that time (9).

In Trumpeldor's group at Migdal, "as a result of the spiritual hardships, and the complex relationships between members of such a small group, one of the youngest and most devoted members put an end to his life" (Tsirkin 364). This reaction was far from unknown in this period among young people whose commitment to their new way of life could make disillusionment literally unbearable. Though more extreme in the psychological sense, it is logically no different from the abandonment of the kibbutz by the individual member. In the case of Migdal, the suicide led to the break-up of the group; and in parallel cases, it happened not infrequently that the number or social importance of those who left was so important as to destroy a particular group.

b) This process of individual disillusionment had its parallel in the collective dimension. There are a number of examples of the abandonment of the utopian dream by whole kibbutzim. In such a case the group might see no further purpose in its continued existence, and simply break up; but there were cases in which collective groups continued to exist as purely economic partnerships, with no special ideology, and no connection with the kibbutz movement. Most of them also left the labour movement altogether, and not a few abandoned Zionism.

c) In a third variation of the abandonment of utopia, the individual remains in the kibbutz, but finds himself alienated from the values of the society in which he lives. Historically, there has been more than one situation in which Eliezer Liebenstein (Livneh)'s words, written in 1927, might apply: "We have among us members who have long since broken off all real connection with the community, and with kibbutz life in general" (Liebenstein, "To the Comrades" 1).[2] And in all periods there have been similar phenomena on the level of the individual; the kibbutz member ceases to believe in the principles of the kibbutz, but, for a variety of reasons – marital or family circumstances, economic or psychological difficulties, health problems, etc. – he exercises his formal right to remain a member of a society whose values he rejects. This is the kibbutz equivalent of "internal emigration" in the Communist totalitarian countries; and, while the motivations and pressures at work

---

2 This refers to a group of veteran members who would have liked to turn kibbutz Ein Harod into a *moshav*. Failing to gain sufficient support for this idea, they eventually left to found *moshav* Kfar Vitkin; but there was a long interim period when they were formally members of the kibbutz, living and working in Ein Harod. A similar incident occurred in Tel Yosef in 1929.

are very different, its results can be no less serious, for individual and community alike.

Thus, we may add a further variation to those we have already described. Before it existed, and in places where it was relatively unknown, the kibbutz has been a conceptual utopia. In the earliest period of its existence it has been (and, indeed, is, for the first members of any new kibbutz frequently undergo very similar experiences) an actualized utopia. And in the eyes of many of its former members, and some who remain part of kibbutz society, it is a dystopia.

All of these variations are interesting in themselves, and each of them has important implications for the kibbutz. But they are not in the mainstream of kibbutz life and thought. For, while the majority of kibbutz members were well aware of the failings as well as the achievements of the society they had created, they remained inveterate utopians. And so, after the initial period of pristine harmony, the kibbutz became – and, in large part, is today – a post-utopian society, in which the utopian vision was not abandoned, but adapted to the changing circumstances of the time and the changing consciousness of the kibbutz community.

This adaptation took three main forms, parallel to those which Festinger described in his account of the Seekers.

The Past as Utopia

In 1951, one of the founders of Degania said:

> Sometimes one can eat something particularly tasty, and its taste stays in the mouth for a very long time, and one uses it as the measure of everything else that one eats. Forty years have passed, and I still have the taste of the beginning of Degania. Ever since then I have compared the present with those days, and used them as my standard. (*Tanhum* 88)

It is not difficult to find examples in the kibbutz movement today of similar attitudes to the distant past. Not infrequently, the memory refines and purifies the historical facts. Indeed, the earliest examples of glorification of the past occur very early in the history of the kibbutz. In 1920, Joseph Baratz spoke of

> the ideal life in Um-Juni[3] in the early days of Degania. Here for the first time was created the idea of self-labour and communal living. If we have carried on in Degania for ten years, it was with the help of our beautiful past in Um-Juni. (Baratz, J. 4)

Historians of the kibbutz movement have written of the seminal effect of the short time – less than a year – spent by the first immigrants of the Hashomer Hatza'ir youth movement in Beitania, above the Jordan Valley, in 1920/1. Three years later Meir Ya'ari, the acknowledged leader of the movement, said:

> Beitania was the fountainhead of our communal life. It was the focal point from which broke forth with immense power all those forces which have saved – and are still saving – our people from sinking in the petty affairs of every day, which prevent their consciences from growing blunt. Beitania gave our kibbutzim their spiritual character. (Ya'ari, "Letters" 21)

In 1951 the American anthropologist Melford Spiro interviewed some of the veteran members of Kibbutz Beit Alpha, and was told that Beitania was still a focal experience in their lives, an example of communal life which they had used as a touchstone of kibbutz life throughout all the ensuing years (Spiro 51–9).

This tendency, to see the earliest years of a particular kibbutz as a utopian period, is widespread in the ideological and historical literature of the kibbutz. A myth of the "golden age" of the kibbutz was created: an age in which the principles of the kibbutz were practiced in full, a period which gave meaning and shape to what came after; and what came after was seen, with various degrees of concern, as a process of decline, or even degeneration.

---

3   The original name of the site later known as Degania.

It is not always possible to test the historical accuracy of the later descriptions of these seminal periods in the life of the kibbutz. But in several cases, and particularly that of Beitania, there are contemporary documents and historical witnesses which attest to internal tensions and qualms, as opposed to the spiritual harmony and completeness which reigned according to the accepted myth. It would appear that, as the original experience receded in time, the doubts and failures which are part of any human enterprise tend to be forgotten. It is, therefore, no exaggeration to call this strategy "the idealisation of the past".

The Present as Utopia

"The *kvutza* needs no artificial idealization" wrote Smetterling in 1930. "Its social, economic, and cultural achievements speak for themselves". In effect, this approach is a continuation of the earliest period of kibbutz history, that of the realization of the utopian dream. The kibbutz is presented as an alternative society – and therefore, in its most important aspects, as fitting the utopian model. In a meeting of representatives of the kibbutzim in 1923, a year of crisis for the whole of the Labour Zionist movement, when the very existence of the kibbutz seemed uncertain, two of the women who were among the founders of Degania expressed themselves in the most extreme terms. Hayuta Bussel said: "People talk about suffering in the *kvutza*. I would like to ask 'Where on earth is life easier?'" (Katznelson, *The Kvutza* 27). Miriam Baratz added: "In my opinion, the *kvutza* has already created a large element of perfection in our lives [...] I have heard the saying, 'In the *kvutza*, nobody can be bad.'" (Ibid.) Five years later, in a discussion on the state of affairs in kibbutz Ein Harod, Hillel Dan explained that the reasons advanced by those leaving the kibbutz were not valid. "The kibbutz gives its member food, accommodation, social life. [...] I don't know who can give more" (Kibbutz Me'uhad Central Committee 615). A year later Yitzhak Tabenkin, the acknowledged leader of the biggest kibbutz movement of the time, said:

> In material terms, the individual in the kibbutz is in a better state than anybody else in the country. Those who leave the kibbutz do not give their true reasons. [...] What do they get in place of kibbutz life? [...] Dubious entertainment in town, cheap films, and so forth. (*Kibbutz Me'uhad Anthology* 150)

These are but two of many similar remarks made at a time when the material standard of life in town was definitely higher than that in the kibbutz, whether it is measured by the numbers who "voted with their feet" and left the kibbutz, or by objective economic standards.

The common assumption of all these arguments is that the kibbutz is indeed "another society", better than that surrounding it – and that it is, therefore, an ideal society, or an approximation to one. Just as the original utopian vision sprang from the negation of existing society, so in these instances, and others, the standard for judging the kibbutz is its superiority to the outside world. It is in comparison with these surroundings that the kibbutz is presented as an ideal society, sometimes, in fact, to an exaggerated degree, by ignoring the realities of life in the kibbutz itself. In Mannheim's terms, utopia becomes ideology.

The Future as Utopia

If neither the present nor the past is idealized, the achievement of utopia may be postponed to the future. In 1921 Shlomo Lavi, later one of the founders of Kibbutz Ein Harod, had laid the intellectual foundations of the modern kibbutz: an expanding society with a diversified economy and social composition, as distinct from the earliest kibbutzim, which were selective in their membership and based on agriculture alone.

All of Lavi's public life from then on was a struggle to realize this utopia; a struggle which never succeeded, as Lavi understood success – even though, as has been said, his model was, in effect, the basis of the modern kibbutz. In 1925 he said:

> Where is the man – if he is truly a man – who does not desire salvation [...] Our struggle must be to restructure society, to conquer the whole of society by example, by the example of rich economic and cultural life ... in an expanding kibbutz, which will encompass as much as possible [...] land, fields, human skills, and every variation of the capacities of the human being. We must conquer everything, everything that is human and natural – even nature itself – on our way to our new society. (Lavi, "Four Years" 336)

Utopia ("salvation", in Lavi's terms) would be brought about by the extension and improvement of the existing framework of the kibbutz. It had not yet arrived; and, indeed, throughout Lavi's very long life he emphasized the imperfection of any form of kibbutz life which did not correspond exactly to his ideal. In this case, and in many others, the future utopia has the concrete form of a well-defined social model. It will be very hard to put these ideas into practice: the flesh is weak, objective conditions are hard, and the society around is hostile. But the blueprint exists. Utopia is defined as a society which corresponds to this model; and, in principle, despite all difficulties, it is possible to build such a utopia.

Side by side with this approach, there appeared at a very early stage in the development of kibbutz thought an alternative concept of the future utopia. Here is an extract from a discussion in 1923:

> When the kibbutz was still only an aspiration. we imagined our future life in simple and beautiful terms. From a distance, kibbutz life seemed to be one part of a lovely and perfect life, of light without shade, an idyll. Only after some years of life in the kibbutz do we begin to realize how long is the road to the life of the true kibbutz, and how full it is of stumbling-blocks which are the result of human nature, and of the tradition of generations – a tradition on which we were educated and in which we grew to adulthood. (Joshua 71)

Utopia will be achieved, not by improving the framework of the kibbutz, but by improving man. A little later, another commentator wrote:

> The "intimate *kvutza*" was the first slogan. It was the first naive expression of the men of the *kvutza* – young and inexperienced as they were. [...] This slogan was based

> on the idea that man is fundamentally good and deserving of friendship [...] it was a sort of utopia, an elevated picture of the society of the future, and of socialist man [...] the concept of the intimate *kvutza* embraces a belief in "self-education" and its ability to achieve a perfect (scheme of) social values. (Smetterling 8)

The expression "self-education" was very widely used by the members of the first kibbutzim. Joseph Bussel, the leader of Degania, said: "We are children of the market-place, and it is hard for us to cast off at once the remnants of our former life." The object of self-education was precisely this – to purify the kibbutz members of the traces of their capitalist past. When this aim was achieved – and the organizational framework of the kibbutz was a necessary condition of its fulfilment – utopia would be realized.

Bussel's contention, that the members of the kibbutz were contaminated by the habits of capitalist society, recurred quite often in kibbutz thought in the early 1920s. It raises a very awkward question: whether this, the first generation of kibbutz members, is capable of purifying itself of these psychological blemishes.

> It may be that, although we have given up our visible possessions and dedicated them to the *kvutza*, nonetheless, in our heart of hearts, deep within us, there are still considerable remnants hidden from our comrades' eyes, and they dominate us despite our conscious will. It is they which call the world of the *kvutza* in question. (Wurm 240)

Realization of the dream was frequently postponed until a generation – even many generations – would have come to maturity within the kibbutz. But even this solution seemed less certain as time went on.

> When we saw our first children in the babies' playpen hitting one another, and even grabbing toys for themselves – we were seized by fear. "In that case" we said, "being educated in a communal society is not enough to uproot all traces of egoism." So, little by little, our original utopian social concepts were destroyed. (Smetterling 9)

Instead. another concept of the kibbutz utopia gradually took shape: "The *kvutza* of today is only the first step on the ladder to the society of the future. The top of the ladder is in the heavens – the perfection of man. And the number of rungs is *infinite* [my emphasis] (Smetterling 27). Here, Utopia is an ideal type, an aspiration which can never be realized completely: not because of the physical and intellectual difficulties in the way of its attainment, and not because of the hostility of the environment, but because of the imperfection immanent in human nature. In this way, the *kvutza*, which, Smetterling says, is "the most fascinating of social laboratories" gives an answer to Thomas More's puzzle. Like More, Smetterling does not believe that men will be perfect "these many years" (or, in fact, ever). But this does not detract from their duty, and their right, to strive for the good society and the good man within it.

What can we learn from all this?

First, a historical assessment. In the kibbutz today there exists a wide variety of cultural elements, political views and groupings, and ideological viewpoints: among them, all the post-utopian attitudes described above. In one widely accepted view, this situation is contrasted with earlier periods, when a monolithic ideology determined the structure and *modus operandi* of the kibbutz community. In many of its versions, this view approximates to the "golden age" variety of post-utopian thought described above. Simply to describe the ideological varieties of the kibbutz in its first two decades is to correct this one-sided view. Virtually from its very inception, kibbutz thought was varied and flexible.

The second conclusion concerns the persistence of utopianism. There is ample evidence to show that the abandonment of utopian thinking means the abandonment of the kibbutz. The individual who takes to thinking in purely pragmatic terms cannot – more correctly, will not – play a full part in the complex process of decision-making which maintains kibbutz society. He will leave the kibbutz, or remain a member, but in a state of alienation from the society to which he formally belongs. Equally, while there is a wide-ranging discussion within the kibbutz movement about the characteristics of the ideal society and the way to achieve it, no kibbutz thinker would deny the possibility or desirability of defining this ideal. "Without vision, the people will perish" says a passage in the Book of Proverbs, much quoted by kibbutz ideologists. There is a sense in which this is the beginning of kibbutz wisdom.

Thus, in the case of the kibbutz, the cognitive dissonance which results from the perception that the utopian moment is, at least in part, an illusion, leads to a variety of attitudes very similar to those described by Festinger. But, both in the classical theory of cognitive dissonance, and in the real historical development of the kibbutz, there is room for many variations within and alongside these categories. In this context, description alone is not sufficient for the practical utopist. There follow, therefore, some critical comments on the various modes of utopistic thinking and practice in the kibbutz.

Post-Utopian Thinking Evaluated

The Past as Utopia

The "golden age" view is clearly deficient as a guide to present-day aims and action. Not only is it intrinsically defeasible as the tools of critical history are increasingly focussed on the kibbutz movement, including its "heroic age". It is also psychologically self-defeating. Members of the first generation can find a certain satisfaction and justification in presenting their pristine creation as unblemished; but they can scarcely fail to be discouraged by the contrast between their past successes and the current, far from perfect, reality. Moreover, this approach may well give succeeding generations a feeling of frustration and even cynicism. For, if it was possible to reach perfection only in the very special circumstances of the early days of the kibbutz (and by the superhuman efforts of the founding generation, who are frequently thought of as an outstanding group of men), what is the point of their less gifted successors' trying to reproduce the same values in completely different circumstances?

But there is another sense of the word "idealization", a sense which is exemplified in some of the passages quoted above, no less than the more usual application of the term. In these instances, the early period of the kibbutz informed and crystallized a world-outlook which gave meaning and direction to the life of the individual and the community for many years after it was over. In this sense of idealization, the platonic origin of the term is dominant: the early kibbutz is not seen as a golden age, compared with which all that comes after is decline and degeneration, but as the embodiment of an idea which convinces all those who come into contact with it of its supreme worth. All the succeeding stages of kibbutz life are of value to the extent that they resemble the original. This is the logic of the "taste" of Degania in its early days, and the power of Beitania. In describing the utopian past as an ideal society rather than a perfect one, therefore, it is presented not as a magnificent but inimitable episode, but as an example worthy of imitation – and which can indeed be imitated in certain essential respects.

During the 1970s there grew up a group of young thinkers and educators in the kibbutz movement who tended to idealize the past in precisely this sense: to present the founders of the kibbutz not as heroes, but as creative thinkers and workers, whose lives and achievements are worthy of study – warts and all. The kibbutz past was seen, not as an ideal state of affairs, but as an educational ideal. One of the most talented and influential exponents of this point of view, Muki Tsur, has written in the course of an article entitled "In Every Generation":

> We were slaves, and the children ask questions. They do not give up [...] One must believe that the Exodus will indeed come. Even though it has already taken place. Even though it cannot return. It will come in another way. In every generation. (Tsur, *Doing It the Hard Way* 23–4)[4]

However, even this modified version of the utopian past is not without its problems. It deals with one of the causes of the end of utopia – failure in execution – by denying it. But something must have gone wrong, or the kibbutz would still be in its original utopian state. What guarantee is there, then, that the same will not happen again? And, in a more fundamental sense,

---

4 The title and symbolism of this passage are taken from the Passover Haggada, the text read by Jews on the eve of Passover, in which the exodus from Egypt is recalled: in every generation, each Jew must feel as if he himself took part in the Exodus.

what are the criteria for deciding whether, in the changed circumstances of today, the reality corresponds to the "idea of the kibbutz"?

One instance will serve to illustrate this. The question of size has always been crucial in discussions of the kibbutz utopia. One of the major differences between the Degania whose "taste" remained with Tanhum Tanpilov all his life and the Degania of today is the steady growth in the size of the population considered necessary and desirable.[5] Surely there is a difference in quality between the intensive social interaction that takes place in a small face-to-face group and that which characterizes a community of two hundred and more. In what sense, then, can Degania of today have the "taste" of the Degania of 1912? Clearly, there are some common characteristics: mutual trust, social equality, mutual aid, and others. But these are personal and social values rather than characteristics of a particular time or place. They are, therefore, logically prior to the actual existence of the pristine Degania; had they not been part of Tanpilov's scheme of values in 1912, he would not have realized that he was in utopia (Cf. Kant II 408–10). As has been said, they also preceded the actual kibbutz chronologically; but this is not essential for the present argument.

The relevant question about the contemporary kibbutz is, then, not whether it is like the pristine Degania, but whether its members live in accordance with the values of Degania in its earliest days. And this is a question which it was appropriate to ask, and which was in fact asked, in Degania seventy years ago. Thus, if the utopian vision is not simply a generalized social critique or *Weltanschauung*, but a defined social structure, it is unlikely that the early kibbutz can be a Platonic model for the later, more complex and sophisticated community. And if it is used as such a model, the result will probably be the victory of the "golden age" doctrine.

On the other hand, there can be no doubt of the authenticity and power of the experience of "utopia achieved". It seems that communal

---

5   In 1919, when the members of Degania numbered 38, they decided that their final aim was to comprise no more than 60 members, and voluntarily relinquished two thirds of their land in order not to strain these limited manpower resources. Today Degania has 240 members.

experiences of this sort can effect a transvaluation of values for those who undergo them. An ideological or ethical predisposition for such an experience will make one more likely to occur, or more effective when it does; but it is not essential. The central factor in the creation of the new set of values is personal experience; an experience which, in the case of the kibbutz, is shared by the whole group. In this sense, therefore, the early utopian period of the kibbutz can be called an ideal society in the Platonic sense, but only for those who actually lived through it.

The return to the early days of the kibbutz can be a source of cultural continuity and psychological identification. It may also encourage later generations to re-enact the experiences of the founders of the kibbutz, and thereby construct their own value system on the basis of a similar experience. But it is not a substitute for such experience. Utopia cannot be lived vicariously.

The Present as Utopia

Utopia is both a perfect society, and different from (indeed, the negation of) those which exist in the real world. These definitions are not equivalent. In the literary utopias, this fact is not emphasized. They assume that it is possible to create a perfect society; and, if they occasionally express doubts as to the feasibility of this project (as did More himself), they are easily resolved by defining utopia as imaginary, or as an unattainable ideal type. But, as soon as an attempt is made to build a utopia in the real world, it is legitimate – indeed, essential – to ask: to what extent has this society, created in accordance with utopian principles, attained the degree of perfection which was expected of it? The simplistic reply, that the kibbutz is indeed a perfect society, is unacceptable. In any historical or contemporary context, the kibbutz is not a utopia in this sense. To maintain that is to run the danger of cognitive dissonance, with all its negative attributes: divorce from reality, self-deception, rhetoric which succeeds in convincing only the speaker.

On the other hand, there is a very real measure of truth in the contention that the kibbutz is "another society", informed by values different from – indeed, often opposed to – those of the world around it. Therefore, a utopian view of the kibbutz, not as an ideal society, but as an alternative society with different values from those of its surroundings, is quite legitimate.

In this connection, it is interesting to note that in recent years there has been a noticeable trend away from the vocabulary of perfection, both in the kibbutz movement and in the literature of the communes. The kibbutz, or the commune, is described as the "other society" or an "alternative society", or the embodiment of the "counter-culture" (Darin-Drabkin; Melville; Shur, *Kibbutz as Another Society*; Clark; Darom). Those who tend to use the utopian vocabulary are, in the main, academics or polemicists who are uncommitted to the kibbutz, or even hostile to it (e.g., Holloway; Diamond; Kallen; Armytage). It would appear that this change in nomenclature is desirable, from the point of view of proper modesty and semantic clarity alike. The kibbutz is far from having attained perfection. But it can claim to be, in many respects, one of the least bad of the many forms of society which exist in the contemporary world.

The Future as Utopia

It seems clear, therefore, that the best strategy for preserving the utopian vision in a post-utopian situation is to project it into the future. This strategy avoids the pitfalls involved in idealizing the past and present; and its proponents can take into account the lessons learned from the processes of change and consequent ideological revision. It permits the construction of a utopian model based on the new conditions which came about after the first period of the existence of the kibbutz, or on a set of values which takes into account the positive and negative experiences of that period. And this model will arise from the thought and experiences of a group of people who have lived together, and together built a different, improved – though still imperfect – society.

This does not apply, however, when the future utopia is a fixed model, as in the case of Shlomo Lavi. For, during the actual development of the kibbutz, the processes which led to the downfall of the pristine utopia will continue to work. Kibbutz society and the world around it will continue to change. There will be differences in world outlook between the different members; their children (and their spouses) will become members; new recruits with varying backgrounds will add fresh points of view, and nuances of the old. And, even were this not so, there is sufficient tension between the original aims and aspirations of the kibbutz to ensure a constant search for the "correct" balance between them.

Nonetheless, it is of the essence of utopianism that not all is open to revision. In the case of the kibbutz, this means not only a consensus on certain basic principles – cooperation, participatory democracy, equality, the centrality of productive work – but a minimal definition of a structural framework which ensures their application. Within this framework, there is much room for trial and error, conscious experimentation, and differences both of opinion and of practice.

However, the structural aim in itself is not sufficient. Side by side with the improvement of the organizational framework of the kibbutz is the attempt to climb the ladder to the perfection of man.

In what respect is man to be perfect (or, more accurately, to aspire to an unattainable perfection)? Of Passmore's ten definitions (Passmore 24) two seem applicable: to be "free of any moral defect" or to "live in the manner of an ideally perfect human being". But the context in which these perfections are defined makes it clear that the morality is, first and foremost, social morality, and that the perfect human being is he who can live in absolute harmony with his fellow men. The revised utopian model is an updated version of J.C. Davis' Arcadia, which postulates "both an abundance of satisfaction and moderation or simplification of desires to a 'natural' level" (Davis 22–6, 382).[6] The satisfactions are to be achieved by "conquering everything: everything that is human and natural – even nature

---

[6] Cf. the slogan, widely held to express the essence of kibbutz ideology: from each according to his ability; to each according to his needs. Davis's categories are in many respects the most subtle that have been suggested by any analyst of utopias. But their terminology, and, to a degree, their content, are attuned more to the author's specific research material than to the critique of modern utopian thought which he attempts in his final chapter.

itself", as Lavi maintained: the moderation and simplification of desires, by the process of "self-education" postulated by Smetterling and others.

From Micro- to Macro-Utopia: The Post-Soviet Model

The ways of thought described in this chapter are not confined to the kibbutz. Examples of similar ways of thinking could be drawn from many macro-utopian societies, from colonial America to modern Israel. Here, I shall concentrate on one example: that of Russia in the early stages of the collapse of Communism, when the model of a socialist society still seemed applicable, though desperately in need of revision.

Prelude: From Utopia to Dystopia

Despite the reluctance of Marx and Engels to use utopian terminology, or to forecast in any detail the structure of post-revolutionary society, there can be no doubt that there are very close parallels between the feeling of "utopia achieved" in the early days of the kibbutz and the atmosphere which prevailed in Russia of the revolutionary and immediate post – revolutionary period. The belief that "the devout Russian people no longer needed priests to pray them into heaven. On earth they were building a kingdom more bright than any heaven had to offer, and for which it was a glory to die" is by no means exceptional in descriptions and memoirs of the period (Reed 259).

It did not take long, however, for utopia to become dystopia even before the horrors of Stalinism. Here again, the parallels are obvious, and even stark: the exile and emigration of many of the Communist intelligentsia, suicides, and "internal exile". The vital difference that the Soviet Union is not a voluntary community but a state, with instruments of legislation and repression, does not affect the similarity of the intellectual and spiritual processes concerned. In each case, utopia realized yields either to dystopia, or to the post-utopian situation.

Moreover, even in the utopian stage there is a clear parallel. Just as the Zionist youth movements built their own conceptual utopias on an exiguous basis of fact, so was the Soviet Union pictured as a utopia by the Communist parties of the world and by a wide range of intellectuals whose utopian propensities triumphed over their critical and scientific acumen.[7]

Geographical Displacement

The analysis of kibbutz thought above was mainly devoted to temporal displacement of the utopian vision. One incident should be cited, however, for the light it throws on non-kibbutz post-utopian thought. In 1927 the Labour Movement was shocked by the emigration of a group of members of one of the most prominent kibbutz movements, Gedud Ha'Avoda (including some of its leading intellectuals) to the Soviet Union. They had reached the conclusion that the communal utopia could not be achieved with the support of a "bourgeois", and largely hostile, Zionist movement, and attempted (in vain, as subsequent history showed) to achieve their aim by building a commune in the "Soviet fatherland" (Near, *Kibbutz Movement* 143).

Here, instead of the temporal displacement which was the most frequent form of post-utopian thinking, was a similar phenomenon, in the geographical dimension; a displacement similar to that of the Communist utopia among those disillusioned by the Soviet Union: from Russia to China, to Cuba – and perhaps other, more distant and therefore less knowable locations. Both in kibbutz and in non-kibbutz thought, this appears

---

7   One of the most extreme cases is Sidney and Beatrice Webb's *Soviet Communism: A New Civilization?* (1935; later edition, 1941, without the question-mark); and cf. *The Truth About the Soviet Union* (1942). But this is just one example of a whole genre.

to be something of an aberration. The main lines of utopian displacement are temporal rather than geographical.

Post-Soviet Utopian Thinking

Micro-utopian thought must inevitably seem irrelevant, even paltry, to those who create or study macro-utopian visions. It is, however, worth considering the development of such visions under the pressure of real historical developments. A case in point is that of Soviet, Communist, and fellow-travelling thinkers in the short period after the twentieth conference of the Russian Communist party, when future developments were unclear, and it looked as if Russian society might still bear some signs of its utopian past: roughly the mid-1970s.

Idealizing Past and Present

There is no need to quote from the official literature of the Communist Party in order to prove that its overall tenor is that described above as idealization, both of the revolutionary past and of the Soviet present. It is virtually impossible to discover to what extent such excesses of praise are simply the product of an oppressive and self-serving regime, and to what extent they express genuine satisfaction with Soviet society which might, under different circumstances, express itself as "idealization of the present". Amalrik (19–21; see also Medvedev, *On Socialist Democracy* 298–9) describes the complexity of the situation at the time, and the virtual impossibility of any attempt at estimating the real state of public opinion in the Soviet Union. Nonetheless, his remarks about the "paradox of the middle class" hint at the possibility that such a phenomenon could well appear under conditions of liberalization and economic improvement.

There is, however, one clear parallel with this variety of utopianism in the kibbutz. This is the tendency to see in the Soviet Union not a perfect society, but an alternative society, free from the gross injustices of capitalism – a society which should, therefore, be criticized only in guarded terms.

Sartre, for example, who believed that the "revolutionary idea became incarnate" (in the USSR in 1917) did not deny the negative aspects of Soviet society, but chose to play them down, since "the USSR does quite clearly still represent the country that abolished the private ownership of the tools of labour" (Sartre 21–3).

Sartre's remark about the incarnation of the revolution hints at yet another parallel with post-utopian thought in the kibbutz. For many radical thinkers, as Melvin Lasky remarks, "the revolution remains their utopia" (Lasky 602), and their interest is more in the destruction of the existing social fabric than in the shape of the new society. But even in such an inveterately revolutionary thinker as Sartre, the concept of "revolution" frequently bears the connotation of the "revolutionary society": in our terminology, the primal macro-utopian state. And here we find common ground between Sartre and a number of other writers whose positive views are radically different from his, but who agree that in one respect at least the Russian revolution in its earliest stage was utopia realized. Leon Trotsky, Daniel Cohn-Bendit, and Roy Medvedev present Soviet democracy in its early stages as the undistorted expression of the will of the masses (Trotsky 100–2; Cohn-Bendit & Gabriel 202–20, 250–1; Medvedev 30, 41, 134–5; for a similar view of other revolutionary situations, cf. Bookchin 250–4, 276–8). In the background of the struggles and speculations of these very different thinkers is the belief in a short-lived but significant "utopian moment".

The Future

Speculations about the utopian future are built into Soviet ideology. The transition from socialism to communism is part of Marxist dogma, and therefore of the official forecast of the future of the Soviet state. But Marx's deliberate vagueness about the lineaments of communist society left a wide field for speculation. Stimulated by Khrushchev's forecast of the "full construction of communism", the lesser ideologists of the USSR filled this vacuum in the Marxist prophecy with a wide variety of speculations (Gilison ch. 1). These prophecies are often marred by the assumption that communism will be no more than a development and refinement of institutions and social structures already to be found in the Soviet Union;[8] an approach parallel to that of the "structural" view of the future kibbutz utopia. Others propound more imaginative views of the future, many of them surprisingly close to the kibbutz utopia – and even to the kibbutz reality – in all its forms.[9] Others again are even more open-minded, and reach such conclusions as that "there will be no end to social development under communism", in a vein reminiscent of the contentions of such kibbutz theorists as Smetterling.

These ideas, and the relative freedom with which they were broached and discussed, stem in no small part from their Marxist setting. But the situation both of the official Soviet ideologists and of those dissident thinkers of whom we have some knowledge is typically post-utopian. It comes as no surprise, therefore, that their ways of thought are not dissimilar to those analysed above. Evgenia Ginsburg retained her basic faith in communism despite her terrible experiences in Soviet prison camps. Solzhenitzyn and others left the Soviet Union, physically or spiritually, voluntarily or under compulsion, just as many left the kibbutz in a variety of ways. Medvedev, on the other hand, explicitly rejected their negation of the revolution. "Rebuilding [...] the decayed elements at the base of the [Soviet social] structure [...] is in no way a question of destroying the values of the October Revolution. Rather we must restore and purify them; they must be reinforced and built upon" (51–4). And the reaction of an English radical thinker to the same situation was very similar (Miliband 67–9).

---

8   For instance: the continued existence of the managerial class (Gilison 111–13), the Communist Party (122), and the division of labour, in increasingly efficient forms (132–5).
9   For instance: communal consumption (Gilison 102–3, 152–8); frequent changes of employment, and managerial rotation (136–45); collective definition and imposition of social norms (147–52, 168–73). Gilison's fundamentally hostile analysis of these aspects of the Soviet utopia springs from his inability to conceive of a voluntary "change of consciousness" (in kibbutz terms: "self education").

Just as we have seen in the case of the kibbutz, the newly formulated utopia was a refashioning of the original utopian vision. And its realization was postponed to an indefinite future – a goal to be striven for, though it would no doubt never be achieved.

Thus, the processes which we isolated on the micro-utopian scale of the kibbutz are seen to apply at least to one example of macro-utopian thinking. Indeed, a case could certainly be made for saying that the ways in which the kibbutz has dealt with the problems of the post-utopian period exemplify universal thought processes, on the macro-utopian and micro-utopian scale alike. For the utopian vision is not only, as has been emphasized here, a model to imitate, avoid, improve, or put into practice. It can also be, in Elisabeth Hansot's phrase, a "thought experiment" (2). Hansot's own analysis emphasizes the value of such "experiments" in criticizing the institutions and values of the age they are set in; and, directly or by implication, in criticizing its utopian constructs.

But the situation of the utopian thinker of today is more complex than that of those of the ancient world, or of the Renaissance. Today's world is post-utopian; and in the background of any utopian construct lies both the assumption that it may be a spur to practical action, and the knowledge that many utopias have already been tried and found wanting. In this respect, Bellamy's remark, that he aimed to construct a model of society "on a basis of equality corresponding to and supplementing [the] political equality" which had already been achieved in the United States (quoted in Hansot 116) is most revealing. For Bellamy lived in a society conscious of its origins in utopian thought and achievement; so that his attempt to adapt and transcend the original utopian model, now shown to be flawed and inadequate, corresponds to the post-utopian situation described above. This is but one instance among many. A detailed analysis of modern macro-utopian thought would surely reveal a repetition on a broad scale of the conceptual themes which appear so clearly in the minuscule world of the kibbutz.

Conclusions and Generalizations

Is there a moral to the story? For the kibbutz, the conclusions seem clear: to avoid idealization of the past, except in the sense of proffering an educational ideal; to prefer "alternative society" language to utopian terminology in relation to the present; and to see the future utopia as an unattainable ideal type, rather than a defined social structure. The concluding section of this essay will deal with a more general question: to what extent are the patterns of thinking described and analysed here of more universal application?

The Persistence of Utopianism

One of the striking factors about kibbutz thought in virtually all its manifestations is the persistency with which the utopian element is preserved, despite all the vicissitudes of its content and context. In some measure, this is no doubt the result of the perspicacity and strength of the first generation of the kibbutz. But there is, surely, an underlying logic to this pertinacity. For a kibbutz is both a micro-utopia in intent and a voluntary society in practice. He who belongs to, or joins, such a society is thereby committed (logically, if not necessarily formally) to participating in the formulation of ends which is called here micro-utopian thinking, and in the constant reformulation which marks the post-utopian period.

This is the essential difference between joining a utopian community and moving to a new town or country. Both cases are declarations of belonging (or the intention to belong) to an existing group, with its present character, structure, and *modus operandi*. But in the case of the utopian (or post-utopian) community, there is, in addition, the element of conscious and directed change. To join such a society is to declare oneself part of this process.

Post-utopian thinking is, then, to no small degree a function of the size of the erstwhile utopia. More exactly, it is a function of the extent to which the members of that society feel that they have control over its development. In this respect, the kibbutz is only one example of a wide variety of intentional societies: among others are the early American colonies, the historical communes of the US, and the pre-state Jewish community of Palestine. As long as the members of these communities were (or believed that they were) masters of their fate, they were also captains of their soul: their ideology was based on the assumption that they could and should mould their societies in the light of a common ideal.

Here, the distinction between micro- and macro-utopias is crucial. There are periods in the process of creating, or attempting to create, a macro-utopia when conscious groups of individuals both are and are seen to be of prime importance: periods of revolution, of democratic decision on central issues, of historic changes which pose real alternatives. But the post-utopian period in such a society is qualitatively different from that in a micro-utopian community. One of the major factors in such a situation is the sheer size and complexity of the society. It is this that frequently leads to the conclusion that any attempt to re-shape society is bound to fail: the factors at work are too many, their methods of interaction are too complex, and the basic patterns of thought and action are too firmly grounded for change. All that can be done is "piecemeal social engineering", or the adoption of "incremental policies", as suggested, or assumed, by Popper, Hayek, and many others. Thus, in small intentional communities post-utopian thinking has a logical compulsion which can be denied with more reason in a larger society. But, as I have shown, in at least one case, even in mass post-utopian societies the same patterns of thought which we have seen in concentrated form in the kibbutz are to be found.

CHAPTER 6

Utopia Reconsidered: The Agrarian Ethos, Then and Now

The industrialization of the kibbutz is in many ways a typical case of post-utopian thinking. The founders of the first kibbutzim were born into Russian Jewish communities whose members had been forbidden to own land for centuries, and lived in the oppressive environment of the Jewish ghetto or *shtetl*. Influenced by the winds of romantic thought which reached the Jews of Russia in the second half of the nineteenth century, they adopted the agrarian ethos common in other nineteenth-century nationalist movements in Europe and the US: the belief that, in Jefferson's words, the small farmer is "the most precious part of a state" (1785). In order to build a healthy Jewish society in Palestine, therefore, it was necessary to create an agricultural working class; and, just as they saw their small cooperative groups as a model for the social organization of the whole of future Zionist society, they considered themselves a model for its economic setup: a purely agricultural society would restore the Jews, long cut off from the wholesome influence of day-to-day contact with nature, to normality and ensure the survival of the Jewish community in Palestine.

This vision was never realized. The Jewish community of Palestine developed along lines which rarely matched the utopian ideals of the kibbutz. But for a decade or more the kibbutzim grew slowly in size and in number, and maintained their agrarian purity. And, despite the fact that many became disillusioned and left the kibbutz altogether, the leaders of the emerging kibbutz movement maintained stubbornly either that they had, in fact, achieved the utopian ideal, or that their original concept remained unchanged and would eventually be realized by dint of hard work and adaptation of the individual to the requirements of the ideal society (in my terms: present and future utopias). To the agrarian ethos and the principles of communitarian socialism they added another, that of "self-labour". According to this concept, kibbutz society was a small, economically self-sufficient community whose members were "neither exploiters nor exploited", in a frequently repeated formulation: as an economically independent community, it would be outside the capitalist nexus, and would neither need workers from outside to maintain it nor have to send its members to find employment in outside society. So important did this principle seem to them that the first kibbutz, Degania, returned two-thirds of the land it had originally been granted by the Zionist movement on the grounds that their community, which they intended to limit to between forty and sixty members, would not be able to work so big an area without hiring workers from outside the kibbutz. It is, perhaps, worth noting in parenthesis that the agrarian ethos did not preclude them from using the most up-to-date farming methods and machinery in their daily work; for instance, before the First World War Degania formed a team to work with one of the most modern pieces of equipment then available – a threshing machine – which worked in the neighbouring farms. In terms more familiar to students of communal societies, they were Hutterites rather than Amish.

In the early 1920s, however, another of the possible variations of cognitive dissonance appeared: not an abandonment of the utopian mindset, but a significant variation of the pristine ideal. In a series of articles and lectures, one of the veterans of the kibbutz movement, Shlomo Lavi, declared himself faithful to the central ideas of the kibbutz: equality, cooperation, and the building of a communal society. But, he said, the practical application of these ideals had led to unnecessary suffering and privation. The desire to build a close-knit, family-type community had led to lack of privacy and unbearable tensions between the members. As a result of this concept of the ideal society, individual kibbutzim had been deliberately kept small, which had restricted their economic development and unnecessarily reduced their standard of living. The ideal of the kibbutz should be to grow, both in numbers, in the variety of its members and in their professional occupations. Unlike the earlier kibbutzim, he proposed an economic model based on a combination of agriculture, handicrafts, and industry.

This ideological stance was adopted by the Kibbutz Me'uhad, the biggest of the three kibbutz movements which were established in the late 1920s and early 1930s. But, although the aspiration to develop industry as an essential element of the kibbutz economy became an article of faith in this movement, for some twenty years it was itself no more than a utopian aspiration; for kibbutz industry began to develop to any significant degree only under the special conditions of the Second World War, when the economy of the Jewish community in Palestine became geared to supplying the Allied forces in the Middle East with industrial products of all sorts, in addition to basic foodstuffs. Although one of the kibbutz movements remained faithful to its original agrarian ethos for several decades, over the years the economic realities began to undermine its ideological purity: many kibbutzim, founded in locations important for security reasons, did not have sufficient land to enable them to derive even a minimal livelihood from agriculture. The idea of kibbutz industry became acceptable throughout the kibbutz movement.

This trend was intensified from the 1960s onwards, when it became clear that although, with the land and water available, it was possible to satisfy the needs of the local population and engage in export crops, agriculture alone would not enable the kibbutzim to maintain the steady rise in standards of living which they needed in order to keep up with the rest of the country and prevent a constant population drain. Kibbutz industry grew exponentially. In 1940 only 815 kibbutz members, of a total of 6,079 working in productive branches, worked in industry; by 1972 this number had grown to 10,591 out of 33,335. Since then, in parallel with the Israeli economy as a whole (and in many respects in its forefront) kibbutz industry has continued to grow, both absolutely and in proportion to the overall kibbutz economy, until in 2004 the 266 kibbutzim then existing owned 303 factories, in addition to seventy-seven "regional" enterprises jointly owned and managed by kibbutzim; in all, kibbutz industrial enterprises employed some 34,300 people (*Yearbook* 17–21).

The development of kibbutz industry, which – once the prohibition on industry as such was abandoned – was largely the result of market forces, cast a huge shadow over the agrarian ethos. This change of emphasis was often given ideological backing in view of the commitment of the kibbutzim to serve the best interests of Israeli society: it was seen as one way in which the kibbutzim could alleviate one of the major problems of Israeli society, by providing employment for members of the general population – particularly new immigrants, and particularly in peripheral areas.

However, this development also meant the end of the principle of self-labour. The market demanded constantly expanding production, and the necessary manpower was not available within the kibbutzim. And as Israeli industry in general developed, so did kibbutz industry; indeed, by the 1970s it was considered to be one of the most efficient and adaptable sectors of the Israeli economy as a whole. In some cases, it was similar to the relatively primitive factories of the 1940s, in that it was based on mass labour, managed by a team of expert kibbutz members; in others, it became more technologically sophisticated, requiring a high degree of expertise which was not necessarily to be found within the boundaries of the kibbutz. In both cases, the pristine ideal of self-labour remained a utopian aspiration; and contemporary kibbutz ideology and practice have abandoned it altogether. By 2004, 67 per cent of the workers in kibbutz industry were not kibbutz members; and in that same year almost 70 per cent of the income of the kibbutzim was derived from industry.

One of the characteristics of the kibbutz as a post-utopian society is that, since it is governed by a system of face-to-face democracy in which each of the members has an equal right to participate, it has from time to time to reconsider its aims and objectives – in other words, its preserved or revised utopian ideal. So what, in this perspective, is the current status of the agrarian ethos?

It may first be remarked that, despite the remarkable growth of industry described above, none of the veteran kibbutzim (those founded before the year 1990, which constitute the overwhelming majority of today's kibbutzim) has abandoned its agricultural holdings, or all of its agricultural economic branches. Moreover, these kibbutzim are still considered, and consider themselves, to be rural settlements, even though several of them are situated on the borders of, and a handful virtually within the bounds of, urban areas. And a number of significant traces of the agrarian ethos may be noted.

Kibbutz culture is to a great extent based on the Jewish religious year. But the traditional festivals have been remoulded, in order to emphasize their non-religious significance as nature festivals, delineating the cycle of the agricultural year: times of sowing and harvest, climatic changes and the like are given precedence over the primarily religious aspects of such festivals as practised in the Jewish Diaspora or in orthodox communities. Thus, for instance, the Feast of Weeks (*Shavuot*) which is traditionally celebrated as the time of the Giving of the Law to Moses on Mount Sinai is marked in most kibbutzim as a harvest festival: the members and their children are conveyed by tractors or other conveyances of the kibbutz in a procession through the fields in order to re-acquaint them with the work being done and the crops being grown; dances symbolizing the change of seasons and the gathering of the crops are performed; and readings from the Bible and other Jewish literary works emphasize the same theme. This sometimes leads to paradoxical situations: for instance, the dates of the Jewish agricultural year, crystallized in Biblical times and unchanged since then, are quite often inappropriate to contemporary agricultural practice: the harvest festival may be celebrated at a time when the main crops of the kibbutz have been yielding their produce for several months; and a special field may have to be sown and saved for the festive cutting of the "first" sheaves. In my own kibbutz the cultural committee, after many years of celebrating the harvest at an unrealistic time, decided to replace the traditional forms of celebration with an exhibition of the huge agricultural implements now in use – tractors, ploughs, implements for feeding cattle, and the like – which rolled past the assembled members and impressed them no less than the traditional trip through the fields. The dancing and singing which accompanied this display were all centred on the joys of spring, the harvest, and the wonders of nature; but on the following day all the members were taken on a guided tour of the new building of the kibbutz's industrial enterprise.

Another, more problematic, aspect of the change in attitude to the agrarian ethos is in the field of education. Kibbutz education in general has always been humanistic, favouring a broad conspectus of learning with a considerable admixture of opportunities for artistic pursuits and the development of artistic skills, rather than being focussed on the acquisition of technical knowledge and skills. On the other hand, agriculture has always been a part of the curriculum; and the children have been required to work, at younger ages in their own "children's farm", and later in the agricultural branches of the kibbutz, until, in their final year at school, they are working a full day every week in the kibbutz farm. But the developments outlined above have made this arrangement seem anachronistic and wasteful: anachronistic because it is widely acknowledged that the great majority of the children will not work in agriculture in their adult lives; and wasteful because this supposedly vocational training could, and in the opinion of many, should be supplanted by subjects more relevant to the reality of the twenty-first century and the needs of the kibbutz: computer skills, for instance, at a higher level than those provided in the normal curriculum. So many kibbutzim – though not all – have abandoned the children's working day altogether.

This tendency has come to fruition in one aspect of the present state of the kibbutz movement. For several years now the great majority of kibbutz-born children have not been returning to their places of birth after their army service: they opt for a variety of university studies, and settle down away from their original homes. The veteran kibbutzim, therefore, face a serious demographic problem, as the average age increases and the members' economic and social burdens are increasingly heavy. The result is an increase in the number of hired workers (including managers from outside the kibbutz). This, together with a number of other factors, has led to deep changes in the system in some two-thirds of the kibbutz movement, amounting in many cases to the abandonment of the basic tenets of the classical kibbutz. In reaction to this trend, over the past two decades there have grown up about a hundred small communal groups which claim to return to the pristine values of the kibbutz; and many see in them the true future of the kibbutz as a communal movement.

There can be no doubt that these groups are utopian, in the sense defined above. They have a clear vision of the ideal society they are striving to build, which is in many respects a replica of the classical kibbutz: they maintain the principles of equality between the members, intense face-to-face democracy, and communal control of the members' incomes and expenditure. But virtually all of them have abandoned the agrarian ethos. They do not derive their livelihood from a jointly owned farm – or, indeed, in most cases, from jointly owned economic enterprises of any sort; their members work mainly in education and in various forms of social work among the under-privileged sectors of the population, and pool the income they derive from these occupations. They are, in fact, more like the communes of America and Europe than the classical kibbutz.

The fact that most of the veteran kibbutzim have undergone a fundamental change in their way of life and livelihood does not mean that they have foregone the utopian element in their thoughts and actions: on the contrary, the very fact of change, and the need to anchor it in formal decisions preceded by a wide-ranging series of discussions, brings the utopian element to the fore; for they are compelled to substitute a new version of their ideal (in many kibbutzim formulated as a "vision" of their social aims) for their previous utopian concept – whether, at the time of the change, they saw this concept as a past golden age, as a near-perfect present, or as an aim for the future.

In very few of these "visions", however, does the agrarian ethos specifically appear. Some of them speak of the "quality of life" and of ecological objectives, but agriculture, if it is mentioned at all, appears simply as one of a variety of means of livelihood – one which is likely to continue to exist, since the kibbutzim already own considerable tracts of land, and have the equipment and know – how to make a profit from it. But, lined up against other means of livelihood, agriculture is having increasing difficulty in proving its financial worth; and the fact that many kibbutzim have devoted large tracts of formerly agricultural land to building projects is a clear indication of this. And in this respect the "communal" kibbutzim – the minority who remain faithful to the classical kibbutz social structure – are no different from the majority of kibbutzim, which have abandoned their former communal and egalitarian methods of distributing income.

Historically, then, the agrarian ethos has undergone radical transformation during the history of the kibbutz. Beginning as an integral part of its founders' vision, it was superseded by a vision of an integrated industrial and agricultural society – a vision which was in large measure realized. But economic developments in Israel and the world led to its gradual abandonment, until today there is virtually no part of the kibbutz movement in which agriculture is seen as any more than a complement to a mainly industrial and technological economy, and sometimes not even that. The agricultural ethos has become utopia abandoned, parallel to the act of leaving the kibbutz; and industry forms part of the future economic utopia of the greater part of the kibbutz movement, with the exception of the young commune-type communities, which implicitly reject the aspiration to create an independent productive economic structure: most of their members earn their livelihood independently, though it is paid into a common pool.

This transformation has not yet been completely assimilated into the educational and cultural systems of the veteran kibbutzim. In these, it may be said that in respect to the agrarian ethos utopia has become nostalgia.

CHAPTER 7

Post-Utopian Women: Changing Concepts of Gender Equality in the Kibbutz

It has often been maintained that the question of gender in the kibbutz is of great importance for gender theory in general. In one version of the historical process, it has been presented as proof that, given the will and the historical circumstances, gender equality is possible; in another, that despite all efforts to the contrary, male supremacy has not been conquered; other theories, all based on supposed analysis of historical processes, speak of the "bio-grammar" of the woman; of the crucial role of economic processes; and more.

Most of these theses are strong on theory, but weak on historical evidence. As a historian, I have looked at the actual course of events during the classical period of kibbutz history – from 1919 to 1948. In doing so, I became convinced of the importance of a factor which, so far, neither scholars nor polemicists have mentioned in this context: the fact that, at least from the early 1920s, the kibbutz has been – and, indeed, still is – a post-utopian society.

The earliest stage in the development of any intentional community may be labelled "utopia achieved". Built according to its members' preconceived concept of a perfect society, in its earliest days it looks as if it is the realization of the utopian ideal. But people are not perfect, and neither is any real community. Sooner or later the divergence of the real from the ideal becomes apparent, and the post-utopian period begins: the aspiring utopians adopt a number of stratagems in order to resolve the cognitive dissonance they now experience (see above, chapter 5).

"Utopia achieved" is succeeded by the post-utopian period, when a good many people abandon the utopian ideal, and leave the community. Here, however, I am concerned with those who stay in the community

– specifically, the kibbutz – and have to find ways of coping with its post-utopian character.

Long before they established the first kibbutz – indeed, before they arrived in what was then Palestine – its founders had a vision of a communal society, egalitarian in all respects – including that of gender. This vision was based partly on their rejection of the values and practices of the Jewish society within which they grew to adulthood, and partly on their reading of feminist literature. In this literature, there are four aspects of gender equality. The first, political equality – women's right to vote and stand for election – was among the principal objectives of feminist movements the world over. So, too, was the demand for women's liberation from economic and legal dependence on their husbands. Feminists also demanded equality of employment: in Bebel's words, the right "to choose her occupation in such field as corresponds with her wishes, inclinations, and natural abilities, and she works under conditions identical with man's" (Bebel 343). In the Socialist-Zionist movement from which the kibbutz sprang, this aspiration was translated into the right of the woman pioneer to work in agriculture by the side of her male comrades. The fourth objective, sexual liberation – in the language of the time, free love – was not universally accepted in the socialist or feminist movements, or, indeed, in the kibbutzim.

In the matter of political and economic equality, in its early days the kibbutz certainly looked like utopia achieved. Participation of women in its general meetings and their right to speak and vote were accepted as matters of course, and women were regarded as independent workers, regardless of their marital status. As for occupational equality, one of the central legends of kibbutz history was the case of Miriam Baratz, one of the founders of the first kibbutz, who won her right to work in the cowsheds by rising before the male workers and milking the herd single-handed. No wonder, then, that in 1919 Joseph Bussel, the leader and ideologue of the first kibbutz, said: "the kibbutz has served [...] to create a life of equality in the economic sense and a life of equality between its male and female members" (quoted in Wurm 237). And this belief was strengthened even further over the next four years, when men and women worked together at the back-breaking task of road-building.

But the utopia was flawed. Despite women's formal right to participate in the kibbutz general meetings and to be elected to any office, men were dominant in its democratic institutions: women spoke less frequently at the general meetings, and constituted a small minority in the kibbutz's central institutions. They rarely assumed executive roles such as farm manager or kibbutz secretary, and only a small number of women participated in the central institutions of the kibbutz movements.

However, for the first ten years of the permanent existence of the kibbutz movement, virtually none of this appeared in its periodical literature. Women wrote articles on matters such as nutrition, the organization of the clothing store, and educational theory and practice. But between 1920 and 1930, the "woman question" simply did not appear. And when it began to be discussed, in 1930, one of the feminist activists remarked:

> It's very common for women to deny the very existence of the question of the woman in the kibbutz: "We are in one kibbutz with the men," they say, "we're equal to them in everything by virtue of this way of life, and there's nothing more to be said." (Artzi 518)

However, as I have said, from 1930 onwards the woman question began to be a subject of public discussion. And even so, five years later one of the leaders of the kibbutz movement said:

> Our women members have finally begun express their bitterness, their yearnings and their aspirations. [...] Half of the members of our movement are women, and they have been pushed aside into a corner. Whether the corner is warm or cold is immaterial, for it is dark and unattractive. (Ya'ari, "On the Way to Equality" 2)

In other words, the first stratagem of women and others in dealing with the failure to achieve and sustain a perfect utopian community is simply denial. "Utopia achieved" may well be a true state of affairs for a short period. But it can last for a very long time as a state of mind.

With the recognition that there are flaws in utopia, the original concept is not abandoned. It is, however, modified in several ways. The first is "utopia deferred". In the kibbutz, while preserving the original concept of gender equality, feminist activists saw it not as a state of affairs, but as a goal to be worked for, and achieved in the undefined future.

This approach seems to have been reasonably effective. In the mid-1930s a group of women in one of the biggest kibbutzim demanded that one third of the seats on the kibbutz committees should be set aside for women. This eventually became a general guideline throughout the kibbutz movement and beyond it. True, there were still "women's committees" – mainly those that dealt with education and the distribution of consumer goods; and executive offices, particularly those in the economic sphere, remained almost solely in the hands of the men. But, from the point of view of the original feminist position, this was a distinct improvement. And similar developments took place in other spheres. For example, until the Arab revolt of 1936, women played little or no part in the defence of the kibbutzim. But, again as the result of the demands of a small group of activists, from then on all the kibbutzim accepted the principle that it was the women's right and duty to take their place at the front, side by side with the men. Here again the advance was limited: in most cases they were given special, non-combatant roles. But it was seen as a clear advance towards the future, egalitarian utopia.

Much the same applies to the sphere of occupational equality, always one of the main preoccupations of those who strove for gender equality. In the early 1920s men and women worked side by side in jobs such as road-building and house-building. They created an image – and a self-image – of the kibbutz as an egalitarian society par excellence. But even during this celebrated period the kitchens and clothing stores were staffed almost exclusively by women. In principle, the child care set-up and arrangements for maternity leave afforded every woman the opportunity to work in agriculture. But the pattern set during the earliest years of the kibbutz, according to which men worked in "productive branches" and women in "service branches," was still dominant in the mid-1920s.

The children's houses were even more "feminine" than the kitchens. The more children there were, the more rapidly the number of women workers in the children's houses grew, and the proportion of women among agricultural workers dropped. The principle of communal child-care was one of the central pillars of the kibbutz society. But the responsibility for putting it into practice rested not on all the community but, first and foremost, on the women. True, demands were made to introduce men into the children's houses, but only rarely and timidly – so much so that they never received a well-reasoned response from the establishment. Moreover, there is considerable evidence of expressions of doubt and derision on the part of male members of the possibility of women succeeding in "masculine" professions. During the entire period of the 1930s there was increasing expression of dissatisfaction in this sphere: in addition to the above, there were complaints about the lack of development and mechanization of the service branches, about the "insulting" distinction between productive and non-productive branches, and so forth.

These developments had their beginnings during the period of "utopia achieved", but received little public notice. However, once the consciousness of the true state of affairs brought the question to the fore, the situation began to improve. Between 1935 and 1942, there was a constant increase in the percentage of women engaged in agriculture, which reached almost 40 per cent in the early 1940s. Again, this was far from equality in its original utopian sense. But it gave credence to what became the accepted wisdom in the mid-1930s: the goal of gender equality had not changed; but it was now an aspiration, not yet an established fact. "Utopia achieved" had given place to "utopia deferred".

Another method of resolving the tensions of "utopia achieved" is by a relative approach: let us call it "utopia preferred". According to this version, the kibbutz is not a perfect society; but is far less imperfect than any other. Here again, this was not far from the historical facts. In the political and personal sphere, by 1910 kibbutz women had the right to vote, and economic independence from their husbands – achievements which were paralleled in most of the western world, and in Jewish Palestine, only some ten or fifteen years later.

In the long run, many of the above stratagems fail to satisfy in any post-utopian community. But the utopian cast of mind remains: she who sought perfection in her youth will often continue to do so, despite all disappointments, in the future. In any intentional society this tendency is particularly marked – not only because of the members' psychological make up, but because even its day-to-day government requires a series of conscious decisions; and in making these decisions, the members cannot help referring to their original aims and ideals. In a sense, all of the public life of the kibbutz is lived in the context of its original utopian concepts.

Hence, the final variation of post-utopian thinking: "utopia revised". A new utopian ideal, forged out of the meeting between the original concept and the experience of the real world, is presented. However, before discussing this I shall say something about the historical circumstances in which the revision took place.

The kibbutz was always a dynamic social organism, continuously absorbing young people from the Zionist youth movements of Europe. As in the early years of the kibbutz, their utopian conception of the kibbutz crystallized in the Diaspora, and continued to affect their perception of reality after they had reached the real kibbutz: every kibbutznik, and every new kibbutz, underwent a period of "utopia achieved". But from the early 1930s onwards the influence of the surrounding world was different from what it had been in the first years of the kibbutz: in Europe, America and Australasia "classical feminism" ("the First Wave" in current terminology) had come to the end of its historical trajectory" with the achievement of the majority of its objectives. In the Soviet Union, a model of a socialist society in the eyes of a great many kibbutz members, a significant change took place with the liquidation of the women's division in the communist party and its return to the traditional familial pattern (Evans). Therefore, the ideological drive to attain the objectives of classical feminism was weakened: it appeared that some of its elements were realized, while others were considered undesirable. Moreover, kibbutz reality was different from that of the surrounding world: the shift to physical work in the fields, the clothing store or the kitchen involved difficulties which were entirely different from the transition to the liberal professions which was the aspiration of classical feminism. This situation "softened up" the attitudes of the leaders of kibbutz feminism. There came about a shift from the first post-utopian stage, in which they strove to realize the pristine utopian ideal, to a process of far-reaching revision, in which their very aims were changed.

In 1946 Lilia Bassevitz, one of the prominent fighters for gender equality in the kibbutz movement, said:

> In the early days of the kibbutz movement the ideal was the pioneer woman who undertakes hard labour side by side with the man, who takes the initiative in economic matters, who rides, dances, and, in short, takes life by storm and achieves her goals. [...] For her, the working day was sacred. She might feel extremely ill, but as long as she had no fever would continue to work until she was totally exhausted. (Bassevitz 351, 357)

In other words: the objective was to resemble men, and even to compete with them in physical labour, in dress, and other aspects of life.

This same Lilia Bassevitz collected material for a very influential anthology, entitled *Women in the Kibbutz* (Ed. Poznanski & Shehori, 1945). It was first published in 1945, when the great majority of women worked not in the fields, but in the kitchen, the clothing store, education and child care. The historical section of the book constitutes a paean of praise to the women of the veteran kibbutzim, who blazed the path to occupational equality. In addition, forty-five vignettes show a picture of women's life in the kibbutz of the 1940s. Thirty-five of them depict work in agriculture and ancillary trades, while only ten deal with those service branches in which the majority of women worked in reality. So this book presented two versions of the kibbutz feminist utopia: "utopia achieved" – a reaffirmation of the classical feminist position, despite its relative irrelevance to the real world; and "utopia past", in which a distant ideal period was presented as a moral or educational example – a utopian myth. The ideological bias is clear. As we shall see, however, it is less certain whether it was in accordance with the desires of the women themselves. For at about the time of publication of *Women in the Kibbutz* another version of kibbutz feminism began to be heard – the beginnings of "utopia revised".

In early 1946, after twenty years of activity in this sphere, this same Lilia Bassevitz published a comprehensive article entitled "The Woman Kibbutz Member". The first part is a tribute to the women members of the kibbutz on their achievements in creating

> [a] form of existence *different* from that of our mothers and grandmothers. And if numerous contradictions continue to gnaw at our souls and there are constant battles between our desire to sit quietly in the corner and our desire to be do battle, between work and social life on the one hand and our inner world, love and children

on the other – we always knew that through these contradictions we could achieve fulfilment. (Bassewitz 345)

She mentioned with pride the women's part not only in agricultural work, but also in purely "feminine" spheres: culture, cleanliness, education and child care, the creation of a national cuisine, and so on. And all of these were presented as the result of a combination of women's will-power and the social structure of the kibbutz. But in the second part of the article she emphasized the price that women members were forced to pay for their achievements. The kibbutz woman, she said:

> [She is] not only *tired* after her day of work; she is *drained* as a result of the character of her place of work, the pace it demands, and the monotony of the work. She is left with little strength or energy for her children, for reading, or for doing voluntary work. This is particularly true when the years take their toll and leave their mark on her health [...] Looking after the room, individual laundry, knitting [...] transform her day of rest into a working day, and add several hours to each work day, particularly when the children are still small. (Ibid. 356–7)

Here we have a significant shift from the accepted ideological line of the time – a line which Bassevitz herself had supported fervently (*inter alia*, when she edited *Women in the Kibbutz*). The "feminine" spheres are not marginal – though essential – sectors of kibbutz society. They constitute a legitimate – indeed, a praiseworthy – part of the kibbutz experience, unique to its women members. Therefore they should be granted legitimacy in the work set-up as well. Bassevitz proposed a series of practical measures to lighten the burden. But at this stage she did not go as far as another woman activist, who proposed shortening the women's work-day, and attaining "equality of opportunity for rest and spiritual development" (S. Frankel 64). It was only in the mid-1960s that this idea was widely discussed, and became the standard in the entire kibbutz movement.

According to Bassevitz, the women of the settlement movement "create, struggle, and dream." (Note the utopian phraseology.) But to a great extent they struggle not together with their male comrades, but against them; and in 1945 their dreams were very different from those dominant in the early 1930s. In other words, they still worked towards a future utopia. But it had now undergone a drastic revision.

This change had another facet. The following extract dates from 1947:

> [In many cases] the personality [of a thirty – forty year old woman] gradually becomes blurred, since she does not dare to be a *woman* [emphasis in original], to bring forth and develop all the positive characteristics of her mature femininity [...] our women members have not yet found the golden way from the charming young girl of the youth movement to the mature woman, who develops spiritually year by year [...]. By ignoring the fundamental laws of nature we block the development of women's potential, and bring them to helplessness, stagnation and depression. (Goldman 85)

"The laws of nature", often mentioned in this context, were not always specifically defined, but they consisted of maternal instincts, aspirations towards cleanliness, order and beauty, and the desire to nurture the family unit. This was "utopia revised" – the second wave of kibbutz feminism. It took two parallel forms: emphasis on the uniqueness of the woman; and recognition that the principle "from each according to her ability; to each according to her needs" is a more egalitarian concept than what was widely called in the kibbutz movement "mechanical [i.e., numerical] equality". These concepts inevitably remind one of the socio-biological theories which were being applied to this question in the 1970s – but also of the work of such feminists as Carol Gilligan (Gilligan; Tiger & Shepher). Although kibbutz feminism took on a new lease of life only in the 1960s, parallel to trends in the US, it looks as if, just as it anticipated developments in the outside world by a decade or more, the kibbutz anticipated these trends of thought by an even greater length of time.

Many of the stratagems adopted by the early kibbutzniks accorded with the processes of post-utopianism, as discussed in the previous chapter of this book. And, even within the small range of events presented here, there is evidence to support any of the narratives I spoke of at the beginning of this chapter: that gender inequality is the result of anthropologically or biologically determined mind-sets; that it can be reduced, or even eliminated, as a result of ideologically motivated effort; or that it stems from economic circumstances, or from men's determination to cling to power. As a historian, I cannot give exclusive credence to any one of these views: the line of development was complex, and resulted from a conglomerate of factors. But I have added one more factor to those usually adduced in this context: the laws of post-utopian development in an intentional community.

PART THREE

Pioneering

CHAPTER 8

The Concept of Pioneering in Zionist Thought

This chapter is an essay in semantic history, a methodological approach deriving from the belief that study of language and its vicissitudes can be an important tool for the historian; and, conversely, that many linguistic developments can be fully understood only against their historical background. I shall illustrate these truisms through an examination of the history of one Hebrew word and its derivatives: *halutz*.[1] The revival of Hebrew as a living language was an important part of the Zionist programme from an early stage; and the general adoption of Hebrew as the *lingua franca* of the Zionist community of Palestine marked a critical stage in the process of nation-building. In the first part of this chapter I shall confine myself to the universe of discourse of a specific sector of the Jewish community in Palestine: the Labour Zionist movement. In the second half, I shall discuss the changes that have taken place in the concept of pioneering since the establishment of the State of Israel.

1   *Halutz* (pl.: *halutzim*; fem: *halutza* but the plural, though grammatically masculine, was always assumed to include women); verbal noun [pioneering]: *halutziut*) is usually translated "pioneer", and in many contexts this is perfectly adequate. In this chapter, however, which deals with the many semantic variations of this expression, some of which could be translated differently, I have thought it better to leave the word in its original Hebrew form.

Pioneering in the Pre-State Period

The word *halutz* occurs seventeen times in the Bible. In every case, it is rendered by philologists and the authors of the standard translations as "soldier", or "armed man" (girt up for battle). But *halutz* was not part of the vocabulary of post-biblical Hebrew before the modern period in this sense or any derived from it.[2] It emerged from this semantic underground only in 1852, as the name of a journal edited by one of the leaders of the radical wing of the *Haskala*[3] (*Hechalutz*). At this point it acquired a new meaning. There are two biblical passages in which a group of armed men precedes the rest of the children of Israel. In the biblical account of the siege of Jericho, the *halutz* goes before the ark of the Lord, which is followed by the *ma'asef* – the rest of the people, or the rearguard. And in one version of the rather unwilling participation of the tribes of Gad and Reuben in the crossing of the River Jordan they go as *halutzim* before the rest of the children of Israel (Josh., vi, 9–13; iv, 12; Num., xxxii, 1–32). Extrapolating from this incident, the editor of the journal wrote of "the *halutz* who goes before the people of Israel in the fight for faith and improvement" (*Hechalutz*, 1). Henceforth the word was incorporated into the language in the sense of "vanguard", or "pioneer", and supported by a spurious biblical quotation: "the *halutz* goes before the host". It was used sporadically from then until 1917. But it really took off in 1917–18, when it began to be applied to the idealistic young immigrants who reached the country in relatively large numbers, most of them members of a movement entitled *Hechalutz*. From now on, it was routinely used to mean "pioneer" in a variety of senses; and this meaning is even applied, *ex post facto*, to some of its biblical mentions by certain modern lexicographers.

2   It occurred only in connection with *halitzat hana'al* – taking off one's shoe, a ritual act connected freeing a man from marrying his dead brother's widow. The standard dictionaries of post-biblical Hebrew until the Haskalah period give only this meaning.
3   The Jewish Emancipation, beginning in the mid-eighteenth century, and lasting about a hundred years.

In effect, therefore, *halutz* was a neologism, though based on a biblical word. So the first question which must be asked is why this term was renewed when it was, and why it gained such wide currency from 1917 onwards. From its first appearance, *halutz* refers to a group, a faction in the cultural struggles then going on in European Jewry. This is a self-appointed elite group which takes on itself the leadership of the rest of the people. Such a concept could only grow up in the late eighteenth and nineteenth centuries: the rigid structure of the traditional Jewish community was becoming gradually looser, and the formation of such groups became possible and socially relevant. Its expanded use during the 1920s and 1930s is connected with the political culture of those it was used to describe. They came to maturity at the time of the Russian revolution, and many of them saw that revolution as a model for their own actions. For them, the *halutz* was an avantgarde; and, indeed, in several of its early appearances the two words are used interchangeably. To take one instance among many: in 1917 the central committee of the Tze'irei Zion movement declared that the *Hechalutz* movement was "the avantgarde of the workers of Eretz Israel". The foreign (by now international) word *avantgarde* was transliterated into Russian.

The political use of the word *avantgarde* as an international term seems to have begun only in the early years of the twentieth century. The idea of the proletariat as a vanguard class was familiar to every socialist; indeed, Katznelson quoted a passage by Lassalle expressing this very idea as a preface to a programmatic speech in 1918 (*Writings* I, 60–1). But it seems that the idea of a vanguard party, and the specific terminology used for it – the word *avantgarde* itself, transliterated into Russian – began to spread only in the early twentieth century. It developed very quickly among the Bolsheviks, and became current linguistic coin in 1917–18. The Bolshevik coup of October 1918 was a triumph for this very concept (Rosa).

The *halutzim* of the period saw themselves as a Jewish vanguard, just as the Bolsheviks were a Russian vanguard: a leading elite, interpreting the laws of history and speeding their operation. But the word they used came into the world with certain associations, culled from its biblical origins. These associations comprise three major elements. First, the individual *halutz* is not alone; he forms part of the vanguard of an army. Secondly, he goes "before the host" – the mass of the people. And finally, in the Bible his actions (both at Jericho and – even more emphatically – at the crossing of the Jordan) are the result of a divine command.

These elements form an essential part of the *halutz* metaphor. But it should be emphasized that it was a metaphor. *Halutz* is one in a long line of military terms which were demilitarized by the Labour Zionist movement, beginning with one of the movement's central concepts – the conquest of labour. The first kibbutz movement was called the Labour Battalion (*Gedud Ha'avoda*), divided into regiments (*plugot*). War (*milhama*) almost always referred to political struggle; and when the *halutzim* actually had to fight – which they did – they evolved a quite different vocabulary to describe it. So these metaphorical soldiers joined not an army but a movement or a collective body – the Hechalutz movement outside Palestine, the Labour Movement (the Histadrut) after their arrival, the kibbutz and the *moshav*. In short, they were a social, not a military vanguard; and they preceded the rest of the people in time rather than in space. Berl Katznelson saw the *halutz* as "the founding father of the future" (loc. cit.): he does today what the whole nation will do tomorrow. As for the divine ordinance, it was translated into social and ethical terms. The *halutz* is not only the agent of divine providence: "The idea of the *halutz* [...] contains first and foremost human and cultural values [...] [*halutziut*] is the opposite of philistinism, of slovenliness, cowardice and servility" (Katznelson, Kibbutz Me'uhad minutes).

The chief duty of the *halutz* was the return to agriculture and physical labour. For this, he needed qualities which well fitted the military origins of the term: he must be tough, disciplined and ready for self-sacrifice. It was not long, however, before the use of the word became routinized, and it lost much of its metaphorical force. Such a phrase as "the *halutz* movement" is little more than organizational description; and this was the first step in a process which led to the current use of *halutz mercazi* to mean centre-forward in a football team. So other metaphors were found to do the same work: *halutzim* were described as "men of stone", who could only acquire the necessary strength and resilience by a painful educational process; and in another widely used formulation, the *halutz* is the dung which fertilizes the soil on which future generations will flourish.

From about 1918 the leaders and ideologists of the Labour Movement adopted the *halutz* concept, and made it peculiarly theirs; and, in fact, until 1948 it was almost exclusively that movement's monopoly. On the face of it, it started as a very simple idea. But, over the years, its implications were expanded, teased out, argued and agonized over – and it turned out to be not so simple, after all. For instance, as early as 1918 the Hechalutz movement decided to be a mass movement, and always thought of itself as such. But, as one can guess from the qualities demanded from its members, it was in fact very selective; and the contradiction between these two concepts led to the creation of several pioneering movements, and constant competition between them. To take another example: the idea of temporal priority only makes sense if one knows the future. So the *halutz* idea had to be assimilated into a broader theoretical framework – for the most part Marxist. Yitzhak Tabenkin, one of the leaders of the kibbutz movement, saw clearly the problems which this involved. He, and most of his comrades, had a more or less Marxist view of history, and were convinced that they, and the whole working class, were the pioneers of mankind. But, Tabenkin remarked, if (*per impossibile*) such thinkers as Nietzsche and Spengler are right, the working class is the most backward section of mankind.[4]

More important in practical terms is the tension between the meanings of *halutziut* as leadership and as service to the nation. Each of them can be – and was – drawn from the original expression, and from its biblical context; and they expressed political and moral conflicts which constituted a central dilemma in Israeli politics and thinking. For instance, shortly after the establishment of the State of Israel Ben Gurion demanded a change in the policies of the kibbutz movements, maintaining that their duty was now to stress the element of service to the state – and, therefore, to abandon or modify their political role. This they refused to do; and many of their arguments rested, implicitly or explicitly, on the concept of the *halutz* as leader or prophet. There is still a similar public discussion over the question of whether the members of Gush Emunim – those who initiated and

---

4 In a seminar at Ein Tiv'on, 1. 12. 1928. Unpublished notebook in Yad Tabenkin archives.

carried out the beginnings of settlement in the occupied territories – are *halutzim*. They are deeply religious, and believe that their acts are "the beginning of salvation" in the Messianic sense. But they also have many of the attributes of the classical *halutz* – devotion, self-sacrifice, service to the nation. Are they *halutzim*? And will they still be *halutzim* if the sporadic peace negotiations now taking place prove them to have been in the margin of historical developments rather than in their centre? The argument is one aspect of the ideological debate raging in Israel today.

The history of this concept illustrates the general truth that the relationship between semantics and history is complex, and far from one-sided. The idea of *halutziut* inspired hundreds of thousands of young people, and deeply influenced their thoughts and actions. But the word itself thereby became part of history, and its meaning was modified, sometimes quite radically, by contemporary events. And this case, history emphasizes that the renewal of the Hebrew language, with its religious history and overtones, is not creation. It can be fully understood only by taking into account the cultural and linguistic – and in this case, also the political – background of those who spoke it. It is also a very cogent example of the power of the semantic past. In its revived form, it began almost as a linguistic *tabula rasa*. But those who used it could not avoid referring to its biblical source; and, in doing so, they opened up a Pandora's box of semantic variety and contradiction. Had they stuck to "avantgarde", the language would have been significantly different; and so too – just conceivably – would the course of history.

In the State of Israel: Ben Gurion

By the time of the establishment of the State of Israel, *halutz* terminology was very widely used both as a generalized expression of approval for the characteristics of the pioneering sector of the Yishuv – mainly members of kibbutzim and *moshavim* – who were believed to be a serving elite, promoting the interests of the Zionist enterprise by their self-sacrificing way of life, and as a more specific organizational term to denote the movements to which these people belonged (for instance, the *halutz* youth movements). In the coming years, while it retained these characteristics it was given different emphases by different personalities and movements.

In the course of his political and ideological campaign to adapt the ways of thinking of the Labour Movement to the new realities of the State of Israel, both David Ben Gurion and his opponents made frequent use of the vocabulary of *halutziut*. The contrast between his views and those of his opponents will, therefore, be a good starting-point for this discussion.

Ben Gurion was not a systematic thinker, but he addressed this subject very frequently, particularly from 1947 onwards. He used almost every semantic variety of *halutz* terminology as it had been crystallized over the previous quarter-century. In particular, he depicted the *halutz* as a revolutionary, "initiating, creative, innovative, breaking out new paths" (*Campaign* 41), But his main emphasis was on the aspect of service to the nation, which he presented as a privilege no less than a duty:

> Nobody who is spiritually a *halutz* envies those who are not *halutzim*, since *halutziut* is a right and a blessing rather than an obligation. *Halutziut* elevates the individual, enriches him, and brings the forces hidden within him to fruition. *Halutziut is the quintessential characteristic of mankind.* (*Vision and Way* 266)

He emphasizes strongly the complex of concepts which are the result of the application of will – power, such as volunteering and mobilization, creativity, initiative, and independence. But, significantly, one of the usages found not infrequently in the discourse of the labour movement – the *halutz* as leader – is virtually absent from his writings.

According to Ben Gurion's conception, which was unlike both that of the artistic avantgarde of nineteenth century Europe and the concept of the avantgarde in the political movements of his time, the *halutz* does not decide freely and independently on his course of action. In his view, the main characteristic of *halutziut* was service: "to put oneself at the service of people and motherland day by day" (253). This ambivalence, of activism and obedience, was well expressed in a speech in 1954: "*Halutziut* is the moral ability and the psychological necessity to live day by day in accordance with the dictates of conscience and the demands of the historical goal" (loc. cit.). In their historical context, definitions such as this assume special significance. It is, in brief, a definition of "state *halutziut*",[5] which was an important element in Ben Gurion's social and political outlook. From a very early period he claimed that the aims of Zionism could not be achieved only by the power of the State (*Vision and Way* 264). "State *halutziut*" is voluntary mobilization of the citizens of the state in order to attain common objectives. But these objectives are decided by the decrees of the "historic mission". To define these decrees and translate them into practical policies is not the function of the *halutzim* themselves, but of those who are in charge of the State's central institutions. Discipline and centralization following a process of democratic decision are essential to any state, and particularly to the problem-ridden State of Israel.

This explains why Ben Gurion laid so much emphasis on the personal qualities of the *halutz*, rather than on his class or movement affiliations. The mobilization of the forces which the State required would be accomplished through the personal volunteering of each individual. True, there still existed such secondary bodies as the Histadrut, the parties and the kibbutz movements, and their activities were desirable in themselves. But they did not fulfill their mission as *halutzim* by creating their own policies; they must mobilize the forces essential to the tasks which the central authority – the state – had defined.

---

5 I have translated the Hebrew term *mamlachtiut* freely. For a rather fuller discussion, see Near, *Kibbutz Movement*, ii, 184, fn. 21.

The Nature and Activities of the *Halutz*

If *halutziut* is connected with individual moral qualities rather than class or movement affiliation, it can be found anywhere in Israeli society. It is not surprising, therefore, that, in addition to his formulation of State *halutziut*, Ben Gurion broadened the definition of those who can be *halutzim* or potential *halutzim*, including in it the early Jewish settlers of Palestine who built villages based on private ownership of the land, and "pioneers of industry" – founders and owners of leading industrial enterprises (*Campaign* iv, 119).

Such statements, and others like them, did not convince most of the leaders of the Labour Movement, and certainly not those of the kibbutz movement. They seemed alien even to many who thought that the popular meaning of *halutz* terminology was obviously correct. This group's reaction was well expressed in a poem of Nathan Alterman, one of the most esteemed poets of the Labour Movement, and on many issues a staunch supporter of Ben Gurion. He wrote sardonically:

> The time has now come, I am bound to relate,
> To sound this clarion call:
> In the great *halutz* project of building the State
> There's plenty of room for *all*!
> That those who go down to the desert to live
> Are *halutzim* we all know well.
> But so is the man who has nothing to give
> But the money to build a hotel.
> (Alterman 206)

To accept proprietors of industrial enterprises into the category of *halutziut*, the holy of holies of the Labour Movement, opened the way to a very broad definition of *halutz* occupations. So Ben Gurion's theory was innovative to an extreme. In 1951 he wrote an important article in which he attempted to sum up his previous social philosophy and develop these ways of thought according to what he saw as their internal logic ("Aims"). He maintained that *halutziut* is a moral value inherent in every human being, and that it can, and should, be made use of for the benefit of the Jewish people and the State of Israel. His words are reminiscent of those of Yitzhak Tabenkin, speaking of the ideal of the *halutz*:

> To be a worker, to be *different* [emphasis in original] [...] The possibility that you, I, he, can achieve, can realize [...] The rumour that there are simple people quarrying stone, and also singing and dancing, and living in a commune [is an inspiration to the young]. (Tabenkin, "Education" 12)

Ben Gurion's conclusions are very different from Tabenkin's. Tabenkin's definition of the *halutz* ideal was narrow: he is a person living in a commune and engaged in physical labour. Ben Gurion completely rejects this interpretation.

> The revolution [...] which came about when we achieved our independence [...] demands of every one of us to make a new reckoning of his life. Our previous ways of life, our accustomed ways of thought, our internal and external relationships, the old values and systems and dimensions, are no longer relevant.
> This demand applies to every trade and profession: civil servants, teachers, lawyers, doctors, army officers, engineers, scientists, authors and artists, and above all to all those in whom the *halutz* spirit burns, whether they are *halutzim* of work, of agricultural settlement, or of the mind. ("Aims" 9)

He broadens the definition of the *halutz* to such an extent that it has little in common with the traditional usage. Moreover, his interpretation of one of the professions on whom he called to act as *halutzim* – civil servants – goes far beyond its conventional significance:

> Workers in field and factory, in the harbours and the airports, in the army and the civil economy, in offices and schools, in trade and handicrafts, in government or private service, workers by hand or brain, directly or indirectly – all of these are creating the foundations of the State of Israel, moulding the character of the liberated nation, and carrying out its historic mission. (Ibid. 22)

Reading this list, one is inclined to ask: "Who, then, could not be a *halutz*?" Every citizen of Israel was a candidate for this title.

The leaders of the kibbutz movements also believed that every Jew was, potentially, a *halutz*. But they believed that the *halutz* potential could only be actualized as the result of a long and difficult process of training and selection. In fact, though not always in theory, their view of *halutziut* was elitist. Unlike them, Ben Gurion defined *halutziut* in more general and less stringent terms, and thereby applied it to a much wider and more varied population.

The Kibbutz Movement: Criticism and Apologetics

For a short while, Ben Gurion believed that the pioneering tasks of the young state could be fulfilled by the kibbutzim (*Vision and Way* 99–100). But during 1949 he displayed increasing disillusion with the kibbutz movement. It reached its peak in a speech in the Knesseth at the beginning of 1950:

> Let me speak, not as Prime Minister, but as one of the *halutzim* [...] The movement which believes in *halutziut* has never disappointed as the kibbutz movement has disappointed [in absorbing new immigrants] [...] Thousands of *halutzim* who have done great things in their own kibbutzim what have they done for the new immigrants? Over the past two years I have been humiliated and ashamed. (*Divrei Haknesseth*, 16. 1. 1950)

Ben Gurion accused the kibbutz movements of several failings. The first was "collective egoism", stemming from their "cutting themselves off from the general public". This accusation was based first and foremost on his condemnation of the politicization of the kibbutz movements, and his demand that they should merge into one all-embracing movement. Now, he claimed that kibbutz members were prepared to work for the development of their own kibbutzim, but not in order to absorb new immigrants. He attacked the political affiliation of the great majority of kibbutzim to the left opposition party, Mapam, and criticized their lack of activity outside the bounds of the kibbutz, particularly in guidance in immigrant camps. And, finally, he was incensed by the refusal of the leaders of all the kibbutz movements to accede to his demand that the kibbutzim employ hired workers from among the new immigrants, in order to create employment and accustom them to physical work. The kibbutz movements rejected all of these criticisms. An analysis of the arguments in this controversy will throw some light on the participants' concept of *halutziut*.

In reply to this speech, one of the ideologues of the leftist Kibbutz Artzi movement wrote:

> It is not only the benefit of the new immigrant of which he is speaking. Here, we can see a repeated effort to harm the standing of the kibbutz movement [...] to undermine the commune in our land, and, indirectly, to cause harm to the party which represents most of the kibbutzim in the country. (Zilbertal 10)

This was certainly true, in the main. This is not surprising, since Mapam was not only an opposition party, but also, in the eyes of many – including Ben Gurion – a potential danger both to the hegemony of his party, Mapai, and to the State of Israel as a whole. The Cold War was at its height, and since early in 1949 the European Communist parties and fellow-travellers had been declaring their loyalty to the USSR, even if this meant the possibility of armed resistance to their own governments. The pro-Soviet ideology of Mapam, and the growing influence of the extreme pro-Communist group within it, gave some support to Ben Gurion's suspicions that Mapam might prove to be disloyal to the State. It is against this background that his efforts to denigrate the majority of the kibbutz movements, which constituted the core of Mapam's supporters, are to be seen. True, in attacking the kibbutz movement as a whole he was doing no small harm to the minority of kibbutz members who were politically allied to him (mainly in the smallest of the kibbutz movements, Ihud Hakvutzot Vehakibbutzim). But this apparently seemed to him to be a small price to pay for an important political achievement.

Absorption and Guidance

The controversy about immigrant absorption was a reflection of two different interpretations of the concept of *halutziut*. The kibbutzim were ready and willing to absorb new immigrants, mainly by educating and training groups of youth movement graduates from Israel and the Diaspora, but also by receiving new members directly from the immigrant camps which were their first stop in their journey from the Diaspora. This was a continuation of the policy which had led to an appalling lack of accommodation from the mid-1930s onwards: absorption of immigrants into the existing community. The kibbutzim also used less conventional methods of absorption, some of which threatened their ideological purity.[6] In general, however, the policy of all the kibbutz movements was to absorb new immigrants into existing communities, or settle them in newly founded kibbutzim. There was, therefore, a certain factual basis to Ben Gurion's contention that they worked for the benefit of their own communities rather than that of the whole Israeli population.

The leaders of the kibbutz movements completely rejected this argument. In their view, the other sectors of Israeli society were absorbing immigrants next to existing communities, and not into them, sometimes in the face of opposition and obstruction by the veteran settlers,[7] and only in the kibbutzim were the immigrants absorbed into the community. This aroused Ben Gurion's ire. He praised the *moshav* movement, many of whose younger generation had volunteered to live in immigrants' *moshavim* and teach their inhabitants how to adapt to harsh Israeli conditions, as against

---

[6] One example is that of the *havurot* – groups of immigrants, usually consisting of whole families, who were to work in a particular kibbutz for a stated period, on the understanding that they would receive pay for their work at the end of that period if they decided to leave.

[7] For instance, many *moshavot* protested at the propinquity of *ma'abarot* (temporary immigrants' settlements) and refused to provide them with municipal services (Hacohen 255 9).

the kibbutzim, which still employed the "traditional" methods of work in the youth movements and immigrant camps, with the intention of recruiting new immigrants to the kibbutzim.

In terms of the analysis presented above, this controversy centred on two different concepts of *halutziut*. Ben Gurion primarily emphasized education: the task of those who worked in the camps and *moshavim* was not to absorb the new immigrants into their society, but to raise the standards of the separate communities (immigrant *moshavim*, development towns and the like) in which the immigrants would continue to live. His approach was elitist, even paternalistic. The ideologists of the kibbutz movements emphasized primarily the interpretation of the *halutz* as precursor: their representatives were not only leaders; they had trodden at an earlier stage the path on which they believed that the immigrants should go.

Ben Gurion's demand of the kibbutz movements to open the kibbutzim to hired labour was an expression of a similar approach, which viewed the kibbutzim as wealthy societies who should devote some of their assets and talents to helping the new immigrants, rather than inviting them to share in the ownership and control of those resources. On this issue he was completely opposed not only by his political enemies, but by almost every sector of the kibbutz leadership, including his political allies. They believed that acquiescence to Ben Gurion's demands would lead to the abandonment of the principle of self-labour, which was one of the foundation stones of kibbutz ideology, and to a process of estrangement from their employees: their approach would be, at the best, a feeling of *noblesse oblige* and, at the worst, simple economic exploitation. Their fears were not without foundation, as was seen from the 1960s onwards (Near, *Kibbutz Movement* ii, 243–7). The kibbutz leadership won the ideological battle, but social and historical forces led to the gradual introduction of hired labour and its eventual acceptance by the whole of the kibbutz movement.

In the Kibbutz Movements

The dominant strain in the *halutz* usage of all the kibbutz movements was roughly similar to that in general use among the Jewish community: it was an extremely positive term, with emphasis on the connection with agriculture and self-sacrifice; but the element of leadership also appears more often than in the popular usage, and, emphatically, more than in Ben Gurion's speeches. Two of the movements – the Kibbutz Artzi and the Kibbutz Me'uhad – were connected with Mapam, a pro-Soviet oppositionist party, and a third World War, which would divide Israel on pro- and anti-Soviet lines, seemed not impossible; so this was a major issue in Israeli politics. As a result, there appeared a new element: the politicization of the *halutz* vocabulary. In 1952, in one of the most extreme expressions of this trend, Ya'akov Hazan, one of the undisputed leaders of the Kibbutz Artzi and Mapam, claimed that, because of the harmful effects of the capitalist environment, neither "economic *halutziut*" nor "social and cultural *halutziut*" by themselves would save the kibbutz from "social and economic failure and bankruptcy". It would be saved from "political degeneration and social deterioration" if it

> sees itself as a fighting cell at the service of the party, and faithfully accomplishes its *halutz* mission [...] Ideological collectivism[8] [...] is an essential condition of the kibbutz's fulfillment of its avantgarde mission within the party. (Hazan 21)

This is thorough-going politicization of the *halutz* concept. Not only is one of the kibbutz's functions – perhaps its most important – to be a leading force within the "revolutionary" party. Hazan also maintains that if it does not perform this task, it will be subject to degeneration in the spheres which were, in fact, the common objectives of the whole of the kibbutz movement – success in production, especially agricultural, and the promotion of the kibbutz's distinctive social and cultural way of life. In fact, there is

---

8   This movement's phrase for "democratic centralism", whereby the individual party or kibbutz member's views are subordinated to the decisions of the leadership.

no evidence to show any correlation between political consciousness and activity and success in these fields; and rank and file kibbutz members of all movements continued to see their economic, social, and cultural activities as expressions of *halutziut*.

With minor exceptions, the kibbutzim of the Kibbutz Artzi never abandoned their constructive activities in favour of revolutionary politics; and, indeed, the ambiguous usage of *halutz* terminology was simply a development of a trend which had been dominant in the movement since its foundation. In a period of uncertainty within the State, and international conflict outside it, both of the meanings of *halutziut* coalesced into a single expression, each of whose parts supported the other: the kibbutz member was part of a social and political elite, which had the dual function of guiding the Mapam party, and through it the whole of Israeli society, in the struggle for a new society, and of strengthening the kibbutz movement both as a constructive force within the state and as a cell of the future ideal society. All of these meanings, intended to strengthen the self-confidence of leaders and rank and file alike, were contained in the Kibbutz Artzi's use of the *halutz* terminology. And to this must be added the almost hypnotic effect of the repetition of phrases in the "private language" of the movement in public speeches and the like, which added much to the rank and file's sense of solidarity.

The leaders of the biggest kibbutz movement, the Kibbutz Me'uhad, also followed this tendency, though with rather different emphases. But within this movement there was a minority of supporters of Mapai, the hegemonic social-democratic party led by Ben Gurion. In 1951 this group left the Kibbutz Me'uhad, and formed a new movement, Ihud Hakvutzot Vehakibbutzim.[9] They eschewed the trend of politicization, and soon began to develop their own interpretation of *halutziut*. This coincided with the beginning of a new answer to the question: what did the kibbutz, as a *halutz* movement, contribute to the State? Levi Eshkol, then head of the settlement department of the Jewish Agency, provided an answer in his speech at the first conference of the Ihud, in 1951:

---

9   Known colloquially, and hereinafter, as "the Ihud".

> The Jewish people and the Jewish state are entitled [to profit from the fact that] [...] in the course of thirty, forty and fifty years a force, or forces, have been created in the country which are, so to speak, called on by history, and have been made ready not to allow the Jewish state literally to starve. (Eshkol 44)

Here increased production is described as a moral obligation of the *halutz* farmer, and first and foremost of the veteran farmers of the State. Over the coming years many leaders of the kibbutz movement justified the employment of hired labour in order to increase agricultural production at any price. In the words of one of the leaders of the Ihud: "We must continue to raise the matter of production to the highest level of national and economic values. We must work at it with heart and soul" (Widler 75). This was not a new trend in the kibbutz movement. Had the very earliest collective groups not ended their first year's work with a small profit, the kibbutz might never have lasted for more than a few months. To take another example among many, in the Second World War those kibbutz members who did not join the fighting forces worked frantically to increase the yield of agriculture and the fledgling kibbutz industry, in order to ensure that there would be sufficient food for the Yishuv and the Allied forces in the area. None the less, the emphasis on productivity as a central moral value was undoubtedly a significant, though not a complete, change, which was emphasized by the Ihud more than by the other two movements.

Summary

In the early years of the state it had to deal with innumerable problems of security, production, absorption of immigrants and many more, and it was clear that the 700,000 new immigrants then reaching the country would be unable to cope with them without the help of the veteran population. The appeal to *halutz* values, and particularly to the values of the kibbutz movement, was one expression of the attempt to mobilize these forces, and the different interpretations of the *halutz* ethos were the result of the ideological differences between the various movements.

Ben Gurion's etatist approach led him to look for the necessary forces in all strata of the population: in an early stage in the kibbutz movement, later in the machinery of government and in a variety of social classes. At each of these stages he supported his demands by changing the application of the *halutz* terminology; and the more he enlarged the circle of those destined to assume the mantle of *halutziut*, the more general and less demanding it proved to be. At no stage did he achieve the success he hoped for. Eventually, when he retired to Sdeh Boker, he returned to the *halutziut* of agricultural labour and personal example; but this move failed signally to increase his political influence or the number of Jewish agricultural workers.

In the decade following the establishment of the State of Israel the attitudes of all the kibbutz movements to the concept of *halutziut* changed perceptibly, if not always overtly. Ben Gurion's attempts to find new definitions of the *halutz* terminology stemmed from the need to deal, in practical and ideological terms, with the realities of the new state. From this point of view, however, his attack on the kibbutz movements was counter-productive. The kibbutz population, who, even according to his own definition, were *halutzim*, were his natural allies in dealing with many of the problems he and the State were faced with; but political differences, to which he attributed supreme importance, prevented him from approaching them directly and seeking mutually acceptable solutions in good will. His blunt and prejudiced style of thought and expression also deterred the kibbutz leadership from making the intellectual effort such an approach might have generated.

Thus, instead of bringing about a fundamental change in the kibbutz leaders' interpretation of *halutz* terminology, Ben Gurion's attitudes encouraged them to use it only in its most general and technical meanings. Instead of seeking new paths, they closed their minds to the significance of the existence of the State, and the changing character of its population. Moreover, Ben Gurion's attacks on the two biggest kibbutz movements intensified the process of politicization both in matters of kibbutz policy and in their interpretation of *halutziut*. Only in the Ihud, which was free of the pressures of the political controversy, was there a slow but perceptible change in its conception of the meaning of *halutziut* in the changing circumstances of the time.

The tragedy of the players in this social and political drama lay in the contradiction between their readiness to accept responsibility for the problems of the Israeli polity and the limited size of their population, which prevented them from doing so effectively. The changes in the interpretation of *halutz* terminology were part of the slow and painful process of accommodation to this fact.

CHAPTER 9

Frontiersmen and *Halutzim*: The Image of the Pioneer in Palestine/Israel and the US

Both Israel and the United States were created in no small measure by pioneers: groups of people who came to areas which were untamed or neglected (or thought to be so), settled in them and cultivated them. In both countries the people concerned in this process, and the period in which it took place, have become central legends in the mythology of the nation. They appear in literary and ideological contexts, have had considerable influence on political thought and action, and form part of a continuous debate about the interpretation of the past.

The subject of this debate is not always clearly defined. Frederick Jackson Turner's primary definition of the frontier was demographic (Turner, ch. 1). Others have emphasized those aspects of frontier life which parallel their own preoccupations; thus, for instance, Lamar and Thompson see South Africa as frontier territory by dint of the confrontation between the existing population and the invading European settlers; and Kimmerling and Shafir, who have interpreted the history of Palestine and Israel in terms of the Turner theory, have emphasized the complementary roles of demography, land ownership, and military activity (and see Winks; Nugent 263).

In this chapter I shall discuss one aspect of Turner's thesis which has received relatively little attention in this comparative research. From his very first article, Turner spoke of the special nature of the pioneer, and its influence on what may broadly be called frontier culture. The pioneer possessed intellectual traits of profound importance [...] coarseness and strength combined with acuteness and inquisitiveness; a practical, inventive turn of mind [...] a masterful grasp of material things [...] restless, nervous energy [...] dominant individualism as well as a political culture which had a profound influence on the development of American democracy. (Ibid. 37)[1]

Like other aspects of the thesis, this view has often been challenged. But it remains a central element in the accepted image of the North American pioneer, and has a firm hold on the popular imagination. And, just as the colonization of North America produced the myth of the pioneer, so did that of Palestine and Israel produce the myth of the *halutz*, a human type with special characteristics springing from the peculiarities of the time and place in which he (and she) lived.

I shall compare the two versions of the pioneer type, and discuss the historical circumstances which led to the creation of the two contrasting myths. It should be emphasized that I shall not attempt to discuss the complex question of the degree to which the myth corresponds to historical reality. Each section opens with a description of the *image* of the pioneer, as it expressed itself in the central cultural tradition of each of these pioneering societies. Subsequently, the historical developments which led to the evolution of the two images are discussed; and here the emphasis shifts to real people and events. Though this comparison may add little to the mass of existing material about the American pioneer, it should contribute to our understanding of the Israeli pioneering myth, which has so far been relatively neglected in the research literature, as opposed to popular legend and history.

Since the two cases are not chronologically parallel, such a comparison cannot be between contemporary processes. In each country there was a "classical" period of pioneering: in Israel, from the second wave of Zionist immigration (Second Aliya) in 1904, until the establishment of the State of Israel in 1948; in the United States, from the beginning of

---

[1] See also "Contributions of the West to American Democracy" in the same volume ch. 9. Detailed descriptions of the pioneer character are to be found in "The Problem of the West" (ch. 7) and "Pioneer Ideals and the State University" (ch. 10).

colonial expansion in the mid-eighteenth century until some time in the second half of the nineteenth. (Turner's date – 1890 – is as good as any for our present purpose.) I shall deal mainly with these periods. Moreover, in the case of Zionist pioneering, the account will be even more restricted; for from the very earliest days of the use of the *halutz* terminology, its use was virtually monopolized by the Labour Movement, and this usage was almost universally accepted by the public at large.

Two Semantic Traditions

I shall begin by justifying my chapter heading. In the surviving American literary sources, the word "frontiersman", first found in 1813, preceded "pioneer" in the sense indicated here by more than twenty years. The root meaning of "pioneer" was of a road- (later also a railway-) maker, at first in a military context, later in civilian pursuits. In 1836 it made its first appearance in the generalized connotation which it bears today. From then on, it seems to have been used almost interchangeably with "frontiersman".[2]

The corresponding Hebrew term is *halutz* [plural: *halutzim*; verbal noun (pioneering): *halutziut*]. Its origin is biblical. In the Book of Joshua there is a description of the manner in which the people of Israel marched round the walls of Jericho: first went the *halutz* (the army: later translated as "vanguard"), followed by the ark of the Covenant, the priests and the people (Joshua, vi, 7–9).

This passage was frequently summarized in Zionist writings in the phrase "The *halutz* went before the host", and the word appears in modern Hebrew in a wide variety of literal and metaphorical usages.[3] So I shall use

---

2 *Oxford English Dictionary*, ad rem. Frederick J. Turner quotes a long passage about pioneers, with no indication that the difference in terminology has any significance (Turner 19–21).

3 For a more detailed account, see ch. 8.

"pioneer" as a generic term of which "frontiersman" is the North American and *halutz* the Zionist species.

This semantic distinction points to one of the ways in which the two concepts of pioneering are distinct. In America the frontier was always an integral part of the pioneering experience. Beyond it there was danger, the primitive, the wilderness in its many forms; within its confines there was civilization, safety, progress. The concept of the *halutz* has no necessary connection with the frontier. Like the American pioneer, the *halutz* was conscious of the contrast between the values of his own civilization and the hostile forces outside it. But there was no physical line dividing them. Indeed, until the early 1920s the borders of the Land of Israel were not clearly defined; and it was not until the mid-1930s, when the partition of Palestine began to be a political possibility, that the border played a major part in the concept of Zionist pioneering.

The word *halutz* had other resonances. The notion of "going before the host" has already been mentioned. The other major biblical source for this word is a passage in the Book of Numbers. On the eve of the invasion of the Land of Israel the tribes of Reuben and Gad, settled and prosperous in Transjordan, ask to be excused from participation in the campaign. Moses is very angry, and demands that they play their part in the invasion, no less than the other tribes. They agree, and "pass over as *halutzim* before the Lord into the land of Canaan" (Num., xxxi, 31–2). Thus, from the very first, the notion of the *halutz* was connected not only with primacy in space or time, but also with acceptance of a divine – or, in the terms used by the men of the Labour Movement, who were secular socialists, a national – imperative.

It could be argued that these are no more than semantic niceties. But there can be no doubt that they formed part of the consciousness of those who founded the Labour Zionist movement, and created the myth of the *halutz* – the young men and women who arrived in Palestine between 1904 and 1923. The majority of their leaders, who created and promulgated the *halutz* terminology, were rooted in Jewish culture, and certainly knew the Bible well. So they were surely well aware of the implications of their use of the word.

However, unlike his biblical counterpart, the modern *halutz* is not a soldier. In Zionist writings the word was always used in a metaphorical sense, as was another widely used term, *kibbush* – conquest: the conquest of land (or a particular piece of territory) – meant its first cultivation; the conquest of work, the entrance of Jews into particular occupations, particularly agriculture; and "self-conquest", a process of self-education to the values of *halutziut*.

In short, whereas the frontier concept refers primarily to the pioneer's physical and military situation, the idea of the *halutz* refers to his/her social context.

Agriculture

One aspect of the pioneering image seems very similar, if not identical, in the American and Zionist versions. Agrarianism was a central *motif* in American pioneering thought. The yeoman farmer was thought to be, in Jefferson's words, "the most precious part of a state" (Letter to Madison), and the motivation of the settlers themselves was to acquire sufficient land to enable them to live the idyllic life of a peasant proprietor.

The Zionist idyll was not very different. From the first, the return to the Land was connected in the minds of Zionist thinkers with the return to, and cultivation of, the land (Near, "Redemption"). And, although the idea of the *halutz* involved readiness to take on any task, during the whole of the period described here the central aim of the graduates of the Hechalutz movement, which educated and recruited young people for immigration to Palestine, was agricultural settlement. Between 1920 and 1923, when there was little land or capital available for such settlement, the new immigrants worked at road-laying, stone-quarrying, and in a dozen other occupations. But as soon as the opportunity arose they created kibbutzim and *moshavim*,⁴ and thus fulfilled the ideal which they had brought with them from the Diaspora. Even when other types of work were acknowledged to be equally important, if not more so, the land had an attraction of its own. In a kibbutz based on the concept of a "mixed economy", in which a relatively high proportion of the members worked in non-agricultural jobs, the members

> have only to smell the odour of the land, and it awakes in them a very strong desire to get closer to nature, to the field [...] how many plasterers, stonemasons and other experts in urban trades have turned into ploughmen, cowmen, and masters of other agricultural skills – not only in Yagur, but in all of our kibbutzim! (Yagur 8)

This attitude was not purely instinctive. The educational work of the major pioneering youth movements was deeply influenced by the doctrines of Aharon David Gordon, who taught that the practice of agriculture, and particularly of physical labour and contact with the land, was uniquely morally elevating.

In this respect, the two pioneering images undoubtedly have many sources in common. The whole of the Zionist movement can be seen as part of the modernizing movement which brought the Jews into contact with European culture; and the concept of the purity of nature, and the nobility of the unspoilt peasant, was an accepted element in this culture by the mid-nineteenth century. But in the Zionist case this doctrine was accentuated by three special factors.

a) The early development of the Zionist movement, and particularly of the Labour Movement, in the early years of the twentieth century, was heavily influenced by Russian populist thought, in which the notion of the superiority of rural life was prominent, if not indeed dominant (Frankel, J.).
b) Both pioneering myths envisaged a "promised land", and referred to the settlers' new homes in biblical terms. In the American version these references were, from the first, metaphorical – often no more

---

4   *Moshav*, pl. *moshavim*, cooperative smallholders' settlement.

than matters of nomenclature. The Zionist ideal was more specific. Based on the Land of Israel described in the Bible, it envisaged the re-creation of a farming community, living in the localities inhabited two thousand years earlier and, by and large, engaging in the same occupations. The very idea of the return to Zion was held to involve a return to the soil. And this standpoint was reinforced during the first twenty years of Zionist settlement, from 1882 onwards. The land available for settlement was, by European standards, under-cultivated and neglected; cultivated land was less open to purchase, and more expensive. Reports from Palestine emphasized this neglect, and fostered the belief that the first task of the *halutz* had to be the renewal of agricultural cultivation. Thus, the phrases which became the clichés of Zionist propaganda – the redemption of the land, making the desert bloom, and the like – were the outcome both of the Zionist myth and the Palestinian reality.

c) For many centuries Jews had been forbidden to own land in most of the countries of Europe. One of the aims of Zionism was to create a new and better type of Jew by changing the occupational structure of the Jewish people. It was widely claimed that the return to the primary industries, in particular to agriculture, would correct the distortions in the Jewish social and psychological structure. The argument for the superiority of the noble peasant was buttressed by proofs based on the social structure of Jewish life.[5]

The persistence and deep roots of the agrarian ethos in the image of the *halutz* are highlighted by the contrast between the image and the reality. At no point during the period under discussion did less than eighty per cent of the Jewish community in Palestine live in towns; from an early stage

---

5   The restructuring of Jewish economic life was widely advocated from the early nineteenth century in Russia (Levin, *Haskalah*). In Labour Zionist circles A.D. Gordon emphasized the moral superiority of physical work, and the constant contact with nature, while Ber Borochov based his theory of Socialist Zionism on a sociological analysis of the Jewish occupational structure.

the biggest of the kibbutz movements proclaimed as its aim the creation of settlements based on "agriculture, industry and handicrafts" (Kibbutz Me'uhad constitution, 1927); and at all stages a high proportion of those who had originally settled on the land, in kibbutz or *moshav*, eventually found their way to the towns. None the less, the tenor of educational material in the youth movements, the propaganda and allocation of funds of the Zionist movement, and the image of the *halutz* in the literature associated with the Labour Movement, all exemplified and reinforced the agrarian ethos. The image flourished even against the background of a quite different historical reality.

There is no parallel to these special incentives to agrarianism in the American experience. Indeed, the semantic development of the word "pioneer" is paralleled by the actual development of the American economy, which from a very early stage exploited mineral resources, and engaged in industry, to an extent unthought of – perhaps even unthinkable – in the Yishuv. Two poems by Walt Whitman, the arch-propagandist of American pioneering, encapsulate the attitude engendered by this fact. "Pioneers! O Pioneers!" opens with the stanza:

> Come my tan-faced children,
> Follow well in order, get your axes ready,
> Have you your pistols? Have you your sharp-edged axes?
> Pioneers! O Pioneers!

The tools used by these pioneers are suited to road-building, hunting and fighting. Agricultural work as such is not mentioned in the whole of the poem. In "A Song for Occupations" Whitman devotes twenty-six characteristically long lines to a list of trades and activities, of which only "the making of [...] reaping-machines, ploughing-machines" has any connection with farming (Whitman 207–14, 223–30).

This section can be summed up quite simply: the *halutz* was, typically, conceived of as being a farmer; in most cases, the frontiersman was not.

Scouts and Settlers

There is more than one type of American pioneer. The first is the solitary hero, exemplified by a long line of semi-mythical figures ranging from Daniel Boone through Davy Crockett and Kit Carson to William F. Cody and the cowboy adventurers (Smith 54–135). He is a hunter rather than a farmer, a trail-blazer rather than a settler. Let us call him the scout.

The settler is no less a pioneer than the scout, but his aspirations and way of life are quite different. He lives in a little house on the prairie, and comes to the West in search not of adventure but of free land. In literary terms he is Judge Temple rather than Leatherstocking. For J.F. Cooper both of these are pioneers. And, indeed, this seems to be common to the historical and literary traditions alike: even at the settlement stage, the pioneer is physically tougher than the Eastern townee, and more egalitarian in his social relationships.[6]

These characteristics, admired by all contemporary observers and image-makers, were carried to excess in the rough, tough, boisterous and hard-drinking type who appeared throughout the period under discussion. The extreme case is the Kentuckian "alligator-horse" of the ante-bellum period, whose cultural specialities were hard work, hard drink and debauchery, as well as constant fighting with friend and enemy alike. Mythologized to the degree of becoming an ideal type, he represents "barbaric individualism [...] the true antitype of institutional man" (Moore 135).

Both scouts and settlers appear in the Zionist historical tradition. But the contrast between their roles in Jewish settlement points up the contrast between the pioneer and the *halutz*.

The *halutzim* of the period before the First World War were noted for their mobility. Long walks in search of work, week-long rambles to get to know the country, frequent regional and national meetings of political parties and trade unions – all these were part of the everyday life of the

---

6   See, for instance, the description of western life in Elias Fordham, *Personal Narrative of Travels in Virginia, Maryland, etc., 1817–18*, quoted in Billington 117–19.

Labour Movement at this time. Though in a smaller area, and at a later date, they could have vied with the American people for the title of "the most mobile and roving people on earth" (G. Unonius, quoted in Still 93–4). Similarly, the romance and challenge of Galilee in the years 1908–10 parallel the "lure of the West" in the United States. In the following extract we can see the myth in the course of creation:

> People would tell wondrous stories of what was happening in Galilee: the attacks by robbers, the malaria, etc. In the evening, after a hard day's work, we would gather in small groups in the workers' restaurant [...] and talk about Galilee. With bated breath we took in every word, and usually dispersed in silence; but deep in the heart of every one was born a fierce longing for Galilee [...] the place where independent Jewish life was being created. (Baratz, J. 5)

In the event, however, Galilee became the area where the idea of the settler ousted that of the scout. The group which founded the first kibbutz, Degania, was originally committed to one year's contract work on the site. But in 1912, when they were offered work in an even less developed region, they decided to make Degania their permanent home. This proved to be a turning-point for the whole of the Labour Movement, and by the end of the first World War the principle of "workers' settlement" – the establishment of kibbutzim and *moshavim* on land belonging to the Jewish National Fund – was generally accepted as one of its central aims. The settler had replaced the scout as the ideal figure of the pioneer.

Many later events in the history of the Yishuv emphasize this development. The ideal of the *halutz* reached its apogee in the late 1930s, when the Zionist movement combated the dual threat of the Arab Revolt and the hostile politics of the British government with the policy known as "strategic settlement": not a movement of forward-thrusting scouts on the American model, but the location of new settlements in positions which would determine the borders of a future Jewish state, combined with continued cultivation and defence of those already in existence.

There are a number of reasons for this contrast between the two countries. The scout/settler dichotomy is at bottom a division of labour. In America unknown country had to be explored, paths blazed, Indians appeased or frightened off. Only after this had been done could the main business of permanent settlement be undertaken. Palestine was a different sort of country. Not only was it smaller and easier to know: the land settled by Jews was often unoccupied, though never unexplored. It was always acquired by purchase, its bounds known and marked. Much of it had been neglected for many years, and the Jews considered it their duty, in the phrase which rapidly became a cliché of Zionism, to make the deserted land blossom. But the skills needed for this were primarily those of the settler rather than of the scout.[7]

In the American and the Zionist case alike, the main skills required for colonization were attributed to the idealized pioneer; but the special characteristics of each country produced two distinctive ideal types.

Toughness and Roughness

The Zionist pioneers needed to be no less tough than their American counterparts: indeed, one of their special problems was the need to adapt to a country, climate, and life of labour for which their upbringing had not fitted them in any way. Whereas many of the American immigrants came from a farming, or at least a labouring, background, virtually all the Jewish immigrants to Palestine originated from lower middle-class families. Poor sanitary conditions, primitive housing, endemic malaria and, above all,

---

[7] In a certain sense, the equivalent of the forerunners, the first wave of American pioneers, may be thought to have been the small group of agents who made the original purchases of land for Jewish settlement. But their skills were in many respects different from those of the American scouting pioneer. They needed to know the country and its people, and often required a high degree of courage and devotion to accomplish their task. But they were not pathfinders or tamers of the wilderness, nor did they need more than the most elementary skills in self-defence. They used diplomacy and commercial acumen, and a knowledge of local customs and laws. In this sense they were closer to Turner's "third wave" of lawyers and businessmen than to the first wave of scouts.

gruelling physical work were the everyday lot of the *halutzim*. The process of acclimatization to all these factors was exceedingly difficult, and many fell by the wayside; in some accounts of the decade before the First World War it is estimated that only one immigrant in ten remained in the country, though a more realistic estimate is about 75 per cent.

From 1919 onwards, the period of preparation and selection took place in the Diaspora, on the training farms of the Hechalutz movement. In the dining-hall of the biggest of these, Klosova, which set the tone for the rest of the movement, was displayed the slogan: "The law of Hebrew pioneering is cruel in its practice, but wonderful in its essence". Toughness, courage and simplicity were the hallmarks of the pioneering image.

The *halutz* had to be tough. But was he also rough, like the Kentucky "alligator-horse" and his legendary cousins? There are a number of myths dating from the early waves of Zionist immigration which seem to point in this direction. Berl Katznelson, one of the leading intellectuals of the Labour Movement, deliberately muddied a new pair of trousers in order to avoid the impression that he had abandoned the life-style of the working class. And the poet Avraham Shlonsky suffered a grave loss of social status among his fellow kibbutz members when a poem was published in his name: he was accused of being an intellectual rather than a real worker. But all this was far from the extremes of roughness of many versions of the American ideal. Berl Katznelson remarked, in the course of a famous controversy on the extent to which "cruelty" was an essential component of the *halutz*'s training:

> The significance of the idea of the *halutz* is first and foremost humane and cultural [...] The opposite of irresponsibility, of sloppiness, cowardice, lack of culture. Everywhere, whether in the kibbutz or the family, we cared about the standard of life – cleanliness, tidiness, productivity. (Minutes of Kibbutz Me'uhad, 1933, quoted in Near, *Kibbutz Movement* 222–4)

Thus, although the cult of the tough anti-intellectual was not unknown in the Labour Zionist movement, it was definitely not part of the mainstream of the tradition. The reason cannot be found only in the economic and political circumstances described above, which militated against the widespread existence of scouting pioneers. The heroes of Kentucky legend, and many other similar types, were not scouts, but workers, paid by contract or for a fixed wage; and the Jewish worker of Palestine was engaged in very similar occupations. "Roughness" was not, therefore, the product of the scout's way of life, and its relative absence in the *halutz* tradition did not stem purely from the Zionist emphasis on settlement.

One reason for this contrast is to be found in the cultural and intellectual background of the Zionist pioneers. Culturally, they were heirs to the Jewish tradition, including at least two elements antagonistic to the cult of coarseness: literacy, and an aversion to drunkenness. The great majority of the *halutzim* had at least a minimal education.[8] And they rarely drank alcoholic liquor. According to the conventional wisdom, Jews drank on Sabbaths, festivals and celebrations, but rarely to excess: Gentiles often got drunk; Jews never.[9] As a result, the cultural expression of the Zionist pioneers, and the release of their frustrations and repressions, took the form of dancing and singing rather than drinking. In all the accounts of social and cultural activities in the Yishuv, those which depict drunken Jews are extremely rare.[10]

There may be a deeper reason for the lack of an equivalent to the cult of the uncouth among the *halutzim*. One of the underlying factors in the motivation of immigrants to America is agreed by many commentators to have been what Arthur K. Moore calls "the garden archetype" (25–43). Millions of Europeans fled from lives of hardship, poverty and persecution in the expectation that they would find a modernized version of the Garden of Eden. When many of the new immigrants failed to find this legendary land on their first stop in America, a high proportion sought it in the West. At this stage, as at the earlier one, their expectations were raised by idyllic accounts of what they would find in this modern version

---

8   The most detailed account of the standards of education in Hechalutz at the time of its greatest expansion in the thirties speaks of "some perhaps close to illiteracy"; but "illiterate" does not appear as a general category in the statistics (Otiker 169).
9   This belief is graphically expressed in the Yiddish folk song, "shikor is a Goy".
10 For one example, see *Isur et al., *Beginning of the Kibbutz* 118. In this account of a party at Degania, the first kibbutz, the writer emphasizes the cultural superiority of the members' behaviour, even when in their cups.

of the promised land. The number of such accounts is legion, and they have frequently been quoted and analysed as an updated version of the myth of Paradise. In the Jewish context, it will suffice here to quote the well-known description of the United States as "di Goldene Medine" – the country where the streets are paved with gold.

Moore and others connect this concept with the image of the Westerner. Among those attracted by the idea of free land to begin a new life of yeoman simplicity, there was also a considerable proportion who thought that they were going to the Land of Cockaigne. These were the people who, despite (or because of) their disappointment with the reality of the West, drowned their sorrows in boisterousness, drink and lawlessness.

No Zionist immigrant expected to find paradise in Palestine. Even before the beginning of Zionist immigration, the state of the country was described in letters to relatives and friends, many astonishingly similar in their message. "This is indeed the Holy Land", they say, "but it has fallen on evil days. It is still waiting for redemption." Similar messages were passed on in appeals for funds, articles and pamphlets, ranging from the barest of descriptions of personal experiences to sophisticated analyses of social and economic phenomena; and this tradition was continued up to the establishment of the State of Israel.

The orthodox Jew would do nothing to hasten the redemption of the Holy Land; it would come about at the coming of the Messiah, and it was a great error – indeed, a sin – to attempt to hasten it. For the secular Zionist, the return of the Jews to the Land of Israel was part of the process of redemption. But only part. The desolate land had to be restored to its former glory and fertility, and this involved work and suffering.

The "garden archetype" helped to create the tough pioneer image in America in two ways. The conviction of plenty was reinforced by the actual conditions of the land in the earliest period of exploration. The hunter and trapper could literally live off the land and its wildlife; the first settlers could take a crop or two and then move on. It was, therefore, natural to act as if they were living on the Big Rock Candy Mountain. In Moore's words:

Frontiersmen and Halutzim

> What the pioneer became in Kentucky was to an appreciable extent a result of his expectation of a paradisiacal situation, that is, an unrestrained existence. Whenever this illusion touches a people, a keen sense of social responsibility is not to be expected or indeed a deep concern with ideas of any noble kind [...] above all else, the rich new land stood for personal freedom and physical satisfaction – hence the indifference to convention and the incidence of spectacular actions. (67)

Not only did this myth shape the thoughts and actions of many American pioneers. It also attracted the type of person who sought a paradise on earth. It served, therefore, as a means of selection; and the people who were selected – at any rate, those who set the tone and created the myth – were adventurers.

The *halutz* neither expected nor found a land flowing with milk and honey. It was, rather, a "land that consumed its inhabitants" (Num., xiii, 32), which could be tamed only by hard work, and the acquisition of the skills and qualities of the settler rather than those of the scout. Moreover, the selection process tended to deter the adventurer, while encouraging the adventurous – particularly those among them who were imbued with "a keen sense of social responsibility" and "a deep concern with noble ideas" (Katznelson, "To the Hechalutz Movement"). In this sense, the westward movement in the US served as a safety valve for the Zionist enterprise. But it did so not within the confines of immigration to Palestine, but by siphoning off those who were not prepared to accept the harsh way of life dictated by external conditions and the Zionist philosophy alike. They went west – mainly to the United States.

The *halutz*, like the frontiersman, could not exist without a high degree of toughness. But his cultural conditioning, his ideology, and the historical conditions in which he lived, all led him to eschew the cult of roughness.

Individual and Community

> [Among] those purposes and fundamental assumptions that have gone to make the American spirit and the meaning of America in world history [...] was [...] the ideal of individualism. This democratic army was not a disciplined army, where all must keep step and where the collective interests destroyed individual will and work. Rather it was a mobile mass of freely circulating atoms, each seeking its own place and finding play for its own powers. We cannot lay too much stress on this point, for it was at the very heart of the whole American movement (Turner 306).

Individualism is, perhaps, the most frequently mentioned trait in the accepted composite image of the American pioneer; and it was thought to apply no less to the settlers, in their simple log cabins, than to the solitary scout. Though all historical portraits of the men of the West mention the existence of such communal activities as bees and log-rolling, in which the whole community turns out to accomplish important tasks, they were never considered to be their most characteristic occupations. By the same token, communal and cooperative settlements existed from an early stage in the conquest of the West. But in the accepted version of pioneering history they are marginal phenomena.

The image of the frontiersman as an individualist has continued to be an integral part of the American cultural heritage until our own day, in scholarly interpretations of history as well as in popular culture in all its manifestations. Among other things, it is held to be one of the ultimate causes of the extension and preservation of democracy in the United States. Despite recent attempts at revisionism in certain respects, it seems that this is still the mainstream interpretation of the frontier ethos in American thought.

If the frontiersman was a loner, the *halutz* (and his female ally, the *halutza*) was a joiner. Berl Katznelson wrote, in an article which deeply influenced the *halutz* movement:

> Unity in work, common expectations of the conditions of life and of common aspirations which will develop in the course of their work together – this great and fundamental unity with regard to the future should unite, educate, and bring about

cooperation between *halutz* groups, despite the differences in their backgrounds and the ways in which they were educated to believe in a creative workers' community. ("To the Hechalutz Movement" 52)

From the early years of the twentieth century the *halutz* joined political parties, professional and trade union organizations and regional groupings. In contrast to the American communes, the kibbutz was not a marginal product of pioneering conditions, but a central part of the Labour Movement. It was only after the establishment of the State of Israel, with the beginning of the decline of the *halutz* ethos, that the form of settlement based on individual holdings – the *moshav* – outstripped the kibbutz in numbers and in its power to attract new immigrants.

In this respect, the contrast with American historical circumstances stretches out beyond the confines of America and Palestine. During the classical period of the westward movement immigrants to America travelled as individuals or in family groups. From 1918 onwards the vast majority of *halutzim* were members of youth movements, or of an overall organization (Hechalutz) which dealt with financial and logistic problems, and maintained an extensive network of branches engaged in educational, cultural and political activities. Moreover, from the early 1920s onward these movements were, in effect, affiliated to the kibbutz movements in Palestine, and the great majority of their members joined kibbutzim on their arrival. The central image of the *halutz* was of "workers, communards, believers in the fraternity of man" (Tabenkin, "Ten Years of Klosova" 7). In short: the collectivism of the *halutz*, no less than the individualism of the frontiersman, was a vital element in the myth.

This contrast is rooted deep in the historical circumstances and ideological background of the two pioneering movements. Neither the frontiersman nor the *halutz* left for his new home without some form of financial and/or political backing. Daniel Boone had his Colonel Henderson, Lewis and Clark their Jefferson. Zionist settlement in Palestine was supported by the Zionist Movement and, from 1930 onwards, by the Jewish Agency. But there is a difference in kind between the two sets of backers. Whereas the American westward movement was supported by individuals or companies seeking their own gain, and hoping to share in the wealth, markets and communications opened up by the pioneers, the Zionist backers were quasi-governmental organizations: their funds were supplied by contributions from all sections of the Jewish people, and were considered to be held in trust for the nation as a whole. The contrast is most striking in the matter of land holdings. In America land was distributed, free or cheaply, to the settlers, whereas in Palestine it was granted on long-term leases, and the Jewish National Fund retained its ownership. Further, the clearing and improvement of land in the new American territories, and the provision of initial capital such as tools and housing, were the responsibility of the settler. In Palestine, basic capital was loaned to the settler by a special national fund (Keren Hayesod), to be returned many years later, when the farm was a going concern.

It is easy enough to point to the historical circumstances which led to this contrast. The American pioneer opened up territories which were, at least in the first stages, rich in natural resources: there he could hunt and fish, obtain quick yields from newly-cleared land, and move on if disappointed. None of these options was available to his Zionist counterpart. Palestine was a land without extensive natural forests and with few rivers. The land available for Jewish settlers was usually poor and neglected, and often needed improvements such as swamp-draining to make it cultivable. Above all, in the arid climate of Palestine it was impossible to achieve yields sufficient for intensive settlement without irrigation projects, and these were usually far too expensive for the individual farmer or settlement group; and, to complete the contrast, land was scarce, and potential settlers many. This necessitated a central authority to determine priorities in the allocation of land, equipment, and money. For all these reasons, the *halutz* needed institutional help long after he had arrived at the place of settlement.

Furthermore, the social and ideological backgrounds of the two pioneering movements were very different. Most of the American pioneers, whether new immigrants or established citizens, migrated as family units; even in the many cases where the head of the household went ahead of his family, the intention was always that they should join him when conditions permitted. The *halutz* was, typically, young and single, and his departure for Palestine often led to a rift between him and his family. Thus, the communalism of the *halutz* was to no small degree a function of his loneliness, and of the need to build a close-knit society which could act as a substitute for the social and psychological support of the family and community he had left behind him.

Ideologically, the individualism of the American pioneer was deeply rooted in the tradition of social and political thought stemming from Locke, and developing through the founding fathers to what may be seen as its extreme form in Jeffersonian Republicanism. Even deeper than this ran the Christian world-outlook, centred on the salvation of the individual. Although the Pilgrim Fathers, and other groups throughout American history, had stressed the importance of the Christian congregation, by the classical period of the westward movement the individualist interpretation of Christian doctrine was clearly dominant.[11]

The Jewish social ethos was different. The individual was regarded throughout Jewish history as part of a community. He prayed with others, and a quorum was necessary for many of the most important ceremonies. His prayers, even on Yom Kippur, when the individual was judged, were couched in the plural, and referred to the community as a whole. Above all, during the years of exile the Jewish communities had developed a network of mutual aid and an ethic of solidarity which stood in strong contrast to the individualist thought of Western Europe since the Reformation.[12]

---

11 The primacy of individual baptism, as against automatic acceptance of those born into the community, had in effect been settled in Massachusetts by the time of the Halfway Covenant in 1662.
12 Alexander Barzel gives a concise account of this element in Jewish life and thought, which he calls *kehilatiut* ("community-ness"), with a broad selection of sources (*To Be A Jew* 120–9). A similar picture emerges from more concrete description of the Jewish ghetto or small town, from which the great majority of the *halutzim* came, for instance, Zborowski and Herzog's *Life Is with People*.

Pre-Classical Periods

All of the above factors made for a collective interpretation of the pioneering situation in the Zionist case, as against the individualism of the American version. But, while they may have been necessary conditions, they were not in themselves sufficient; for, in both societies, many of them were also present before what I have called the classical period of the pioneering image. The terminology and image of Zionist pioneering was crystallized in the first quarter of the twentieth century (Near, "What is a Pioneer?"). But there was Zionist settlement in Palestine before that period. Some thirty Jewish villages were established between 1881 and 1904, all of them supported by philanthropic bodies which raised their funds in the Diaspora, and all based on family holdings – a capitalist structure not essentially different from that of the villages of the American settlers (Eliav & Rosenthal 25–83, 179–206). Equally, the spirit and practice of the founders of the first American colonies was collectivist rather than individualist. In both cases there is a marked contrast between the early period of settlement and that described here as the classical period, during which the main lines of the pioneering image became fixed.

The major difference between the two periods seems to be in the nature and ideology of the settlers themselves. From 1904 onwards Jews arrived in Palestine imbued with a variety of socialist, anarchist and revolutionary views derived in large measure from the social and political ambience of the society in which they had grown up. Moreover, the constitutions of the Jewish National Fund and the Foundation Fund, which supplied their land and capital, were deliberately contrived in order to prevent the sale of land and resources to private farmers. This was done in deference to the views of a number of Zionist leaders, themselves socialists or influenced by socialist ideas, who insisted that the basic resources of Jewish society in Palestine (primarily land and water) should be nationalized. These included Theodor Herzl, Menahem Ussishkin and Franz Oppenheimer, in the first rank of the Zionist leadership (Shilony 10–11, 96–101).

The parallel change in American society came about with the mass immigration and territorial expansion which began in the early nineteenth century. It was no longer dominated by small groups whose origins were marked by joint religious beliefs encapsulated in their communities. From now on, while the motivation and ideology of the immigrants and pioneers was varied, the dominant motif was the urge to achieve material success for the individual and his family. The relative homogeneity and communal-mindedness which had marked the earliest period of settlement gave way to pluralism and individualism (Hansen; Jones).

The individualist image of the frontiersman was the result of a combination of practical and ideological factors, which reinforced each other in the course of the westward movement. The collectivist ethos of the *halutz* was no less the product of the specific historical circumstances described above. But it was reinforced by a background of national and social ideology which rejected the capitalistic world-view of the earliest Zionist settlers.

Post-Classical Pioneering

In both societies the pioneering period proper came to an end at a more or less specific date: in the US, with the closing of the frontier, in Israel with the establishment of the State. But the concepts generated in the classical pioneering period lived on, and continue to do so.

In the US, the pioneering ethos was generalized and attributed to the nation as a whole, under the name of Manifest Destiny. This term originated in the classical pioneering period, but the attitudes it embodied continued to be influential long afterwards; indeed, it has been convincingly argued that, in religious or secular form, they continued to inform American foreign policy throughout the twentieth century, right up to the US intervention in the Balkans in the 1990s and the wars in Iraq and Afghanistan (Weinberg; Stephanson). In Israel, for the two decades following the establishment of the State it looked as though the concept of pioneering was outmoded. But it was revived by the movements which created new settlements in the territories conquered in the 1967 war – particularly the religious settlement movement known as *Gush Emunim* (The Bloc of the Faithful).

The parallels between this movement's ideology and the concept of Manifest Destiny are very striking. In both, the pattern of human history is decided by divine providence. In both the nation is seen as the embodiment of righteousness; and its right to territorial expansion (or, in the current version, military intervention) is derived from these two characteristics. Both were derived from doctrines embodied in the mainstream views of their respective nations: in the case of the US, Puritan Christianity; in the case of Zionism, a secularized form of Jewish Messianism. And both of them had a utopian vision in which the righteous rule over conquered territory, in preference to those who formerly owned it, thus bringing about salvation – in the American version, the triumph of righteousness and true belief, in the Israeli version the coming of the Messiah.

In Israel, as in the US, this claim is far from being universally accepted.

In 1998 the then prime minister of Israel, Binyamin Netanyahu, paid a visit of condolence to a family of settlers in the occupied territories one of whose children had been killed by Palestinian terrorists. "You", he told them, "are the true pioneers of today." In reply, there appeared an article by a veteran kibbutz member comparing the present-day settlers with the classic Zionist pioneers. They, he maintained, came to Palestine in order to earn their living by physical labour, giving up better conditions in the Diaspora to do so. They created agricultural settlements by the sweat of their brow, without employing others and with no help from outside sources, and fought in defence of their homes – often in defiance of the authorities. They aimed to create a homeland for the whole Jewish people, and therefore gained the admiration of all the nation.

The present-day settlers, he said, are quite different: by settling in the occupied territories they forgo nothing of their standard of life, and receive governmental support in many spheres, from economics and health to education and defence. They do not engage in agriculture, and employ others to do the hardest and dirtiest work. Moreover, he concluded:

> The present-day settlers [...] are emissaries only of their own messianic faith, and therefore they cannot be considered an important part of the Jewish people as a whole. Present-day settlement is no more like pioneering than a caricature is like the original. (Modan 11)

The accuracy of many of these statements, which constitute a succinct embodiment of what may be called the protest myth of the Israeli Left, may well be called into question: for instance, Jewish settlement was supported by the Zionist movement in very many ways almost from its very beginnings. But they certainly have some foundation in truth with regard to settlement in the occupied territories from the 1980s onwards. In one of the few research papers published on the subject Goldberg argues that unlike previous settlement movements, which created self-supporting socio-economic enterprises in the spirit of the *halutz* ethos, most of those who had settled in the conquered territories in recent years were white-collar workers – an urban population, with no local initiative or productive capability. It seems likely to the author that this massive migration has taken place primarily because of the availability of superior housing and a high standard of services, while the settlers continue to be dependent on their sources of income in pre-1967 Israel (Goldberg).

There are many differences between the post-classical pioneering concepts of the US and Israel – the main one being the contrast between Christianity, a missionizing religion, and Judaism, which has traditionally eschewed any form of missionary activity. In short, however, the advocates of Manifest Destiny proved to be true pioneers in the short run, with the US's successes in absorbing Oregon, Texas, Louisiana, and Hawaii, and conquering the Philippines, Cuba and Puerto Rico. But in the long run it seems that in going beyond the bounds of continental North America they led the nation along a false path, although it may be said that on certain contemporary manifestations of this concept, such as the Gulf War, the US intervention in Yugoslavia and the war in Afghanistan and Iraq, the jury is still out. As for the contemporary Israeli settlers – this brings us back to Binyamin Netanyahu and his critics.

The earliest settlers of Gush Emunim, in the late 1960s and early 1970s, bore a distinct resemblance to those of the 1920s and 1930s; and in many respects – their way of dress, their readiness for personal self-sacrifice, and, until the Begin government of 1977, their defiance of authority – they deliberately adopted this model. But, as we have seen, few of the settlers of the 1980s and 1990s have embraced this way of life. Moreover, neither in their aspirations nor in their practice do today's settlers share the utopian vision of their predecessors. Far from being socialists, they have established a society which, apart from the special beliefs and practices of its many orthodox communities, is entirely Whitmanesque. Like much of Israeli society, the utopian dream has been Americanized.[13]

Nonetheless, it seems to me that the critique quoted above, which echoes ideas very often heard on the Israeli Left, misses the point. Netanyahu's central claim was not that the present-day settlers are like the classical pioneers in the degree of their self-sacrifice, or even the sacrifice of their children: he has never described the victims of terrorism within Israel's pre-1967 borders as pioneers. Rather, he was saying that they are pioneers in the pristine sense of the word – forerunners, influencing the movement of history by their actions: just as the pre-State pioneers defined the borders of the state by "creating facts", in the often-heard phrase, the new settlers are redefining those borders, and thereby bringing about their own divinely defined utopia – a state of affairs which, for a variety of reasons, many Israelis would consider positively dystopian.

So who are the true and who the false pioneers? The attempts to achieve peace in the Middle East will no doubt continue, and it has more than once been shown that political considerations can lead to the abandonment of land occupied and settled by Israelis "as of (often: divine) right" – for instance, the evacuation of the settlements in Sinai in 1981, and those neighbouring the Gaza Strip in 2000. And at the time of writing it looks as if the US may well continue to pursue its not entirely manifest destiny in Iraq and Afghanistan. What will be the final map of Israel? And will right, as conceived by US policy-makers, triumph over evil in other parts of the

---

13 The high proportion of orthodox American Jews among the settlers is one factor in this process, though far from the only one.

world? The true pioneers have history on their side, or manage to bend it to their ends. Who they will prove to be – only time will tell.

Comments and Conclusions

Myths such as those described here are central to the culture of nations. They define and circumscribe accepted aims and norms, providing grounds for pride in times of success, inspiration in times of emergency, and disillusion in times of failure. Their relationship with other elements in the national character and heritage is complex: they may be a powerful influence on the course of events, or an expression of national characteristics formed by more general circumstances, or both.

In this chapter I have attempted to present the image of the pioneer and the *halutz* as functions of the historical development of the two nations concerned. As I remarked in the introduction, my prime aim has been to highlight the special character of the *halutz* image by comparison with that of the frontiersman, rather than to attempt a new analysis of the pioneer legend of the United States. So I shall confine my remarks in this section to the place of the *halutz* image in the development of Jewish Palestine.

Pioneering as construction

We have seen that the *halutz* is conceived of less as a fighter than a builder, more as a settler than a scout. This image, and the underlying attitudes it reflects, has had an immense influence on Zionist ideology. Throughout the period of the British mandate land was acquired by purchase, and its former tenants compensated financially or by the offer of alternative holdings. The concept of "redemption by labour" became part of the basic creed of the Zionist movement. And all of the *halutz* movements shared the doctrine of "constructive socialism", which saw the creation of wealth by cooperative labour, rather than its just or equal distribution, as the central aim of their movement.

Agriculture

The agrarian bias, rooted deeply in the Zionist idea from its inception, was confirmed and strengthened by the development of the *halutz* movement and its success in developing Jewish agriculture. This bias was expressed in the emphases of Zionist propaganda, and the allocation of land, financial resources and manpower, virtually until the end of the Mandatory period. While it is true that during this time the urban sectors of the Yishuv grew apace, this fact was reflected neither in the public statements of the leaders of Zionism and the Yishuv nor in the consciousness of the general population (Troen). It was only with the establishment of the State of Israel that the prestige and priority of non-agricultural pursuits began to equal and surpass those of agriculture; and the transition was effected in the face of a tenacious ideological struggle.

"Softness"

The fact that the *halutz* was not thought of as "rough" in the sense defined above had far-reaching effects on the development of the cultural forms and mores of the Yishuv. The ideologically motivated use of Hebrew, which involved a deliberate effort to learn the language, as against the "natural" speaking of Yiddish, the mother-tongue of most of the *halutzim*, is but one example. Another, no less important, is the development of new ways of celebration of the Jewish festivals, which were very largely invented and promoted in the kibbutzim and *moshavim*. It was also in this sector that the special types of folk dancing and song which became hallmarks of the Zionist community in Palestine were fostered, and spread throughout the Yishuv largely through the agency of the pioneering youth movements. The proclaimed ideal of the kibbutz movement – to create a "cultured peasantry" – was a direct expression of the image of the "soft" *halutz*. The same ideal can be traced up to the present day, in the educational syllabus of most kibbutz schools, in which humanistic subjects play a role quite out of proportion to the social and economic needs of the kibbutzim. The kibbutz movement's educational values are fundamentally opposed to any conception of the *halutzim*, or their children, as rough untutored sons and daughters of the soil (see chapter 10, below).

Communality

It was remarked above that this is the chief distinguishing feature of Zionist pioneering. Of its many expressions in the life of the Yishuv, only one need be mentioned here: the centrality of the kibbutz and the kibbutz movement in public life and, indeed, in many versions of the Zionist ideal (Near, *Kibbutz Movement* I, 389–99). Among other results of this phenomenon was its deep effect on the nature of the democracy of the Yishuv, and later of the State of Israel, which was much closer to the ideal type of "unitary" than to "adversary" (in historical terms: Jeffersonian) democracy.[14]

Theoretical implications

One of the main conclusions of this chapter is that the cultural ambience within which the pioneers grew up, and which they carried with them to their new land, was a prime factor in the creation and persistence of the two pioneering ideals. If this is so, it has much wider theoretical implications than the matters discussed here. For one of the underlying assumptions of the Turner thesis, as developed by later exponents of frontier theory, is that like causes lead to like effects: demographic, military and cultural

---

14 J. Mansbridge's *Beyond Adversary Democracy* distinguishes between unitary democracy – "the democracy of friends based on equal respect" – and adversary democracy – "the democracy of citizens based on equal rights". Two discussions of this aspect of Israeli political culture, each dealing with a small sector of the Yishuv at a particular period, may be quoted: Ben Eliezer, and Near, "Authority and Democracy".

phenomena, first discerned and analysed in the case of the American frontier, are repeated, though with significant variations, in other parts of the world. I have presented an alternative definition of pioneering: not as the ideological reflection of the frontier situation, but as an effort of man to conquer nature, and in doing so to create a new civilization. Viewed in this light, it seems that the different versions of the pioneer image do not stem only from objective circumstances such as those emphasized by other scholars. They are also, and perhaps even more, the outcome of a multitude of cultural attitudes and historical circumstances created as different peoples, each bearing the mark of its own history, moved to their new lands. Any attempt to universalize the idea of the pioneer must give due weight to such factors.

CHAPTER 10

Youth Movements and the Kibbutz

The history of the kibbutz and the kibbutz movements is intimately bound up with that of the Zionist youth movements – so much so that it is doubtful whether the kibbutz movement would exist today at all without the support and reinforcements which they have given it over the years. From their very earliest days the kibbutzim have been subject to loss of members through disillusionment, illness and death. Until the early 1960s, when kibbutz-born adults began to be a significant demographic factor, constant recruitment was needed simply in order to maintain the population at a viable minimum, and the constant growth and absorption of new members from 1920 to 1948 was largely the result of recruitment through the Zionist youth movements. Moreover, the idea of the youth movement, its methods of organization and its educational approach, have always been central elements in the educational systems of all the kibbutz movements. Youth movement concepts were applied to the education of the kibbutz-born differently in each of the kibbutz movements; but their influence is clearly to be seen throughout the educational system.

In addition to these two direct channels of influence, both the kibbutz movements and the youth movements had an indirect effect on the society within which they functioned. The structure of the movements was pyramidal; members dropped out at all ages and educational stages, in increasing proportions as they approached the age of eighteen when they were required to join a training farm or working group and commit themselves to a life on the kibbutz. But these "drop-outs" had been subjected to movement education for anything up to a dozen years, and many of them retained the attitudes and values which they had acquired during this time. In the words of one of the leaders of the kibbutz movement some eighty years ago:

> Our pioneering education will not be wasted, even in the case of those who cannot join the kibbutz for various reasons. It will make them faithful to the realization of Zionism and Socialism, and give them respect for and understanding of cooperative living wherever it may be. (Liebenstein 13)

This "indirect" educational effect was also thought to apply in much broader areas, such as the imparting of Jewish and general humanistic values. Thus, although the two major functions of the pioneering youth movements were recruitment to the kibbutz and the education of the younger generation within it, their influence on society was not confined to these spheres alone.

Definitions

The youth movement – indeed, the very concept of youth as a distinct social category between childhood and adulthood, as against a situation wherein the transition takes place quickly, usually with a short initiation ceremony – seems to be specific to the modernizing, industrialized world from the early twentieth century onwards. Moreover, it seems to have been confined, at least in its early stages, to young people of the middle classes, freed for the first time in modern history from the necessity of making a living in early adulthood, and able to use the relative freedom and leisure of high-school life for the intellectual and social ventures which are typically part of this phase of modern life.

This description fits the movements which are known in Jewish historiography as the "classical" youth movements, as well as the archetypal movement, the German Wandervogel, which influenced them deeply. But many other organizations, some of which shared these characteristics only in part, have an equal claim to be called youth movements; for example, the British Boy Scouts and Girl Guides, whose members were mainly working-class boys and girls, though most of the leadership was recruited from the middle and upper classes. The same dichotomy existed within the Zionist youth movements: the biggest of them, Hechalutz (The Pioneer), claimed to be a mass movement (as against the other, more selective, movements) and deliberately aimed at recruiting young people from the working class.

No less pertinent to the questions I shall be asking here is the matter of age. Hechalutz was, essentially, a movement of young adults, on the threshold of decisions about their future lives: whether to stay in Europe or emigrate to Palestine, whether to join a kibbutz or follow some other occupation. In terms of chronological age, this period usually covered the years from about seventeen to twenty-one. The other youth movements also dealt with these questions, but as the culmination of an educational process which began very much earlier, usually at about the age of thirteen, and ended in young adulthood – eighteen to twenty. In this sense, the period of the youth movement is parallel to that of adolescence, according to one of its classical definitions – the interval between the ages of physiological and social maturity: between the time when young people are able to father or bear children and that at which society permits or enables them, in legal, moral and/or economic terms, to do so. In recent years the term "youth" has also been applied to what is described as a "post-adolescent" phase – the time of university studies, as opposed to that of high-school age in the definition current before the Second World War. My definition still seems to be valid, however; for the young people described, for instance, by Keniston are still not "mature" in the eyes of the world or, in many instances, in their own eyes. They remain "young" until they have made a decision about future careers, or until their academic attainments enable them to support themselves and their present or future families. This is social maturity (Keniston 17–19).

History

The beginnings of the kibbutz movement were chronologically almost parallel to those of the youth movements. The first kibbutzim were founded in the first decade of the twentieth century, and by the outbreak of the First World War the handful of kibbutzim which then existed were a recognized part of the Jewish community of Palestine. But, although the founders of the early kibbutzim were young – many of them scarcely out of their teens – the connection between the kibbutz and the youth movement as such began only after the First World War, when the British mandate in Palestine, with its declared intention of promoting a national home for the Jewish people, was established. This connection was a prime factor in the growth of the kibbutz movement. The very existence of the kibbutz was a central element in the process whereby young people, most of them graduates of the youth movements of Eastern Europe, joined existing kibbutzim and created new ones during the 1920s. From the late 1920s onwards this process was strengthened and institutionalized by the formation of three major kibbutz movements, each with its own ideological and political orientation, and each receiving reinforcements from one or more youth movements in the Diaspora. Those who joined a particular youth movement in the town or *shtetl* of Eastern Europe and stayed in its ranks received agricultural training in a "training kibbutz" in the Diaspora, and then joined a group destined to settle as a new kibbutz, or to reinforce an existing one. The organizational and educational links between the kibbutz movements and the youth movements of the Diaspora were many and varied. The established kibbutzim provided top-level educators and organizers, as well as a great variety of educational material. No less important, they presented a coherent world-outlook offering hope of escape from the ghetto to a meaningful and productive life, and provided role models and a focus for the positive aspirations of these young people.

From the mid-1930s onwards, historical circumstances – primarily the need for increased absorption and settlement in the face of persecution in Europe and the possibility of the establishment of a Jewish state in part of Palestine – turned the kibbutz into a focal point of the Zionist movement and, to no small degree, of the Jewish people as a whole. Sectors of the Jewish people and the Zionist movement which had up to then had little or no connection with the kibbutzim began to create links with the kibbutz movement: it became more varied in its politics, its attitude to religion, and in the national and cultural origins of its members. One very significant development was the creation, and the affiliation to the kibbutz movement, of a number of Jewish youth movements in Palestine. But despite this variety, which often expressed itself in bitter political and ideological rivalry, they shared a number of basic principles.

From its earliest days, the kibbutz movement had two major objectives. Its internal structure, based on communal ownership, direct democracy and a far-reaching degree of equality, expressed the aspiration to build a new society, free from the tensions and injustices of the capitalist society in which all of its members had been born and educated. But its members also saw themselves as a serving elite, dedicated to advancing the major goals of the Zionist movement and of the Jewish people. The aspiration to serve society was called pioneering (Hebrew: *halutziut*) and the kibbutz youth movements were called pioneering youth movements (see chapter 8, above). Despite the many political and ideological differences between the kibbutz movements, this consensus on the aims and nature of kibbutz society remained constant until the establishment of the State of Israel in 1948.

The Philosophy of the Youth Movement: Juventism

A major part of the youth movements' ideology, whatever their political complexion, was their claim to have effected a revolution in educational methods. Typical of this approach are two articles which appeared in the early, formative years of one of the major movements, Hashomer Hatza'ir, and were frequently reprinted, as complementing each other, in subsequent years.

Until now [educators] have looked on young people as unfinished creatures, always requiring guidance on the part of adults. This fits the notion of education: the shaping of the character of the young on the basis of the experience of grown-ups, who aim to shield them from the dangers and difficulties which they themselves experienced [...] They prepare the young for their lives in the future as if they had no independent lives of their own in the present. They cut young people off from the surrounding world, and from real life. They show them the clear blue sky, harmonious human relationships, permanent and universal laws and ethics which prevail in the adult world [...] and what they cannot hide, they suppress with the use of certain catch-phrases – "heretics", "enemies" and the like [...] In the life of the youth a new force has come into play: the youth movement. Within it is concentrated all the life of the youth, and it provides answers to all the unresolved questions of the past. Youth fashions its life according to its own aspirations and needs, and realizes that the time of youth is not an "introduction" to life.

In the youth movement there flourishes the pattern which is most fitted to this period: the youth group. In the movement the young person ceases to be an object of education, and becomes simultaneously its subject and object. Many young people come to the youth movement stupefied by home and school, lacking any independent thought; in a short time they become free and confident, constantly striving to complete their transformation into active human beings. Thus, the youth movement frees its members from the curse of materialism and gives them the chance of freely directing their own destiny during a most significant stage in their lives. The youth movement has presented its members with an ideal of spiritual activity and self-education that will be part of them for all their lives [...]

[As against education in school and home], our methods are suited to the innermost needs of youth, and express its most vital aspirations. Our movement is motivated by the consciousness of our inner reality: it is this that enables us to grow and gain strength in the spirit of our young members. Each of us would quickly become disillusioned and despair if left to ourselves: but being united we do not fear such a fate.

♦ ♦ ♦

The significance of life [in our movement] is that it springs directly from the fountainhead of youth. Our ambition is not to create a "decent" person, with all the traits of the good citizen. We ourselves, the youth, are our own objective. Our life is not an ante-chamber to the life to come. I believe that any form of tendentious education, even that which puts forward Jewishness as an educational objective, falsifies our character, just as any tendentious emphasis can spoil a work of art.

We have nothing in common with the educational reformers except our rejection of the old pedagogics. We live in the company of young people, and our life together determines its nature. "Presumption, *chutzpah*" we shall be told. But we are not ashamed to declare that we are presumptuous enough to prefer the spirit of youth above all: the values of youth are the quintessence of culture.

Today we are entering into a new period in our movement's life. We are young and strong. It is of the nature of youth to aspire continuously to new forms of human thought – infinite yearnings for the highest and most exalted. What we achieved yesterday is of no interest to us today. Tomorrow is our future, that for which we yearn. We were educated in the Diaspora, but our ambition is the Shomer in the Land of Israel: a young Hebrew, fearless, striving for freedom and regeneration. In the heart of nature, in field and forest, we shall awake to new life and free ourselves from the slough of the Diaspora. We shall love labour, for only in labour shall we achieve our future. (*Book of the Shomrim* 43–4)

These two documents together give a clear picture of a great part of the educational ideology of the classic Zionist youth movement as envisaged by its members and, in particular, its leaders. The youth movement is contrasted with the school. Its members are "both the subject and the object" of education – they teach themselves and learn from themselves, rather than from their elders, and thereby become active human beings rather than passive recipients of accepted doctrines; and their educational experience "springs directly from the fountainhead of youth" as against the external motivation of the dominant trend in conventional education.

Despite the fact that one of the authors denies any far-reaching affinity with "educational reformers" these short statements can be seen as the epitome of some of the fundamental principles of progressive education: paedocentricity, the emphasis on the child's active participation in the educational experience, and the highlighting of process as against content.

However, the youth movement ideal is a more extreme version of these principles than many progressive educators would accept. Paedocentricity (more exactly, "juventocentricity") is grasped here not simply as an educational tool, but as a philosophical principle: the values created, or discovered, in the youth movement are both more suited to the needs of young people and more valid than those in whose light they are educated in the school system and in their homes. Independent thought leads to literally revolutionary conclusions: denial of the social and moral precepts of the existing society, and a desire to build a new society grounded in their own, self-generated ideals. It is this process which "gives answers to *all* the unresolved questions of the past" [my emphasis, to stress the fact that the questions are not only educational]. This, in my phraseology, is juventism.

These manifestos also stress two of the main educational tools of the youth movement: the central role of the movement as such, over and above the content of its education; and its characteristic organizational pattern – "the youth group". The theme in both cases is the being together which forms an important part of the social development of the adolescent. In the case of the movement it is generalized and ideologized. But, as one of the authors points out, belonging to such a movement is a potent source of spiritual strength. The "youth group", involving the intensive interaction of a small number of people, gives even stronger emotional support – to the point of being seen as a (superior) substitute for the family unit.

Thus, in certain respects the youth movement was almost a model of progressive educational methods. It focussed on the needs of the young person, fostered independence and active participation in the educational process, and created frameworks for the acquisition of social skills and mutual interaction between peers. Some other aspects, not directly dealt with in the above texts, should also be mentioned. All the movements emphasized the importance of nature in the process of growing up: rambles, camps and similar activities were an essential part of their ambience. In this context they also developed methods of physical education, through games and the like. And in each movement there developed a distinct cultural style, which was seen to be the outcome of the principle of simplicity and the rejection of urban values. Folk singing and dancing were practiced both for their own sake and with an ideological overlay. Clothing, whether in the form of uniform or of a stress on simplicity, was also part of this special cultural ambience.

All of these aspects of youth movement education can be viewed as natural developments of the principles of progressive education, if not necessarily essential components of it. Juventism, by contrast, is the claim that youth creates special values, superior to those of the society around it.

Progressive educational elements were common to virtually all the organizations which called themselves, or were described by others, as youth movements before the Second World War, from the Boy Scouts and

Girl Guides to the German Wandervogel and the religious and political movements which derived from it. Not all of them adopted juventist ideas, however. The "mix" between the different elements described here, and the emphasis given to each of them, differed between the various movements, and this, no less than their overt ideological differences, formed part of the special nature of each movement.

Content

Even a superficial scrutiny of the texts I have adduced as being typical of the classical Jewish youth movement will show that they contained a basic contradiction, of which the authors themselves were apparently aware: the contradiction between the outright rejection of "tendentious" education and the message of the final paragraph, which accepts Jewish and Zionist principles as an educational aim. This seems to be true of almost all youth movements, and the exceptions were "non-tendentious" only for a very short period of their existence. They proclaimed the principles of spontaneity and absolute self-expression, but these ideals were realized within a pre-determined ideological framework. All youth movements, with the possible exception of the Wandervogel, have had quite clearly defined political, religious and/or cultural aims. Even the Boy Scouts, which claimed to be non-political and to have no aim other than the creation of good citizens, had a clear political bias: the good citizen was loyal to monarch and Empire, in an age when these very virtues were being called into question by socialists and democrats. Indeed, apart from their special educational methods all of these movements had one characteristic in common: they promoted that love of country and people which was variously called patriotism or nationalism. In the ideology of the Zionist movements nationalist ideals were linked firmly with their educational practice: the rebellion against the "classical" values imposed by school and society led them to seek new, "natural" forms of cultural expression. These they found in their national traditions – national folk-song and dance – and in reviving folk-tales, symbols and heroes specific to their people's history. These symbols were different from those of the people around them because their history was different: young Jews in Germany found their inspiration in legends created on the banks of the Jordan rather than the banks of the Rhine. Similarly, their leaders proclaimed that they were socialists because of the ideals of fraternity and equality which they had created in their educational units, in their camps and rambles: the notion of universal solidarity was simply an extension of the principle that "a scout is a brother to every other scout". And, in Zionist terms, the desire to create Jewish agriculture and a class of Jewish farmers in Palestine/Israel was derived from the return to nature, from camps and rambles, and the rejection of urban life and urban values.

This picture of spontaneous activity by groups of active, self-governing young people which jelled into moral and political guides for their adult life was, however, no less myth than it was historical reality. One of the classical analyses of the development of the Zionist youth movement reveals a common morphology, which can be seen, with variations, in other such movements, Jewish and non-Jewish (Schatzker).

In this schema, the beginnings of the movement are far from spontaneous: the Wandervogel, for instance, was originally created by a few schoolmasters seeking new after-school activities for their pupils. Similarly, virtually all of the Zionist movements were initiated by students or young members of the local Zionist organization, who were concerned to find ways of invigorating the adult movement and attracting young people to its ranks. These movements had no "pre-Zionist" or "pre-ideological" period: their very names – Hashomer (The Guard), the symbol of Jewish heroism in modern Palestine, Blau-Weiss (Blue and White [the colours of the Zionist flag]), Tze'irei Zion (The Young People of Zion) – reveal their Zionist ideology.

In the formative period, therefore, a group of older people with clear doctrinal and organizational allegiance laid the foundations of the movement. But in many cases the first generation of young people who had undergone the process of education rebelled against their elders, and took over the movement in the name of the independence of youth. It was during this period that the philosophy of juventism was crystallized, and became a central tenet in movement thought and practice. The growth in numbers and self-confidence which this period brought about was enough to enable the movements to break free from adult supervision, and become independent financially and organizationally. The revolt of youth was epitomized in the revolt of the youth movements. They became independent entities, encouraging their members to continue the "way of the movement" in their adult lives – in the case of the pioneering Zionist movements, to strengthen the kibbutzim and kibbutz movements which they played a vital part in creating and reinforcing.

This, however, was not the end of the historical process. Each of the youth movements became, in effect, part of a kibbutz movement, and the connection between them was institutionalized: the very movements which continued to declare themselves spontaneous and self – regulated were now controlled by leaders who, while themselves youth movement graduates, were far from being young. They continued to use the educational tools which had been developed at an earlier period – the small educational group, their characteristic cultural activities, and scouting in a variety of forms – in order to educate to "good citizenship" of a very special sort – immigration to Palestine and agricultural settlement (Margalit, *Hashomer Hatza'ir* ch. 9). And much the same applies to the Palestinian youth movements which grew and flourished during the 1930s and 1940s; even the most independent and distinctive among them affiliated to a kibbutz movement at an early stage of their development.

Thus, from fairly free associations of independent, spontaneous groups of young people, the youth movements became organizations for recruiting youngsters to the kibbutzim, and educating them to accept kibbutz values. In this process, too, there were a number of internal tensions, even contradictions. For instance, the fact that the main educational unit, the small group, was controlled by leaders appointed from above tended to limit the application of democratic principles. The structure of the movement – councils, conferences and the like – was democratic; but it tended to be a guided democracy, in which leaders (present and past), advisers from the kibbutz movement, and the movement establishment in general, had sufficient influence to settle virtually every issue. And this situation was replicated in the relationship between the youth movements and the kibbutz movements, as the leaders of the latter grew in age and in public stature, in contrast to the perpetually renewed youth of their affiliated movements.

There were some movements which rejected the concept of juventism. In the words of Pinhas Lubianiker, the founder and leader of Gordonia, one of the most influential of them:

> It is true that youth is a world unto itself, different from that of the parent generation. There is no doubt that the young have a distinctive psychological make-up [...] for their individuality has not yet been subjected to the stultifying influence of the social framework. But it is a mistake to think that youth has any special ideals which mark it off from the society in which it lives. The very fact that the youth movements are divided on the basis of the same national, social and religious ideals which divide the older generation proves that this concept is illusory. *Youth is a psychological category, not an intellectual one.* Its function is not to introduce new ideas, but to create new attitudes towards existing concepts – not to originate goals, but to achieve them. (Luvianiker 327)

This movement, however, no less than those which continued to use the language of radical juventism, employed the traditional methods of scouting and intensive social interaction in the educational group. And its leaders, and a great many of its ordinary members, reached much the same conclusion: the logical end of youth movement activity and education was to join a kibbutz.

The founders, graduates and educators of the youth movements became the founders, leaders and educators of the kibbutz movements. They applied youth movement principles and practices within the kibbutz, but the ways in which they did so differed as between the three major kibbutz movements: in the Kibbutz Artzi of Hashomer Hatza'ir, by the use of progressive methods in the schools, and the establishment of "educational institutions" (boarding schools) which were meant to provide a youth movement type of experience for the kibbutz-born; and in the other movements, through the "children's society", the "youth society", and spare-time activities according to the youth movement model. In all of the movements the kibbutz groups were also formally attached to nation-wide youth movements.

Principles and Practice

The Classical Period

For something like a generation it looked as if these principles provided a solid foundation for both stages of the system: the pioneering movements of the Diaspora and Jewish Palestine educated young men and women to be committed Zionists and socialists and, in their adult lives, to practice the principles they had acquired in their early years; while within the kibbutz, itself built on those principles, there grew up a generation most of which adopted kibbutz values and the kibbutz way of life – for until the mid-1970s the great majority of kibbutz-born youngsters returned home after their military service and became members of the kibbutz.

Even at this early stage, however, the system worked less effectively than it aimed, and often claimed, to. During the 1930s the pioneering youth movements in Europe afforded a way of escape from persecution and poverty for tens of thousands of young Jewish men and women, who flocked to the training farms and swelled the movements to numbers never achieved before or later. But even in this, their peak period of membership and activity, they never reached more than about eight per cent of their potential membership in the appropriate age-groups (Near, *Kibbutz Movement* I, 233–4). Even Hechalutz, which deliberately aimed at mass membership, was in fact a small minority among Jewish youth, chosen by a stringent process of selection according to physical, social, and ideological criteria: it was, in short, an elite. While their achievements were impressive in themselves, they seem less so when contrasted with their declared aim of conquering the whole of Jewish youth.

By contrast, the effectiveness of the kibbutz educational system seemed at this time to be unquestioned. But here again, it must be remembered that the kibbutzim themselves were a minority within the Palestinian Jewish community – never more than eight percent of the total population. They, too, constituted an elite group, which became even smaller at times of prosperity in the surrounding society, as many of those recruited through the youth movements succumbed to the temptations of town life.

It is, of course, very difficult to assess success and failure in matters of value education such as those with which we are dealing here. In this case, however, there is a crude but easily measurable criterion: the degree to which the movements succeeded in the aim which they set themselves – recruitment to the kibbutz. As we have seen, they recognized the existence of "educational by-products" such as the inculcation of a socialist or Zionist world-outlook, simplicity in dress, and directness and honesty in human relationships. But the prime object of their education was the creation of pioneers, in a very clearly defined sense of this term: kibbutz members; and in the years of the classical youth movement, before the establishment of the State of Israel, both the urban youth movements and the kibbutz educational system achieved a remarkable degree of success. This was, of course, not only the result of the educational process. In the case of the urban movements, two historical factors increased their power and influence: those in the Diaspora were a convenient – indeed, often the only – way for young Jews to escape from poverty and persecution; while the Palestinian movements grew in prestige and size from the mid-1930s onwards, when the kibbutz movement was almost universally seen as the avantgarde of the Zionist struggle, and its affiliated movements enjoyed both widespread approval and institutional support. As for the kibbutz-born, the values which they had derived from their education were reinforced both by their emotional ties to their home and the public status of the kibbutz.

The Post-Classical Period

Shortly after the establishment of the State of Israel a major change came over the urban pioneering movements in Israel and the Diaspora. After the mass immigration to Israel of Holocaust survivors and Middle Eastern Jews, the Jewish communities of the Diaspora were now tiny compared with their pre-war numbers, and most were no longer subject to the exigencies of extreme antisemitism and economic distress. In consequence, the objective of immigration to Israel, once a clear imperative of the Zionist movement, was called into question. This was doubly true since, after the destruction of European Jewry, the majority of the youth movements were now situated in countries such as the US, Britain and South America, where co-existence with the non-Jewish population was one of the facts of Jewish life. Young people were more concerned with questions such as the quality and purpose of Jewish life and culture, or the possibility and desirability of assimilation into the surrounding society, than with ways of escape from poverty and persecution. Within Israel, many of the former objectives of the kibbutzim were taken over – actually or potentially – by organs of the state, and the status and prestige of the kibbutz decreased drastically. Though all of the movements continued to see recruitment to the kibbutz as one of their central aims, the number of recruits dropped sharply, and has continued to decline until the present day. There was also a gradual change in educational emphasis: elements which had previously been considered "by-products" were now seen as no less important than the creation of pioneers, and sometimes even more so. The existence of the movements was justified in the Diaspora by their role in affording Zionist and general Jewish education to a broad segment of Jewish youth, regardless of their future plans; in Israel, their function was defined in terms of political education to the Labour Movement and its values, and preparation for citizenship.

In the kibbutzim, the change came about at a later stage. Until the early 1970s, the number of kibbutz-born men and women returning home after their army service was eighty per cent and more. From then on intergenerational tensions began to be felt strongly within many kibbutz communities, there was a widespread decrease in faith in the mission of the kibbutz within Israeli society, and many began to doubt the validity of socialist values. The result was a demographic decline no less serious than that suffered by the youth movements. The number of kibbutz-born returnees is today somewhere between twenty and thirty per cent; certainly not enough to ensure demographic growth or even stability.

It would not, however, be true to say that the educational systems discussed here were failures. On the contrary: there is plenty of evidence to show that, by less stringent standards than the simplistic one of kibbutz recruitment, they have enjoyed considerable success. The urban youth movements in the Diaspora were influential in educating generations of young Jews to be active in their communities, and particularly in the Zionist movement, while the Israeli movements have educated tens of thousands of young people to a world-outlook based on social solidarity, justice and service to the country.

The Urban Youth Movements

In the light of the above account, we can now attempt to answer the following questions: To what extent is education in the youth movements I have described progressive? Is it effective in terms of the declared aims of the educators – or in any other terms? To what extent are successes and failures in these spheres the results of youth movement education, and to what extent are they the outcome of other historical and/or societal developments?

In effect, the first of these questions has been answered, to no small degree. Camping and scouting, song, dance and play, educational work in small groups, democratic conduct of the affairs of the group and the movement, and the "learning by doing" which is the essence of education to work in the kibbutz educational system – all of these are consonant, even identical, with the spirit and practice of progressive education.

In schools and other formal educational organizations, these methods are used to promote ends decided and controlled by the educators; and this is no less true in the youth movement, whether the educators be called leaders, advisers, or scout-masters. Historically, they were seen as part of a single complex. Analytically, however, the two strands of which it was composed – juventist ideology and practice, and progressive educational methods – are separable; and, indeed, many youth movements (notably the Boy Scouts and Girl Guides in most parts of the world) have used progressive means while eschewing the ideology of youth. Their aim is education for citizenship: that is, to acceptance of the values of the surrounding society, rather than rebellion against it in the name of "the values of youth" and the like.

The outcomes of these two elements in the classical pioneering youth movements can be analysed in similar terms. In the Western Diaspora (primarily the English-speaking countries, as well as Germany and Czechoslovakia before the advent of Hitler), progressivism was an effective tool in the area of what may be called Jewish citizenship: promoting Jewish consciousness, bringing young people to appreciate Jewish culture, support for Palestine/Israel, activity in the Jewish community, and so forth. Juventism was also effective, but with a very limited number of young people, a high proportion of whom acted as leaders and organizers of the younger age-groups: an elite within the elite. It became more effective, not as a result of more efficient education or more intensive ideological activity, but through external circumstances. In the face of persecution and catastrophe, to immigrate to Israel and join a kibbutz was seen by the surrounding community not as rebellion against the established order, but as a reasonable way of solving the basic existential problems of Jewish youth.

The Youth Aliyah scheme of the 1930s and 1940s is a paradigm of this phenomenon. This was an organizational framework for transferring young people (mainly from Germany) to Palestine, where most of them completed their education in kibbutzim. Most of these youngsters were youth movement members, and the great majority joined the scheme with the encouragement (or, at least, the agreement) of their parents. Though they spoke the language of juventism, this step was not a revolt against adult values, but the culmination of education for what I have called above Jewish citizenship. When the two elements coincided – namely, when the overt juventist message received the (not necessarily explicit) blessing of the surrounding society – the youth movements reached their maximum effectiveness.

This analysis applies equally to the situation of the movements in Palestine/Israel. From the mid-1930s until 1948 the kibbutzim had a special place in the implementation of a widely approved political and military strategy, and the social status of the kibbutznik was close to the head of the prevailing scale of social values. For the first quarter-century of its existence the kibbutz movement had been a self-appointed elite. Now it received the approval of a very great part of the Jewish community, and most of those youth movement graduates who joined the kibbutzim won the admiration of that community, including their own parents.

Thus, the socializing function of the youth movements led to the strengthening of the kibbutz movement. Juventism was still part of their accepted ideology; but the "revolt" which they preached led, in practical terms, to the kibbutz, which had become one of the most prestigious sectors of the Jewish community of Palestine.

From 1948 onwards, however, the nature of Israeli society began to change. The status of the kibbutz, as well as its numerical proportion in the Jewish population, declined rapidly: with governmental agencies now available to fulfil many of the functions it had performed in the pre-State period, many (including many in the political establishment) considered it an anachronism; and, though the leaders of the kibbutz movements claimed that they were still of major importance in fields such as defence and agricultural settlement, the Holocaust had destroyed their manpower reserves in the Diaspora. As a result, the proportion of youth movement graduates joining the kibbutzim has undergone a steady decline over the past sixty years.

What, then, of the youth movements? They continued to fulfil their socializing function. But from the 1960s onwards the society for which they prepared their members was very different from that of the pre-State period: it was marked by increasing class differentiation, individualism and materialism. The situation was now not very different from that of the early 1930s, when the values and aspirations of the kibbutz movement contrasted sharply with those of the great majority of the Yishuv; in other words, the kibbutz was again in large measure a counter-cultural society. It is not surprising, therefore, that the proportion of youth movement graduates joining the kibbutz dropped steadily. For the majority of their members the movements' function was to ease their entry into adult life, and develop a network of attitudes and relationships which would aid their progress in middle-class society. Only a very small minority of activists took the juventist pretensions of the movements seriously, and joined kibbutzim – and most of them for a short period only (R. Shapira et al.).

Thus, the tension between juventism and progressivism had different results at different periods of history. In the "classical" youth movements, as we have seen, the reasons were in part inherent in the nature of such movements, and in part the result of historical developments over which the movements and their leaders had little control. In recent years they have also been deeply affected by a complex psycho-social development. During the twentieth century, the limits of adolescence in the Western world have broadened: boys and girls reach physical maturity today two or three years earlier than they did at the time when the youth movement phenomenon began, and society now demands of young people of all social strata – especially of the middle and upper classes – an increasing period of training and education before they are ready to enter the employment market in the fields considered appropriate to them. The result is "extended adolescence": forms of thought and behaviour normally considered to be appropriate to the adolescent stage are continued until the mid-twenties and even later. At this stage, as a result of a growing awareness of self and of interpersonal relationships, the search for identity and the tendency to criticize the world around and the parental generation, the "revolt of youth" becomes meaningful to the adolescent boy or girl. Usually the revolt is short-lived, and the young person finds his or her own way to fit into the adult world. But in a minority of cases youthful rebellion leads to a permanent change of values; and, when the historical circumstances are appropriate, it is encapsulated in movements bearing the banner of youth.

All this applies to Israeli youth – including kibbutz youth – no less than to the rest of the Western world. But the process is complicated by a major factor, that of military service. In many respects this period – three years for young men, two for women, from the age of eighteen – leads to a cessation of development – in Yehezke'el Dar's terms, a "latency period" (Dar). So, despite the continued juventist element in the ideology of the Israeli youth movements, the combination of military service with the pattern of their members' psycho-social development has until recently ensured that their real function was progressivist rather than juventist: education for citizenship rather than the development of an alternative world-outlook.

In about the mid-1980s, however, almost coinciding chronologically with the massive changes which have fundamentally changed the character of the kibbutz movement, there began a new development. A minority of youth movement graduates began to establish small "communes" in development towns and other socially distressed areas, which engaged in educational and social work. This was a development of the "year of service" performed by many kibbutz youngsters as part of their military service, extended to encompass the period after their release from the army (cf. Dror). These are not kibbutzim: most of them have no communal means of production and there is a great variety of ways of life and degrees of communality among them. But they have in common two of the major characteristics of the classical kibbutz from its very beginnings: the centrality of the communal experience in their common life-style and social philosophy; and the aspiration to help Israeli society solve some of its most burning problems – poverty, social and ethnic tensions and educational backwardness – rather than settlement, economic production and security as in the classical kibbutz. They consider themselves, and are considered by the kibbutz movement, to be part of that movement, and many see them as its best last hope for growth and renewed vitality in the future. As has been remarked, they are only a minority within their own age-group (in 2009 they numbered about a thousand), but they are organized and encouraged by the youth movements, including those of the kibbutzim. This is the contemporary realization of their juventist philosophy.

Kibbutz Education

Though the kibbutz educational system requires a rather different analysis, it is in many respects similar to that of the Israeli youth movements. Here, the juventist aims of self-development and independence of thought and action are exemplified and institutionalized in the "youth society", in which the extra-curricular activities of the young people of a given kibbutz are organized on a democratic basis. Though the founders of kibbutz education believed that this would give kibbutz-born children experiences similar to those which had been so important in their own lives, there are two major differences between this system and the urban youth movements. As we have seen, the very nature of the youth movement requires it to be selective. But the kibbutz educational system aimed at embracing every kibbutz-born child, and succeeded in doing so in all but a tiny minority of cases. Thus, it was forced either to adapt its activities to the needs and desires of the majority, and thereby weaken the juventist message, or concentrate on the activist minority and run the risk of alienating the majority. In fact, the kibbutz youth movement has oscillated between these two poles during most of its existence.

Even more important than this, however, is the fact that the institutionalization of the kibbutz movement within the overall Israeli educational framework emphasizes and exacerbates the inherent contradiction between the juventist and progressivist approach. Despite the overt emphasis on the independence of thought and action of youth, the task of the educator, and of the system as a whole, was, in the words of one of the standard works on the subject, "educating the successor generation" (Messinger). The educators of the older generation encouraged their children to develop their own ideas and ideals. But in their own rebellion against the bourgeois world of their parents they themselves had developed ideals which they considered to be universal; it was, therefore, scarcely conceivable to them that independence of thought should lead to rejection or drastic modification of these ideals.[1] So, in general, youth movement activities in the kibbutzim fulfilled much the same function as those in the towns: character education, and inculcation of the values of good citizenship – in other words, of the surrounding society: the kibbutz.

---

1   The one major incident in which juventism was put into practice was in 1951, during the split in the Kibbutz Me'uhad on political lines, when several groups of young people left their parents' kibbutzim and joined kibbutzim which shared the political views these young people had formed in the kibbutz youth movement. But this was a quite exceptional case.

Nonetheless, there was a change of values among the younger generation. It began to be felt in the early 1960s, and has been gaining strength ever since. But it was only indirectly the result of juventist education. Its causes are to be found partly in the differences in world-outlook which stemmed from the contrasting life experiences of the two generations, and partly in the weakening of kibbutz ideology as a result of the post-State crisis. It was reinforced in those kibbutzim (about two-thirds of the whole kibbutz movement) which had adopted a pro-Soviet ideology. The disillusionment with the Soviet Union which became prevalent during the 1960s led, in many cases, to a widespread scepticism towards ideology of any sort.

This scepticism chimed well with the spirit of the age, the time of the "end of ideology" in the western world. And when the pace-setters of the younger generation of Europe and America reverted to ideological thinking, one aspect of their thought was well suited to the mindset of kibbutz-born youngsters. The Marxist shibboleths of the 1960s meant nothing to them: they felt them to be part of their parents' world. But they had been brought up to believe in the "revolt of youth", and to practise the principles of self-determination and autonomous decision-making in the "children's society" and the "youth society". They now applied these ideas to their own case, and formed a set of values significantly different from those of their parents. One central issue was the question of "self-realization"; their interpretation of this concept was more individualistic, less concerned with service to the community and more with the satisfaction of private needs. Many concluded that these needs could not be satisfied within the kibbutz framework, and left for town. Others stayed within the kibbutz, but made – and are still making – significant changes in its social set-up.

These developments were intensified by the social trends prevalent in Israel from the 1970s onwards: the previously accepted ideals of socialism and a welfare state economy were gradually replaced by norms of individualism and capitalist development. Such ideas reached the younger generation through their many contacts with the outside world, especially at the time when they were most impressionable, during their army service and immediately after it.

Here, in the kibbutz context, was expressed one of the most critical differences between the youth movement experience and that of the younger generation in the kibbutz. As a result of the long-term changes mentioned above, by the 1970s the phenomenon of "extended adolescence" was recognised and even institutionalized within the kibbutz movement. But the fact that the doubts and self-examination associated in the 1930s with the late teens now took place between five and ten years later meant that at precisely this critical period the influence of surrounding society on the kibbutz-born generation was at its height. It was felt in the armed forces, in the universities, and on their world-wide wanderings. And at just this time they, unlike their parents, lacked the focusing and directing influence of a movement which could help them find their way back to the kibbutz. Moreover, the effects of the communal experience often led to denial of the kibbutz ideal; and this fact in itself, in addition to all the factors unfavourable to demographic growth which have already been mentioned, leads to a steady process of attrition, Thus, the decreasing curve of kibbutz-born returnees reflects elements common to kibbutz education and the non-kibbutz youth movements – elements which have been of increasing force since 1948, and are still prevalent today.

In order to bring this description up to date, however, it should be added that from the early years of the twenty-first century a new demographic trend has set in. In many kibbutzim there has been an influx of married couples in their late twenties and early thirties. Most, if not all, are kibbutz-born people who did not return to the kibbutz after their army service, but began to carve out a career for themselves outside the kibbutz, married, and have now "returned home", while, usually, still practising their professions outside the kibbutz. In many kibbutzim there is a waiting-list for such couples, until accommodation becomes available. It is too early to know how long this trend will last, or make an informed guess as to its reasons;[2] but it exists virtually throughout the kibbutz movement – in "communal" and "privatized" kibbutzim alike – and has changed the atmosphere and expectations of survival of many kibbutzim.

2 But see Karolina Rab, "Privatization: Collapse of Kibbutz Ideals or a New Chance for this Community?", lecture at ICSA Conference, Jezre'el Valley College, June 2010.

Summary

The historical outcome of the symbiosis between the Zionist youth movements and the kibbutz movement can be summed up succinctly: without the youth movements there would have been no kibbutz movement. There were certain crucial historical periods when the youth movements changed the course of kibbutz history, and very many failing kibbutzim have been rescued by reinforcements from the youth movements.

Today, the great majority of the members of every kibbutz are either graduates of a youth movement or children of such graduates. So, from this point of view, the symbiosis between youth movements and kibbutzim is a remarkable success story. None the less, the final reckoning is not unambiguously favourable in all respects, and I shall permit myself some reflections on various aspects of this remarkable partnership.

One of the most dearly cherished aspirations of the Labour Movement, in Palestine/Israel as elsewhere in the world, was political and social unity. In principle, all the kibbutz movements also shared this aspiration. But until the first decade of the twenty-first century it was never even remotely realized: the movements were divided ideologically, in their concepts of the ideal structure of a kibbutz, politically – whether because a particular movement was an independent political force or whether it supported one of the major parties in the Yishuv or State – and organizationally, in that the structure of each of the movements was different in some vital respects. And this lack of unity was to no small extent the result of structural factors. Members were recruited at an early age – sometimes between eight and ten years old – for reasons which in most cases had nothing to do with ideology, but with scouting, song and dance, and social activities. Many chose a particular movement because it was close to their home, or its activities were held at a convenient time, or because friends or relatives were members. From that moment onwards the young person entered a path which led from a branch of the movement in a *shtetl* or the Jewish quarter of a European town to the movement's training farm, and thence to a working or training group in Palestine and to his/her eventual permanent home in a kibbutz – very often not of his/her own choosing, but decided by the "advice" of the movement's central institutions. This track was to a great extent sealed off from outside influences, including that of other, parallel movements. In most of the countries with sizeable Jewish populations (with the partial exception of Germany, Russia before the Bolshevik revolution, and the English-speaking countries) there was no free market of conflicting views, but parallel, largely self-contained, paths.

Yitzhak Tabenkin posited as one of the aims of the *halutz* movement the elimination of these differences, particularly those which stemmed from the social or geographical origins of the young pioneers. "Anything which reminds a person that he comes from a 'bourgeois' or 'working-class' home, that his educational background is Hebrew or Yiddish speaking or Polish/Russian diminishes and weakens him", he declared (*Kibbutz Me'uhad Anthology* 157). But the ideal of a unified movement in which all the variations resulting from differences of home background, country of origin or movement were abolished was never achieved: the movements demanded continuity in absorption of new immigrants, and their graduates concentrated in kibbutzim whose character was strongly influenced by their country of origin: thus, there are today "Polish", "Hungarian", "English", "Brazilian" and "Argentinean" kibbutzim. The differences between them are expressed in many different ways, from the food provided in the dining-room to styles of socializing and varieties of democratic culture. These, however, are usually ignored in statements of their explicit ideological stance, which generally conforms to that espoused by the movement.

The results of the separation of paths were expressed clearly in two different historical events. The first was in politics. When the Kibbutz Me'uhad movement split in 1951, the ideological differences between the two camps were clearly defined, in terms of sympathy for or rejection of Communism and the USSR. But the camps which adopted these attitudes had been well defined years before the split. The common denominator of each group was movement loyalty, and their ideological loyalties matched the national origins of their members almost exactly. They had been crystallized in the youth movements.

Another example is the controversy about "communal sleeping": whether children should spend the night in the children's houses or in their parents' homes. The change from "communal" to "private" sleeping first took place in the early 1960s in five kibbutzim most of whose members originated in English-speaking countries. The reason for this is still a matter of controversy. But it is unquestionable that these women (and their male partners), with a common social and cultural background, received their movement education together, arrived in the country together, and settled as more or less homogeneous groups in several kibbutzim. And a later wave of pressure for "family sleeping" was largely prompted by young kibbutz-born parents. This, a harbinger of the fundamental changes of the 1980s, can be seen as one result of the "revolt of youth" which was one of the facets of juventist philosophy. So both structural and ideological elements connected with the youth movement played a part in changing the face of the kibbutz in the twenty-first century.

It should be added, in conclusion, that all the youth movements connected with the kibbutzim were known as "pioneering" (*halutz*) movements. Though this appellation rarely led to deviations from what I have called the popular usage (chapter 8), this element was prominent in their ideology, with all the variations and interpretations discussed above. But the youth movement's special contribution to the philosophy of education has always been, as it still is, the concept of juventism.

PART FOUR

Looking Outwards

CHAPTER 11

Paths to Utopia: The Kibbutz as a Movement for Social Change

One of the major assumptions behind the thought and actions of all the major kibbutz movements has always been that the kibbutz can, and should, influence the rest of society. Ways and means have varied greatly. All of them, however, aim at applying the values of the kibbutz – Zionism, self-labour, equality, democracy and mutual responsibility – to the State of Israel (or, before 1948, to the Jewish community of Palestine) as a whole. These ways and means form the subject of this chapter.

Over the past eighty years, the kibbutz movements have developed some thirteen different strategies for social change. I shall describe and classify them, with some comments on the historical circumstances in which they evolved. One would, of course, also like to know to what extent these strategies were effective. This is a complex question, and I do not believe that it can be fully answered in the present state of the research. Here, I shall only ask which of the strategies described are considered by the members of the kibbutzim to have been successful in the past or relevant in the present, and which have been explicitly or tacitly abandoned. In my concluding comments I shall suggest that some of these strategies were conceptually flawed, and therefore bound to fail; some became outmoded in the course of history; while others seem *prima facie* to have been relatively successful.

Kibbutz Holism

Before discussing the strategies themselves, I shall say something about aims. The first countrywide kibbutz movement, Gedud Ha'avodah, aimed at establishing a "general commune of all the Jewish workers of the Land of Israel." Open to all who were willing to accept its principles and very stringent way of life, it aimed to expand until it included the whole of the working class; and, since the "general commune" would eventually cover the whole of the Jewish economy, it would thus become the Socialist Zionist society (Shapira, Anita).

I shall call this variety of ideology kibbutz holism. Today, when the kibbutz numbers less than 3 per cent of the population of the State of Israel, this aim may seem ludicrously over-ambitious. But it was not always so. In 1939, when the kibbutz population had grown from 2.7 per cent of the Jews of Palestine to 5.3 per cent in less than three years, and more than 100,000 young members of the Jewish pioneering movements in Europe were waiting to join them, it certainly did not seem an impossible dream. Indeed, although Gedud Ha'avodah ceased to exist in 1929, this dream informed the ideas and actions of its successor as the major kibbutz movement – the Kibbutz Me'uhad – right up to the early 1950s. Throughout this period, the very existence of the belief in holism was a source of strength to the kibbutz movement. Under conditions of poverty, political weakness and military danger, the vision of a future all-kibbutz society created a confidence which was certainly not self-evidently grounded in the real situation of the kibbutz.

Whether the holistic vision could ever have been realized we shall never know. Any possibility of unlimited growth of the kibbutz was cut short by the Holocaust, which destroyed its reserves of manpower viciously and completely. Although during the period of mass immigration to the State of Israel in the early 1950s the kibbutz movements declared themselves willing to absorb unlimited numbers, the social composition of the new Israelis – survivors of the Holocaust, and Jews from the Arab countries – led to a drastic reduction of the kibbutz population in relation to the State as a whole. Today, all are agreed that in any foreseeable future the kibbutz will be one sector in a pluralistic society. Kibbutz holism was one of the myriad unseen victims of the Holocaust.

Kibbutz Marxism

In some versions of kibbutz ideology, the emergence of the holistic kibbutz society is called "the kibbutz revolution". One of them, which I shall call "constructive Marxism," was current in the Kibbutz Me'uhad in the 1920s and early 1930s. The Marxist schema of class struggle and revolution was translated into terms of the formula generally accepted in the Labour Zionist movement: constructive socialism. According to this theory, the Jewish community of Palestine would be built as a socialist society, thus obviating the necessity of class struggle in the usual sense and the destruction of the old society. In the interpretation of this doctrine adopted by the Kibbutz Me'uhad, class struggle became competition between various social forms: the kibbutz; the *moshav* (a village made up of individual leaseholds on nationally-owned land); the town; and the *moshava* (a village comprised of privately owned farms on private land). The revolution would consist in the victory of the kibbutz; in other words, the achievement of kibbutz holism (Near, *Kibbutz and Society* 94–100).

Another kibbutz movement, the Kibbutz Artzi, achieved a different synthesis of Marxism and kibbutz theory. According to the "Theory of Stages", the immediate task both of the kibbutz and of the Labour Movement as a whole was to build a Jewish society in Palestine, in collaboration with the bourgeoisie, and, indeed, with all sectors of the Jewish people. The revolution would come about after the fulfillment of Zionism. Under such circumstances, the immediate strategy had to be a combination of constructivism (that is, building kibbutzim) in the present, and political and educational work which would prepare the kibbutz members and all those they could influence for the future revolution (Margalit, 1971, 135–49, 303–4).

In a third variant of kibbutz Marxism, adopted by the left wing of Gedud Ha'avodah, the kibbutz is "the avantgarde of the revolutionary movement [...] a fighting, conquering unit that expresses the collective will of the Labour Movement" (Horowitz 279). On this view, the chief task of the kibbutz is political education and organization, and its social and economic activities afford a material basis for this revolutionary activity. The kibbutz is an avantgarde in the classic political sense of the term, a Leninist revolutionary party. Many members of the kibbutz movement which adopted this view became Communists, abandoned Zionism – and Palestine – and made an unsuccessful attempt to rebuild their commune in the Soviet Union (Margalit, *Kibbutz, Society and Politics* 234–82, 382–7).

These three doctrines have been eliminated by history no less than the idea of kibbutz holism. No kibbutz group or movement today would rely on the simplistic Marxist formulae of the 1920s, 1930s and 1940s, or on the inevitability of any sort of revolution. All contemporary kibbutz ideologies assume that we live in an age of uncertainty. The future may hold a socialist revolution, or a holistic kibbutz society; but nobody is prepared to base a strategy for social change on the assumption that it does.

Commendatory Holism

Holism as I have described it so far was couched in the prophetic mode: it was both a forecast of the future and an expression of approval of that future. It also existed, however, and still exists, not as a forecast, but purely as a value judgment: whether or not the kibbutz will encompass the whole of society, this version of holism says that it should do so. I shall call this attitude commendatory holism, to distinguish it from the prophetic variety previously described. Any version of kibbutz theory and practice must take into account the need of the kibbutz to survive, and, therefore, to shepherd and increase its resources. Commendatory holism says much more than this. It sees the reinforcement and expansion of the kibbutz as the only permissible aim. All of its relationships with the outside world – in politics, in the educational sphere, in the struggle for governmental support – are directed to this end. This view was expressed in 1979, in the course of a discussion between the leaders of two kibbutz movements: "Even today, the uniqueness of Israel lies in the existence of the kibbutz. This is the quintessential expression of the idea of 'salvation' in Judaism. [...] It's only the kibbutz that gives the country whatever it has that's special."[1] If this is so, only one strategy can be relevant: the strengthening of the kibbutz by any means possible.

Such an attitude is by no means uncommon today. It is also found in much earlier periods, when the kibbutz had much greater confidence in its ability to influence the society around it. A pertinent example is the attitude of the leaders of the kibbutz to the *moshav*. The most extreme of the kibbutz movements, Gedud Ha'avodah, opposed its acceptance by the Histadrut on the grounds that it was a capitalist form of enterprise. This view was rejected both by the majority of the Labour Movement, and by all the other kibbutz movements; but, throughout the 1920s and 1930s, the question of the legitimacy of the *moshav* arose in various forms. In 1924 Ben Gurion addressed the conference of Hechalutz, the comprehensive organization of Jewish pioneers. He demanded that the enthusiastic young delegates should see the *moshav* as a legitimate part of the Labour Movement, even though, in his view as in theirs, it was "not sufficiently Zionist and not sufficiently socialist" (Near, *Kibbutz and Society* 151). Nonetheless, in practice if not always in theory, the *moshav* was always in the position of a stepchild in the Hechalutz movement.

---

[1] The speaker was Yehiel Shemi, a well-known sculptor, and at the time secretary of Kibbutz Kabri. Shemi's remarks seem to have evoked no particular reaction from the other speakers, from which it may be inferred that they were not thought particularly eccentric (*Dialogue on the Unification of the Kibbutz Movements* 19–20).

The attitude of the leaders of the Kibbutz Me'uhad, which held a dominant position in Hechalutz, was also not substantially different. Since their underlying philosophy was prophetic holism, they believed that the moshav had no future, and was therefore undeserving of the support of the Zionist authorities. By the early 1930s the theory of constructive Marxism was in temporary abeyance, and the Kibbutz Me'uhad was learning to live in a pluralistic society. This, however, did not prevent it fiercely opposing the expansion of the *moshav* movement, on the grounds that it was a capitalist social form. This attitude was encapsulated in the punning phrase adopted by Yitzhak Tabenkin, the leader of this movement: the *moshav* must enjoy equality of rights; but it should not be viewed with equanimity.[2] Clearly, if the *moshav* was considered inferior to the kibbutz, and not worthy of political or financial support, the same must apply, *a fortiori*, to the rest of the *Yishuv*. There could be no more unequivocal statement of the principle of commendatory holism.

It seems, however, that this concept of the place of the kibbutz in society has certain built-in disadvantages. In 1926, one of the leaders of the kibbutz movement suggested that the tendency of the Histadrut bureaucracy to rigidity and insensitivity to the real needs of the workers could be corrected by sending its officials to the kibbutzim, to renew their contact with the working class and its essential values. This suggestion was castigated by one of the leaders of the Labour Movement as "kibbutz imperialism". Again, in the struggle of interests between the kibbutzim and the *moshavim* in the early 1930s, the kibbutz was described by its opponents as a "sect", or a "faction". (Near, *Kibbutz and Society* 212–14) Naturally, these terms aroused the ire of the kibbutz members, who were convinced that it was "only the kibbutz which gave the country whatever it had that was special." Simply to state this, however, is not necessarily to convince.

This situation is even more critical today. Not only is there wide acceptance of the fact that the State of Israel – and, within it, the Histadrut-owned enterprises known as the "workers' economy" – is a pluralist society, encompassing a wide variety of social forms, but there is also no longer the

---

2   In interview with author and Baruch Ben Avram, 1975.

wide consensus on social values which was held by most of the population of the *Yishuv*, according to which the kibbutz was indeed the embodiment of ideals theoretically accepted and admired by society at large. Moreover, the very success of the kibbutz has led it to acquire resources and rights, and to establish positions of social strength. In short, it has become part of the Israeli establishment, and must, therefore, compete with other sectors of that establishment for economic and political power. Thus, what may seem to the kibbutz members themselves to be "the expression of the idea of 'salvation'" may well be, in the eyes of those outside the kibbutz, the struggle of one interest group among many for the preservation of its rights and privileges. A contemporary example is the dilemma of the kibbutz movements in the economic crisis of the 1980s. In a situation of runaway inflation, it was virtually impossible for them to preserve the value of their resources and provide individual kibbutzim with working capital without recourse to the money market and the Stock Exchange. Such activities are in conflict with the traditional principle – and the accepted image and self-image – of the kibbutz, that it must live on the products of its labour alone. Thus, when certain kibbutzim, and some officials of the kibbutz movement, were found to have been making speculative, and even ethically questionable, deals this was widely held to prove that the kibbutzim were "no better than the rest of the country": and this was often said with no small degree of *Schadenfreude*.

Pioneering and Revolution

Most of the strategies adopted by the kibbutz do not assume a holistic approach, of either type. The next three to be described were historically often associated with the Marxist analysis. In fact, they are logically independent of Marxism; and, as we shall see, they were often couched in non-Marxist terminology. All of them, however, derive from a firm belief in a new, revolutionary, socialist and Zionist society. In 1932 Israel Bar Yehuda, one of the leaders of the Kibbutz Me'uhad, said: "We are not teachers or leaders. We are merely pioneers (halutzim), going along the road before the host" (9). In this use of the term halutz, the kibbutz is a forerunner of the new society, doing on a small scale today what the whole of the people, moved by the ineluctable forces of history, will do in the future (see chapter 8). Close to this view, though not identical with it, is the idea that the kibbutz is a "growing-point" of the new society. The kibbutzim seek "new spiritual sources, and arouse hidden cultural forces which will be the basis of the new society". In the words of Meir Ya'ari, the leader of the Kibbutz Artzi movement, there will be a progression "from commune to communism" (Margalit, *Hashomer Hatza'ir* 135–49).

I find no contemporary version of the concept of the forerunner; scepticism is too deeply embedded in our way of thinking for it to seem feasible. Yet that very scepticism about a future perfect world has bred what may well be interpreted as a variant of the "growing-point" concept: the belief that the kibbutz, and similar scattered communes throughout the world, can be the basis for reconstructing the world after an ecological or nuclear or social catastrophe. This is, of course, very far from the orthodox Marxist prognosis. Yet, like that theory in its time, it reaches out beyond the local – Jewish, Zionist, Israeli – concerns of the kibbutz, and links it with universal ideas and problems.

The Kibbutz as a Reference Group: Models and Prototypes

Historically, the earliest theory of social change in the kibbutz movement is expressed in the phrase used by the members of the very first kibbutzim: they were attempting to create an exemplary society. The individual kibbutz aims at perfection in the relationships between its members, in economic progress, and in its social and cultural activities. If it is successful, others will see this perfection, and do likewise. The result will be, in the words of one of the earliest kibbutz writers, "a Land of Israel sown with kibbutzim"

(Shatz 92). Joseph Baratz, one of the founders of Degania, the first kibbutz, said in 1923:

> The question of the place of the kibbutz in mass settlement has never greatly concerned me. On the one hand, our way of life is suitable for the masses – and, indeed, for all mankind. But, equally, it is obvious that the masses (including the so-called mass immigration to Palestine at the present) are not yet suited to communal life. (quoted in Katznelson, *The Kvutza* 19)

The kibbutz must improve its social, moral and economic standards, and wait until historic conditions produce a generation which will live up to them. Then it will become, in contemporary terms, a model for others to copy.

Related to this view, but significantly different, are two other versions of kibbutz ideology. The first is a moderate form of the "exemplary society" doctrine. At various periods, and particularly in the 1950s, at the nadir of the kibbutz's status in Israeli society, there was much talk of "radiation of values". In this view, as in the concept of the "model", the kibbutz influences by being; however, here it is not the kibbutz as a model of society which is being imitated, but particular aspects of its social being: the existence of kibbutz democracy has a positive influence on Israeli society as a whole; kibbutz members working together with new immigrants, themselves members of *moshavim*, educate by example to such values as social equality, self-labour, agriculture, Jewish cultural forms; and so forth. Third in this group of strategies is the concept of the kibbutz as a prototype: a view embodied, for instance, in the constitution of the Kibbutz Artzi movement as long ago as 1927 (Margalit, *Hashomer Hatza'ir* 303). Note that a prototype is not simply a model, but a model that may be amended: if anything goes wrong, one can always go back to the drawing-board. The difference was exemplified in the mid-1930s with the establishment of the first *meshek shitufi*, a village where production is organized as in the kibbutz, but income is distributed according to family units. The founders of the first *meshek shitufi* saw their society as a sort of kibbutz; so much so, in fact, that they applied for affiliation to the Hever Hakvutzot kibbutz movement. Their application was rejected; the leaders of the kibbutz movement still saw the kibbutz as a model, to be imitated but not changed (Ben Avram 127–8). It was only in the 1970s that the Ihud movement accepted some *meshakim shitufiim* into its ranks, and thus acknowledged that they are a legitimate variant of the kibbutz idea.

What is left of these three doctrines? The idea of the model is certainly still alive, if one is to judge by the number of times kibbutz writers echo Buber's well-known phrase "an exemplary non-failure".[3] There are also some theorists who speak of the possibility of increasing the handful of Israeli cooperatives and communes which derive their inspiration from the kibbutz, but experience seems to teach that there is little prospect of such communities' being established on anything more than a very small scale. The "model" terminology appears most frequently today in discussions of the relationships between the kibbutz and its neighbours in the relatively underprivileged "development towns," and, in particular, those who are employed in the economic conglomerates owned by the kibbutzim and *moshavim* in different regions. One suggestion is that kibbutz members, instead of engaging in various forms of social and charitable work in the development towns, and thus creating a relationship of patronage, should act as "agents of change", helping the people of the development town to create networks of mutual aid and cooperative organizations. The final result will be, according to this theory, a complex of cooperative units based on the kibbutz model. Similar ideas have been proposed for solving the problem of the cooperative conglomerates, which would be integrated into an overall regional organization in which each enterprise would be controlled by its own workers. Here again, the concept of the "kibbutz model" frequently appears.

This concept does not appear only in an Israeli context. Such phenomena as the Harvard University Project for Kibbutz Studies, or the triennial conferences on kibbutzim and communes of the International Communal Studies Association, bear witness to the considerable interest in the kibbutz on the part of the very widespread (and highly differentiated)

---

3 "Exemplary" is better than the standard translation, "a signal non-failure," (*Paths in Utopia*, 1949, 142) since it points up the echo of the phrase frequently used by the ideologists of the early kibbutzim, "an exemplary society" (*hevra le-mofet*).

movement of communes, workers' cooperatives and other forms of workplace democracy. In the deliberations of such groups, the word "model" is often used. In terms of my analysis, however, this is a terminological error in both the regional and the international context. When one of the theorists of the German communal movement expresses the hope that the kibbutz will "free itself from its Zionist ideology", or when a leader of the American communal movement finds that the kibbutz has failed to solve the problem of the woman, neither of them sees the kibbutz as a model.[4] It is, rather, a prototype, which they study in order to learn from its mistakes, or adapt its social system to their own circumstances. Similarly, there is no real expectation that the new social forms to be created in and around the development towns will actually be kibbutzim. Rather, they will be adaptations of the kibbutz idea to the circumstances and wishes of their members. And even the currently relatively flourishing urban kibbutzim and communes emphasize that they are variants of the kibbutz original, and not copies.

The phrase "radiation of values" is still sometimes used. For instance, in Alexander Barzel's *Categories of Social Existence*, published in 1984, we find:

> Can [the kibbutz] exist in a world whose principles are opposed to those of the cooperative community? [...] If the answer is positive, the basic alternative [...] is an attempt to radiate the communal idea [...] into a world dominated by the philosophy of atomism. (182–3)

It is far from being self-evident, however, that this radiation can take place without some more active policy to help it. In this connection, the speech of the deputy minister of agriculture, Avraham Katz-Oz, one of the founders and leaders of the United Kibbutz Movement, at that movement's conference in 1985, is instructive. He emphasized the importance of the social morality of the kibbutz and the kibbutz movement as an essential element in their relations with the outside world, and particularly the

---

4   Both views were expressed in an informal discussion group at the conference of Utopian Studies Society, Europe, Plymouth, UK, 2007.

political system. Without this, he maintained, the kibbutz would not enjoy the esteem which was essential for it to influence the world outside. Yet he did not see the moral superiority of the kibbutz as in itself ensuring this influence; on the contrary, he demanded more intensive political and educational activity.[5] Neither he, nor any contemporary leader of the kibbutz movement, believed that the kibbutz can change the world around it simply by existing.

Leadership and Service

The next two strategies to be described have been viewed, historically, as variations of the halutz concept. I have noted the change from prophetic to commendatory holism. A similar progression can be seen in the interpretation of the notion of the halutz. In one formulation, he goes, not before the host, but at its head: showing the masses not necessarily where they will go, but where they should go. In other words, the kibbutz has often been thought to have a function of leadership, even outside the Marxist avantgardist context.

Naturally enough, this strategy has frequently been applied in the area of politics. Three kibbutz movements have initiated and played a leading part in political parties or factions. The fact that their members rarely achieved more than minor office may be the result of electoral failure rather than refusal, on ideological grounds, to join a governmental coalition. Nonetheless, it is true that, historically, the kibbutz has always been hesitant about playing an independent role of leadership in politics. Its typical roles have been either that of a left-wing opposition within the Labour Movement, or of a minor partner in a coalition led by the major party in that movement (Mapai or the Labour Party). Typical ministerial positions

---

5 At conference of United Kibbutz Movement, 1985. Minutes in Yad Tabenkin archives, Ef'al.

of kibbutz members have been education, health, and transport; and a typical political function, that of party secretary at a period of inner tension between competing factions: a status of honest broker rather than policy maker. This applies no less to the Kibbutz Artzi, whose political rhetoric has been revolutionary in the extreme, than to the other movements.

When discussing the political power of the kibbutz, it is usual to emphasize its overrepresentation in the elected institutions of the *Yishuv* and the State of Israel; for instance, the fact that the strength of the kibbutz movement in the Knesset between 1951 and 1965 was between 3.7 and 4.3 times as great as its proportion in the population, and that even in the mid-1980s, when its influence had greatly declined, it was overrepresented by 250 per cent. The question asked here, however, is not whether the kibbutz movement had political power, but for what purpose this power was used. From the first government of Israel until the defeat of the Labour Alignment in 1977, the total number of months for which all cabinet ministers served was 5,823. Of these, kibbutz members served for a total of 1,100 months (19 per cent of the overall total). If we divide the ministerial positions of the kibbutz members between policy-making ministries (prime minister, deputy prime minister, foreign minister, defence minister, and finance minister), and all other ministries, kibbutz members served in policy-making positions for 241 months, as opposed to 859 months in other positions (Near, *Kibbutz Movement* ii, 256–60, 327–31).

In a sense, this analysis is purely formal, and does not take into account the possibility that kibbutz members played a leading role in policy-making in such informal groupings as that known during Levi Eshkol's term of office as "our ministers", and Golda Meir's as "Golda's kitchen". Until the aforementioned critical account and detailed research is available, this question must remain open. It may be said, however, that in the accepted version of the events only Israel Galili (of Kibbutz Na'an and the Ahdut Ha'avoda party) appears to have wielded any substantial influence of this sort, as a result of his personal influence with the Prime Minister, Golda Meir.

It seems, therefore, that the political function of the kibbutz has less frequently been leadership than another of the connotations of the term *halutz*: the idea of service. "To be a *halutz*" said Ben Gurion in 1924, "does not mean to demand rights, but to amass duties" ("I Icchalutz in Russia" 17).

An extreme version of this view is the saying, widely in use in the 1930s, and considered an expression of pride, that the current generation of *halutzim* is "dung for the fields of Israel" (see chapter 8, above).

The implications of this idea are, of course, far wider than the political sphere. To take one example among many: the "heroic age" of the kibbutz was undoubtedly in the late 1930s and the 1940s when the kibbutzim played a major, and generally admired, role in settling and defending the borders of the future State. In the changed circumstances of the State of Israel, the concern for security was (and still is) epitomized by the part played by kibbutz members, and especially the younger generation, in the Israeli Defence Forces. In both cases, the kibbutz has contributed to the physical security of the wider community far beyond its numerical proportions; and it is rewarded in a variety of ways, from prestige to political and economic support. This example could be repeated in many other spheres: particularly those of agricultural settlement, economic development, and culture. For the kibbutz has always prided itself on its contribution to Israeli society, and considered itself to have earned whatever special status and privileges it has by this contribution. Indeed, were one to sum up in quantitative terms the relation between the kibbutz and the outside world as perceived by its members, there is little doubt that this approach would predominate. The kibbutz, in this view, is, and aims to be, a serving elite.

It should, perhaps, be stressed that the service done to Israeli society as a whole is not considered by the kibbutz members to be a by-product of their achievements in building a viable socialist community. On the contrary, the desire to create a Jewish society economically stable and militarily secure, imbued with the values of love of physical labour and of the land, and creating a modern Hebrew culture, was part of their social vision from the very first. It is part of the conventional wisdom of the kibbutz that, at any rate until the establishment of the State of Israel, it was largely successful in promoting these aims; and that in some of them – particularly settlement, security and economics – it still enjoys no small measure of success.

As I have implied, both of these strategies – leadership and service – and the immanent tension between them are an intrinsic part of current kibbutz ideology. In the political field, the state of affairs when this essay was first written, in July 1986, is almost a textbook illustration of this conflict. For many years, the two major kibbutz movements – the United Kibbutz Movement and the Kibbutz Artzi – had aspired to leadership in the Labour Movement; indeed, one of the reasons for the formation of the United Kibbutz Movement was the dissatisfaction of the two movements which united to create it (Ihud Hakvutzot Vehakibbutzim and the Kibbutz Me'uhad) with their lack of real political power, and their desire to assume a role of leadership within the Labour Movement. Still, in terms of practical politics and their place in the system, they consistently served rather than led. Thus, in the general election campaigns of 1973, 1977 and 1981 they provided a major part of the logistic support for the Labour Alignment: volunteers for door-to-door canvassing, special teams for outdoor propaganda, transport on polling day, and many other organizational functions. There is no evidence that they received positions of political power commensurate with this effort: in fact, it seems certain that, in terms of their public image and influence, they actually lost. For the realization of their importance in the Labour Alliance's political effort led the anti-Labour Likud bloc to attempt to delegitimize them, and to present them as "arrogant millionaires" with no common language with the real working class. In the election campaign of 1984, the Labour Alignment tended to assume that this effort had been successful, and deliberately played down the part of the kibbutzim in the campaign.

These conflicting aspirations – to leadership, and to service – exist within each of the kibbutz movements, and can be seen in almost every discussion of tactics or of general policy. In general terms, however, it may be said that kibbutz ideology has, on the whole, not succeeded in adapting itself to the social realities of Israel, which have been so dramatically reflected in the political situation since the first right-wing party to achieve power (the Likud) took office in 1977. In this respect, the kibbutz is widely seen – by its members no less than the rest of the populace – as part of the economically ascendant Ashkenazi establishment. Many of the strategies which seemed feasible in the past – leadership, example, value radiation – assumed a national consensus on aims and values. It is far from clear that such a consensus exists today. Indeed, in the political sphere it looks as if the efforts of the kibbutz movement, whether they aim at leadership or at service, are directed mainly at what may be called its own social constituency. The recently increased emphasis on strategies which reach out to international circles and universal problems is, in effect, only an extension of the same constituency. For, while it can certainly be argued that the communal movement is concerned with problems which affect all of mankind, it speaks mainly to the educated, middle-class citizens of the developed world. The parallel is too obvious to need emphasizing.

Education

From the mid-1930s on the kibbutzim began to use the educational forces which they had developed in order to help absorb and educate young refugees from Nazi repression in the framework of what is still known as Youth Aliyah, although now it has become a scheme for educating young people from underprivileged areas of Israel. Only a small proportion of these young people actually become kibbutz members; and this and similar schemes are normally looked on as methods of education for citizenship – another variant of the concept of service.

Youth Aliyah recruits are almost all Sephardi Jews; and all the youth movements follow a policy of ethnic integration, particularly with regard to the Nachal (Agricultural Corps) groups which join the kibbutzim after their army service. Thus, one of the results of the educational work invested in both types of organization is to effect a slow change in the ethnic composition of the kibbutz population. In both of these schemes, however, a conscious attempt is made to educate to the specific values of the kibbutz; and there is some evidence that their graduates retain these values after they leave the kibbutz, and attempt to apply them in their new circumstances (Avnet). Thus, education is seen as a tool – slow, but perhaps the most effective that the kibbutz possesses today – for changing the values of the surrounding society (see also chapter 10, above).

Conclusions and Comments

In conclusion, I shall sum up the processes and conceptual categories described here, and add some more general comments. For, even though the state of the research may not yet enable us to reach final conclusions, both history and logic can help us to make a tentative evaluation of their effectiveness. Let us start with kibbutz holism.

I have said that the major factor in the defeat of holism as a realistic aim of the kibbutz was the Holocaust: in other words, the very specific historical circumstances of the destruction of the pioneering youth movements, and the foundation and growth of the State of Israel. I also added that, had things turned out differently, the holistic aim was not altogether unrealistic. Nonetheless, few if any kibbutz members or ideologies would today advocate kibbutz holism, even as a distant aspiration.

Doubts about whether kibbutz holism is a possible aim do not only spring from the events of the past fifty years. The founders of the kibbutz movement had an almost unbounded belief in the perfectibility of man. Over the past century this belief has been eroded, not as a result of philosophical argument, but in the light of the actual experience of the kibbutz. Many of the founders of the kibbutz believed that a combination of a non-competitive environment and an educational system attuned to it could produce a generation entirely suited to kibbutz life and values. Today, most kibbutz members would agree that, even in the best kibbutz, with the most effective educational system, a certain proportion will be found not to be suited to kibbutz life. If this is true of those born in the kibbutz, then it is so *a fortiori* of non-kibbutz society. In that case, a holistic communal society is indeed an impossible dream, not because sociological and historical developments will always prevent its realization, but because of the nature of man.

Have we, then, advanced no further than the ideological confrontations of the early days of the kibbutz, when the possibility, inevitability or impossibility of the kibbutz's survival was argued from general, and sometimes irreconcilable, philosophical premises? I think not. The very fact that kibbutz members themselves have changed their ideological stance as a result of their experience points to a change in the logical status of the question. It is seen as being arguable on empirical grounds. On these grounds, the current conventional wisdom is a pluralistic view of human nature: some people are suitable for kibbutz life, others not, and it is far from clear how such tendencies are established. It may be that a further examination of the evidence, or advances in the social and educational organization of the kibbutz, will cast doubt on this view, and reinstate the concept of holism as a possible aim. The achievement of the kibbutz so far has been no more than to provide some of the empirical evidence on which such assessments and reassessments can be based.

Commendatory holism raises a number of quite different problems. Both in the past and in the present, this principle is, in effect, a moral protest by the kibbutz against the direction taken by a predominantly individualistic society – including, not infrequently, the Labour Movement which theoretically supports the kibbutz idea. It has two basic flaws, however, as a theory of social change. In the first place, if the holistic prophecy is abandoned, commendatory holism in itself has no suggestion for dealing with that part of society which will in all probability remain outside the kibbutz. Also, as we have seen, while the moral superiority of the kibbutz may be self-evident to its members, it has certainly not always been so to all other Israelis, or even to the rest of the Labour Movement.

There is a third flaw in commendatory holism which is even more fundamental than these; for it raises doubts about the very state of affairs which is to be commended. Historical circumstances never required the leaders of the kibbutz to give a direct answer to the question: "Do you want *all* Israelis to join the kibbutz?" It is clear that most kibbutz members would answer in the negative, for the kibbutz is, and always has been, a voluntary society. In kibbutz literature, the kibbutz is more than once contrasted with the *kolkhoz*,[6] not only in terms of the differences between their respective structures, but because the kibbutz depends on the will

---

6   Collective farm in Soviet Russia.

of its members to live this way of life.⁷ A holistic kibbutz society would eliminate this element of free choice, and would radically change the nature of the kibbutz. So it is no accident that, though the kibbutz movement has always attempted to ensure the backing of the Zionist and Israeli authorities, it has never contemplated the possibility of enforced expansion by means of legislation.

All three versions of kibbutz Marxism seem to have been consigned to the rubbish-bin of history. During the 1950s, both the Kibbutz Artzi and the Kibbutz Me'uhad revised their pro-Communist stance in world affairs, and to a large extent abandoned their Marxist ideology. As in other parts of the world, the abandonment of Communism was often followed by the adoption of various forms of neo-Marxian ideology, but these are not dominant in any part of the kibbutz movement today. On the other hand, it is certainly relevant to the current situation of the kibbutz that what I have described as the surviving remnant of the revolutionary prophecy – the survival, or post-catastrophic, theory of communal life – seems still to be alive in certain circles. Prophecies of doom are perhaps the most rational estimate of the future of man in the twenty-first century; so it may be that this is the best hope that kibbutzim (and similar types of communes) have to offer in a world with small grounds for hope.

Models, prototypes and sources of value radiation are all positive reference groups; and we have seen that the only concept among them which seems still to be relevant to the kibbutz is that of the prototype. The kibbutz was once seen as the embodiment of the values of a united *Yishuv*; but today it is almost universally perceived as a component of one sector in a society divided both in economic and ethnic terms and in terms of national and social values. So it is not surprising that it no longer functions as a reference group for Israeli society as a whole. There is a target popula-

---

7 Robert Nozick maintains that "under conditions as ideal as the real world can produce, nine per cent of the people would choose to shape their lives in accordance with socialist principles" (22–3). Nozick's article is scarcely more than a *jeu d'esprit*; but the question which it raises is legitimate, and merits more serious consideration.

tion for the prototype concept: but it is today to be found largely outside Israel, in sectors which share its overall scale of values.

The same problems bedevil any attempt to use the traditional terminology of pioneering in relation to the kibbutz. Even if we disregard the ethnic element in Israeli society, there is a deep rift on such questions as relations with the Arabs, and the future of the occupied territories. Under these circumstances, it is not surprising that the "hawkish" element of the Israeli public relates to such groups as Gush Emunim as the majority of the *Yishuv* related to the kibbutzim in the late 1930s. In the eyes of those sectors which approve of their political aims, such groups are seen as pioneers in all senses of the word. By their refusal to support the Likud government's plans for settling the occupied territories in the last two decades of the twentieth century, the kibbutzim lost the virtually unanimous approval which they once enjoyed.

Even though the terminology of pioneering may no longer be relevant to the current circumstances of the kibbutz, the distinctions which have been drawn in the course of this analysis are certainly so. For the tension between an attitude of service and an aspiration to leadership seems to be one of the dilemmas immanent in the situation of any small group which aims to influence the society around it, and certainly of a socially oriented intentional community.

Finally, a few words about education. Many leaders and thinkers of the kibbutz movement believe that this has been its most successful stratagem in the past, and that the main thrust of its activities in the wider society should be in this sphere. Many social movements have proclaimed their belief in the "revolt of youth", and seen this period in life as the best opportunity for the basic change in the fundamental attitudes and values without which no social revolution can take place. It has always been the boast of the kibbutz movement that, in contrast to other youth movements which either disintegrated, lost their ideals, or became corrupt with the transition to adulthood, the kibbutz found a way of translating the essential ideals of "youth culture", such as equality, community, self-realization, and the love of nature, into the realities of adult life (see chapter 10, above). There is a very real sense in which this still applies: indeed, any increase in the numbers and influence of the kibbutz in the near future seems likely to come from this source; and the growth of the "communes", initiated and nurtured by the youth movements, which are today a small but dynamic part of the kibbutz movement, confirms this view. Education is still the kibbutz movement's last best hope.

Afterword

In outlining a possible philosophy for a communal society, I began by emphasizing the centrality of the communal experience. I claimed that it is in itself sufficient ground for a social philosophy justifying the maintenance of a communal way of life like that of the kibbutz, though this view is not held in many societies which are superficially similar to the kibbutz. I added that communalism may lapse into totalitarianism if not linked to a firm belief in and practice of democratic values (see chapter 3). It is neither an expression of a universal "world-soul" nor of a series of face-to-face encounters; it entails a moral imperative which can be – and, historically, has been, and still is – a sufficient and, in fact, essential foundation for the existence of a kibbutz or a kibbutz-like community.

When such a society comes into existence, it can properly be called utopian, since it is the realization of the aspirations of a group of like-minded people. But no utopia lasts forever, and any such society will inevitably arrive at a post-utopian stage, involving a variety of reactions on the part of its members, but not shrugging off the effects of its utopian origins. I have given examples of post-utopian patterns of thought, both within the kibbutz and outside it. Post-utopianism involves the reference to a possible ideal state of affairs whenever a community undergoes, or is considering undergoing, a fundamental change in its way of life.

Most communal societies which have lasted for a reasonable length of time have set themselves goals beyond the maintenance and livelihood of their own community: some religious or spiritual, some political, some philanthropic. The kibbutz is an eminent example of this rule, which was expressed in kibbutz philosophy in the cluster of concepts associated with the term *halutziut* – pioneering – a concept with a whole array of meanings, ranging from service to the broader community to social and political leadership. In my analysis of this concept, and my description of the kibbutz as "a movement for social change", I have outlined a vital aspect of the kibbutz movement's political philosophy – the varying concepts of the relationships between the kibbutz and the outside world. The dominant view, that of the kibbutz as a serving elite, led to a long-term contract with the Zionist and Israeli authorities, whereby it received financial, territorial, moral and political support without which it is doubtful whether it would have survived. And, conversely, in its role as a serving elite it provided support for the Jewish community in Palestine and in the early days of the state without which it is doubtful whether the state would have come into being.

Is this of any importance beyond the telling and analysis of history? The very fact that I have chosen to deal with philosophical aspects of kibbutz thought shows that I believe it is; for philosophical discourse is (or claims to be) meta-historical, and relevant to periods and places beyond those where it originated. And the background against which this book appears emphasizes its relevance; for the past three or four decades have seen an unprecedented growth in the number and variety of communes, cooperative communities and intentional communities, some with crystallized world-views, others "seeking their way" in a globalized environment inimical to the social and political philosophies presented above (Oved, 2009). If this book is directed to any particular address, it is to this growing protest movement of communities built by people who have chosen, as have kibbutz members over the years, to put their ideals into day-to-day practice.

Such communities cannot be called "communal" without the bonding ingredient of the communal experience. They will, no doubt, undergo the process I have described, from pre-utopianism through the utopian moment to post-utopianism, which involves the testing and re-definition of their original aims in the light of their experience; but if they reject any effort to make the communal experience a guiding principle of their community life, they will not be communal societies. Many of them will have aims and philosophies of life beyond communalism: religious, spiritual, political, ecological, and more. But if my arguments in the first section of the book are correct, these are logically independent of the philosophical basis for communalism grounded in the communal experience: ashrams, monasteries, churches and political parties can exist without any communal element;

and, conversely, a communal society does not need any of their doctrines to justify its existence, though they may certainly serve to strengthen it.

The first two sections above present arguments which can readily be seen to apply to any form of cooperative community. The third, which discusses the concept of pioneering, seems at first to be more specific to the kibbutz. As I have remarked, however, pioneering terminology can be interpreted to mean any aim which the community sets itself beyond the concern for its own livelihood and the maintenance of its social principles and structure. Its adoption within the kibbutz movement has led to a wealth of discussions and definitions probably unparalleled in any other communal movement; there, the intellectual energy devoted to pioneering in the kibbutz has been devoted to matters specific to the "external" aims of the community, whether theological, spiritual, political, ecological, or social. This is a field of endeavour logically separate from communalism, but, apparently, vital to the self-confidence and survival of many communal societies.

Chapter 10 deals with a matter which seems to be characteristic only of the kibbutz movement: its educational philosophy. Although other social movements have been largely composed of young people, the specific doctrine of the kibbutz youth movements – juventism – does not seem to be a feature of any of them. Nor have any, except those which maintain their own elementary schools (primarily the Hutterites and the Bruderhof) built any organization parallel to the kibbutz youth movements in order to ensure demographic growth. Their success has not led other communal societies to imitate them, and it seems that the number of adult recruits to the kibbutz has now settled down at a much smaller proportion than in the classical period. Its major present-day success in the kibbutz movement has been in the establishment of the "communes movement", a numerically small but vigorous offspring of the main kibbutz movement. In the schools, progressive educational methods are finding it hard to hold their ground in competition with more utilitarian approaches. But, though it is not universally accepted by kibbutz thinkers, and scarcely exists elsewhere, juventist educational philosophy seems to be alive and active.

Finally, "looking outwards". The most ambitious expectations of the social and political philosophy of the kibbutz, such as kibbutz holism and its variants, have long been abandoned. Nor have its attempts to influence the political system on a broad scale been particularly successful. And this certainly applies to the communal movement in general. What remains is the attempt to influence outside society on a local level, by varieties of social and educational work, and by "radiating values" – showing, by being, that an alternative life style is both possible and desirable. All of this applies both to the kibbutz of today and to communal and intentional communities the world over. Whatever the doctrines avowed by these communities, they serve the double purpose of strengthening the community within and influencing outside society, albeit on a small scale, but often to a significant degree. This would seem to be a common pattern of thought and activity for kibbutzim and communes alike in the twenty-first century.

Thus, the communalist movement embarks on the twenty-first century with expectations diminished, but in the certainty that, even if it is no more than a relatively small movement of protest against a commercialized and alienated world, it will continue to keep the spark of human brotherhood, equality and mutual aid alive, and draw inspiration from the thought and achievements of its predecessors.

Works Cited

An asterisk *, here and elsewhere in the book, indicates that the publication was originally in Hebrew; translations are by the author.

The inconsistency in the numbering of some kibbutz publications such as *Mibifnim* is due to occasional alterations of the system as editors changed, new series were begun, etc. The dates, volumes and issue numbers are given as they appear in the originals.

*Admati, M. *Youth on the Rise: Hanoar Ha'Oved 1924–1933*. Tel Aviv: Am Oved, 1974.
*Alon, H. *Jewish Scouting in Israel (1919–1969)*. Tel Aviv: Am Hasefer, 1976.
*Alterman, Nathan. *The Seventh Column*. Vol. 1. Tel Aviv: Am Oved, 1972.
Amalrik, Andrei. *Will the Soviet Union Survive Until 1984?* New York: Harper & Row, 1970.
Armytage, W.H.G. *Heavens Below: Utopian Experiments in England, 1560–1960*. London: Routledge, 1961.
*Artzi, Fania. "The Isolation of the Woman Member". *Mibifnim* 47 (1930): 518–19.
*Asaf, Y. "The Political Conflict in Hakibbutz Hame'uhad". PhD thesis. Tel Aviv University, 1987.
Avineri, Shlomo and de-Shalit, Avner (eds). *Communitarianism and Individualism*. Oxford: OUP, 1992.
*Avnet, L. "The Influence of Kibbutz Education on Youths of Oriental Origin". PhD thesis. Bar-Ilan University, 1983.
Baldwin of Ford, *Spiritual Tracts*, Trans. D.N. Bell. Kalamazoo, Mich.: Cistercian Publications, 1986.
*Bar Yehuda, I. "With the Stream or Against It?". *Mibifnim* (December 1932): 8–12.
*Baratz, Joseph. "The First Two Years." *Hapoel Hatza'ir* 18 July 1920: 4–7.
*Baratz, Miriam. "My Wedding Day". *Work and Life* (house journal of kibbutz Degania Aleph), 1937: 1–2.
Barber, Benjamin J. *Strong Democracy*. Berkeley: University of California Press, 1984.
*Barzel, Alexander. *Categories of Social Existence*. Tel Aviv: Am Oved, 1984.
Basil, St. "The Longer Rules. VII". *The Ascetic Works of St. Basil*. Ed. W.K.L. Clarke. New York: Macmillan, 1925.
*Bassevitz, Lilia. "Woman in the Kibbutz". *Mibifnim* 11.3 (1946): 344–63.

Bebel, August. *Woman under Socialism*. Trans. D. De Leon. New York: New York Labor News Co., 1917.
Bellamy, Edward. *The Religion of Solidarity*. Yellow Springs, Ohio: Antioch Bookplate Co., 1940.
*Ben Avram, B. *The Social and Ideological Development of Hever Hakvutzot*. Tel Aviv: Am Oved, 1976.
*Ben Eliezer, U. "Political Practices and Leadership in the Youth Movements of the Yishuv during the 1940s". *Jewish Youth Movements in the Struggle for Statehood, in the Diaspora and in Palestine*. Eds O. Makover & O. Shiran. Ef'al: Yad Tabenkin, 1986. 91–104.
*Ben Gurion, David. "The Characteristics of the *Halutz* in Preparation for and Immigration to Palestine". *Hechalutz* (world organization edition) 6 (1932): 37–9.
*—— "Hechalutz in Russia". *Kuntress* (10 February 1924): 11–14.
*—— *In the Campaign*. Tel Aviv: Am Oved, 1957.
*—— "The Aims of the Spirit and *Halutziut* in the State of Israel". *Government Yearbook, 1951/2* (1951). 2, 7–31.
*—— *Vision and Way*. Tel Aviv: Am Oved, 1953.
Billington, Ray Allen. *The Western Movement in the United States*. Princeton: Van Nostrand, 1959.
*Bitman, I. (ed.). "Ben Gurion's Articles on Kibbutz". *Hakibbutz* 9–10 (1984): 12–51.
Blasi, Joseph R. *The Kibbutz and the Utopian Dilemma*. Norwood, PA: Norwood Editions, 1980.
Book of the Shomrim [no author cited]. Warsaw: Hashomer Hatza'ir, 1934.
Bookchin, Murray. *Post-Scarcity Anarchism*. Montreal: Black Rose Books, 1982.
Bradley, F.H. *Ethical Studies*. Bristol: Thoemmes, 1972.
Buber, Martin. *Between Man and Man*. London: Routledge and Kegan Paul, 1947 [Includes: "Education" (1926); "Dialogue" (1929); "The Question to the Single One" (1933); "What is Man?" (1938)].
—— "Drei Sätze eines religiösen Sozialisten". *Neue Wege* 22 (1928): 327–9 [Hebrew version in the new edn. of *Paths in Utopia* (1983). 180–2].
—— *Hope for Our Time*. New York: SUNY Press, 1999.
—— *I and Thou*. Trans. Walter Kaufman. New York: Scribner, 1970 [1st edn 1922].
*—— *Paths in Utopia*. 1st Hebrew edn. Tel Aviv: Am Oved, 1947.
*—— *Paths in Utopia*. New Hebrew edn. Ed. Avraham Shapira. Tel Aviv: Am Oved, 1983.
—— *Paths in Utopia*. London: Routledge and Kegan Paul, 1949.

*——*Selected Writings on Judaism and Jewish Affairs.* Vol. 2. Jerusalem: Zionist Library, 1961 [Includes: "The *Halutz* and His World" (1936); "The Regeneration of a People's Life" (1939)].
——*The Way of Man.* London: Vincent Stuart, 1963.
——*Zwiesprache.* Berlin: Schocken, 1934.
*Bussel, Joseph. "Letter to a Friend" [1919]. *Sefer Bussel.* Ed. Shalom Wurm. Tel Aviv: Am Oved, 1960. 239–40.
Christy, Arthur E. *The Orient in America Transcendentalism.* New York: Columbia University Press, 1932.
Clark, David. *Basic Communities: Towards an Alternative Society.* London: SPCK, 1977.
Cohn-Bendit, Daniel and Paul, Gabriel. *Obsolete Communism: The Left-Wing Alternative.* New York: McGraw-Hill, 1968.
Dar, Y. "Youth in the Kibbutz: The Prolonged Transition to Adulthood." *Israel Social Science Journal* 8 (1993): 122–46.
Darin-Drabkin, Haim. *The Other Society.* London: Gollancz, 1962.
*Darom, Dov. "Changing Values in Kibbutz Society." *The Kibbutz: Interdisciplinary Review* 9 (1982–3): 214–39.
Davis, J.C. *Utopia and the Ideal Society: A Study of Utopian Writing, 1516–1700.* Cambridge: Cambridge University Press, 1981.
*Dayan, Shmuel. *Degania at Its Half Jubilee.* Tel Aviv: Stiebel, 1935.
De Waal, Esther. *Seeking God: The Benedictine Way.* Collegeville, Minn.: Liturgical Press, 1984.
**Dialogue on the Unification of the Kibbutz Movements.* Kiriat Anavim: Ihud Hakvutzot Vehakibbutzim, 1979.
Diamond, Stanley. "The Kibbutz: Utopia in Crisis." *Dissent* 4 (1957): 133–40.
Driscoll, Martha E. "Reflections on the Document 'Vision of the Order 2002.'" *Cistercian Studies Quarterly* 39.2 (2004): 181–200.
*Dror, Y. (ed.). *Communal Groups in Israel.* Ef'al: Yad Tabenkin, 2008.
Dworkin, Ronald. "Liberal Community." *Communitarianism and Individualism.* Ed. Shlomo Avineri and Avner de-Shalit. Oxford: OUP, 1992. 205–23.
Ehrenpreis, Andreas. *An Epistle on Brotherly Community as the Highest Command of Love.* Delhi: I.S.C.K., 1992.
*Eliav, M. and Rosenthal Y. (eds). *The First Aliyah.* Vol. I. Jerusalem: Yad Ben Zvi, 1982.
*Eshkol, Levi. [Speech at conference of Ihud Hakvutzot Vehakibbutzim]. *Niv Hakvutza* 1 (January 1952): 44.
Festinger, Leon. *When Prophecy Fails.* Minneapolis: University of Minnesota Press, 1956.

Flohr, P. & Susser, Bernard. "'Alte und Neue Gemeinschaft': An Unpublished Buber Manuscript." [1900] *AJS Review* 1 (1976): 41–9.

Flohr, P. "From *Kulturmystik* to Dialogue." PhD thesis. Brandeis University, 1974.

Frankel, Jonathan. *Prophecy and Politics: Socialism, Nationalism, and the Russian Jews, 1862–1917*. Cambridge, UK: CUP, 1981.

*Frankel, S. "Correcting Injustice." *Hedim* (April 1947): 63–4.

Frothingham, O.B. *Transcendentalism in New England*. Boston: American Unitarian Association, 1876.

Fry, T. et al. (eds). *The Rule of St. Benedict in English*. Collegeville, Minn.: Liturgical Press, 1982.

*Gadon, Shmuel. *Paths of the Kvutza and the Kibbutz*. Tel Aviv: Am Oved, 1958.

Gerson, Menachem. "Martin Buber and the Kibbutz Movement." *Shdemot* (English edn) 19 (1982): 80–3.

Gilison, J.M. *The Soviet Image of Utopia*. Baltimore: Johns Hopkins University Press, 1975.

Gilligan, C. *In a Different Voice*. Cambridge, Mass. & London: Harvard University Press, 1982.

*Goldberg, A. *The State of Settlements in the West Bank and the Gaza Strip, 1992*. Tel Aviv: Centre for Peace, 1993.

*Goldman, S. "Comments on the Question of the Woman in the Kibbutz." *Hedim* 3–4 (Sept. 1947): 85.

*Gordon, Aharon David. "People and Labour." [1911] Trans. in A. Hertzberg (ed.), *The Zionist Idea*. New York: Atheneum, 1989. 372–4.

Green, T.H. *Prolegomena to Ethics*. Oxford: Oxford University Press, 1890.

*Hachlili, B. *Invitation to a Talk*. Tel Aviv: Hakibbutz Hameuhad, 1993.

*Hacohen, Dvorah. *The Seed and the Millstone*. Tel Aviv: Am Oved, 1998.

Haffner, Sebastian. *Defying Hitler*. London: Phoenix, 2003.

Hansen, Marcus L. *The Atlantic Migration, 1607–1860*. New York: Simon, 2001.

Hansot, Elisabeth. *Perfection and Progress*. Cambridge, Mass.: M.I.T. Press, 1974.

Hazan, Y. "The Kibbutz and the Party." *Hedim* 2 (April 1952): 12–25.

Hechalutz: Journal for Research, Criticism and Jewish Knowledge 1 (Lvov, 1852).

Hillery, George A. Jr. *The Monastery: A Study in Freedom, Love and Community*. Westport, Conn.: Praeger, 1992.

Holloway, Mark. *Heavens on Earth: Utopian Communities in America, 1680–1880*. London: Turnstile Press, 1951.

*Horowitz, D. "Kibbutz and Party." *Mihayeinu* 67 (1926): 278–80.

James, William. *The Varieties of Religious Experience* [1929]. New York: Collier Books, 1961.

Jefferson, Thomas. *The Republic of Letters: The Correspondence Between Thomas Jefferson and James Madison, 1776–1826*. Ed. J.M. Smith, J.M. New York: Norton, 1995.
Jones, Maldwyn A. *American Immigration*. Chicago: University of Chicago Press, 1960.
*Joshua [no family name cited, untitled contribution]. *The Kvutza*. Ed. Berl Katznelson. Tel Aviv: Cultural Committee of the Histadrut, 1925. 71.
*Kafkafi, E. *Truth or Faith*. Jerusalem: Yad Ben Zvi, 1992.
Kallen, H.M. *Utopians at Bay*. New York: Theodor Herzl Foundation, 1958.
Kant, Immanuel. *Grundlegung zur Metaphysik der Sitten*. Riga: Hartknoch, 1792.
Kateb, George. *Utopia and Its Enemies*. New York: Free Press, 1963.
Katz, Steven T. (ed.). *Mysticism and Philosophical Analysis*. New York: Oxford University Press, 1978.
Katznelson, Berl (ed.). *The Kvutza*. Tel Aviv: Histadrut Cultural Committee, 1924.
—— "Towards the Coming Days." *Writings*. Vol. 1. Tel Aviv: Hapo'el Hatza'ir [n.d.]. 60–86.
—— "To the Hechalutz Movement." [1917]. *Collected Works*. Vol. I. Tel Aviv: Mapai, [n.d.]. 52–3.
—— Minutes of Kibbutz Me'uhad central committee, 23 October – 6 November 1933. Cyclostyled transcript in Yad Tabenkin archives.
Kehiliateinu. Anthology published by the Kibbutz of Hashomer Hatza'ir on the Haifa-Jedda Road, 1922.
Keniston, K. *Youth and Dissent*. New York: Harcourt Brace Jovanovich, 1971 [1st edn 1960].
Kibbutz Me'uhad Anthology. Tel Aviv: Hevra, 1932.
*"Kibbutz Me'uhad Central Committee, 25. 7. 1927." *Mibifnim* 28 (4 August 1927): 609–33.
Kimmerling, Baruch. *Zionism and Territory*. Berkeley: Institute of International Studies, University of California, 1983.
Kol, M. *Youth Aliyah: Past, Present and Future*. Jerusalem: F.I.C.E., 1957.
Krook, Dorothea. "The Triumph of Rationalism." *Politics and Experience*. Eds P. King & B.C. Parekh. London: Cambridge University Press, 1968. 309–40.
Lamar, Howard and Thompson, Leonard (eds). *The Frontier in History: North America and Southern Africa Compared*. New Haven: Yale U.P., 1981.
Lasky, Melvin J. *Utopia and Revolution*. Chicago and London: University of Chicago Press, 1976.
*Lavi, Shlomo. "Four Years." *Mibifnim* 17 (1925): 336.
*—— "On Our Work." *Selected Works*. Tel Aviv: Am Oved, 1944. 1/–22.
Levi, Peter. *The Frontiers of Paradise*. London: Collins Harvill, 1987.

*Liebenstein [= Livneh], Eliezer. "To the Comrades." *Mibifnim* 29–30 (October 1927): 1–5.
*—— "For Unity." *Mibifnim* 42 (August 1929): 13.
*—— "The Spirit of Buddhism." *Moznayim* 2 (1956): 89–90.
*Likever, Y. "The Table." *The Book of Ginegar*. Ginegar, 1947. 136–8.
Lindsay, A.D. *The Modern Democratic State*. New York: Oxford University Press, 1962.
Livneh, Eliezer. See under Liebenstein.
Lunn, Eugene. *Prophet of Community: The Romantic Socialism of Gustav Landauer*. Berkeley and Los Angeles: University of California Press, 1973.
*Luvianiker (Lavon), Pinhas. "The Principles of Gordonia as a Youth Movement." *Hechalutz Anthology*. Warsaw: Hechalutz, 1930. 327–8.
Mannheim, Karl. *Ideology and Utopia*. London: Routledge, 1936.
Mansbridge, J. *Beyond Adversary Democracy*. Chicago: Chicago University Press, 1983.
Manuel, Frank E. & Manuel, Fritzie. *Utopian Thought in the Western World*. Cambridge, MA: Harvard University Press, 1979.
*Margalit, Elkana. *Hashomer Hatza'ir: From Youth "Bund" to Revolutionary Marxism*. Tel Aviv: Tel Aviv University & Hakibbutz Hame'uhad, 1971.
*—— *Kibbutz, Society and Politics*, Tel Aviv: Am Oved, 1980.
*Marshak, Benny. "Contribution to Discussion." *Mibifnim* (June 1933): 75.
Matarasso, P.M. (ed.). *The Cistercian World: Monastic Writings of the Twelfth Century*. Harmondsworth: Penguin, 1993.
Mavrodes, George. "Real versus Deceptive Physical Experiences." *Mysticism and Philosophical Analysis*. Ed. Steven T. Katz. New York: Oxford University Press, 1978. 235–58.
Medvedev, R. "Problems of General Concern." *Detente and Socialist Democracy: A Conversation with Roy Medvedev*. Eds Y. Craipeau et al. Nottingham: Spokesman Books, 1975.
—— *On Socialist Democracy*. New York: Alfred Knopf, 1975.
Melville, Keith. *Communities in the Counter-Culture*. New York: Morrow, 1972.
*Messinger, Y. *Educating the Successor Generation*. Tel Aviv: Am Oved, 1973.
Miliband, Ralph. *Marxism and Politics*. Oxford: OUP, 1977.
*Modan, R. "*Halutzim*, for Heaven's sake!" *Hakibbutz* 8 June 1998: 11.
Moore, Arthur K. *The Frontier Mind*. New York, Toronto, London: McGraw-Hill, 1963.
Murphy, John W. *The Social Philosophy of Martin Buber*. Washington: University Press of America, 1983.

*Near, Henry. "The Actress's Wisdom and the Author's Beauty." *Shdemot* 63 (1980): 102–9.
*——— "Authority and Democracy in the Kibbutz, 1935–1942." *Yahadut Zemanenu* 7 (1992): 37–66.
*——— "Could There Be a 'Torah' of the Kibbutz?" *Issues in Education and Training* (Oranim) 1 (1981): 145–57.
——— "Kibbutz Education: An Historical Approach." *Interchange* 13. 1 (1982): 3–16.
*——— "The Language of Community." *Hatsionut* 13 (1988): 123–46.
*——— "What is a Pioneer? Semantic Changes in the Terminology of Pioneering in the Labour Zionist Movement, from 1917 to 1939." *Tura* 2 (1992): 228–48.
*——— *The Kibbutz and Society, 1923–1933*. Jerusalem: Yad Izhak Ben Zvi, 1984.
——— *The Kibbutz Movement: A History*. Vol. 1. Oxford: Littman Library & OUP, 1992; Vol. 2. London & Portland, Oregon: Littman Library, 1997.
*——— "Redemption of the Soil and of Man." *Redemption of the Land of Eretz – Israel*. Ed. R. Kark. Jerusalem: Yad Yitzhak Ben Zvi, 1990. 33–47.
*——— "The Kibbutz and the Outside World." PhD thesis. Jerusalem: Hebrew University, 1977.
——— "Elephants." Paper read at New College Essay Society, Oxford, January 1951.
Nozick, Robert. "Who Would Choose Socialism?" *Reason* (May 1978): 22–3.
Nugent, Walter. "Frontiers and Empires in the Late Nineteenth Century." *Western Historical Quarterly* 20 (November 1989): 393–408.
*Otiker, I. *The Hechalutz Movement in Poland, 1932–35*. Lohamei Hagitaot: Lohamei Hagita'ot Museum, 1972.
*Oved, Y. *Communes and Intentional Communities in the Second Half of the Twentieth Century*. Ef'al: Yad Tabenkin, 2009.
——— *The Witness of the Brothers*. New Brunswick and London: Transaction, 1996.
Passmore, John. *The Perfectibility of Man*. London: Duckworth, 1970.
Reed, John. *Ten Days That Shook the World*. New York: Boni and Liveright, 1919.
Rees, Daniel et al. (eds). *Consider Your Call: A Theology of Monastic Life Today*. London: SPCK, 1978.
Rosa, Alberto Asor. "Avanguardia." *Enciclopedia Einaudi*. Ed. G. Einaudi. Vol. 2. Milano, 1977. 195–231.
Rosner, Menachem. "The Philosophy of Martin Buber and the Social Structure of the Kibbutz." *Shdemot* (English edn) 19 (1982): 34–44.
Sartre, Jean Paul. *Politics and Literature*. London: Calder and Boyars, 1973.
*Schatzker, Haim. "Jewish Youth in Germany, 1900–1933." PhD thesis. Jerusalem: Hebrew University, 1969.
Schmalenbach, Herman. *On Society and Experience*. Chicago: University of Chicago Press, 1977.

*Schweid, Eliezer. "Between Martin Buber and A.D. Gordon." *Martin Buber: A Centenary Volume*. Eds Y. Bloch, H. Gordon & M. Dorman. Tel Aviv: Hakibbutz Hame'uhad, 1981. 229–43.

Shafir, G. *Land, Labour and the Origins of the Israeli-Palestine Conflict, 1882–1914*. Berkeley: University of California Press, 1996.

—— "Changing Nationalism and Israel's 'Open Frontier' on the West Bank." *Theory and Society* 13.6 (November 1984): 803–27.

*Shapira, Anita. "The Dream and its Shattering: The Political Development of Gedud Ha'Avoda, named after Joseph Trumpeldor, 1920–27. Part 1." *Baderech* 3 (December 1968): 34–63.

Shapira, Avraham. "Meetings with Buber." *Midstream* (November 1978): 45–54.

*Shapira, R., Adler, H., Lerner, M. & Peleg, R. *Blue Shirt and White Collar*. Tel Aviv: Am Oved, 1979.

*Shatz, Zvi. *On the Border of Silence* [1917]. Tel Aviv: Tarbut Vehinuch [n.d.].

*Shilony, Zvi. *The Jewish National Fund and Settlement in Eretz-Israel, 1903–1914*. Jerusalem: Yad Ben Zvi, 1990.

*Shlonsky, Avraham. "In Gedud Ha'avodah." *The Third Aliya Book*. Ed. Y. Erez. Tel Aviv: Am Oved, 1964. 892–4.

*Shtok, Dov. "Lines." *Ma'asef Hechalutz,* Warsaw: Centre of the World Hechalutz Movement, 1930. 149–56.

Shur, Shimon (ed.). *The Kibbutz as Another Society*. Tel Aviv: Kibbutz Artzi, 1975.

*—— "The Evolution of the Idea of Equality in the Kibbutz Movement." *Hakibbutz* 9–10 (1983/4): 162–96.

Simhony, Avital. "Green's Notion of the Morally Justified Society: An Interpretation of Self Realization and the Common Good." Unpublished paper. St. Antony's College, Oxford, 1982.

*Smetterling (Gil'ad), David. "Apophthegms on the Kvutza." *Niv Hakvutza* 1 (1930): 27–9.

*—— "Conclusions." *Niv Hakvutza* 7 (1933): 8–11.

Smith, Henry Nash. *Virgin Land*. Cambridge, Mass.: Harvard University Press, 1971.

Spiro, M. *Kibbutz: Venture in Utopia*. New York: Schocken, 1971.

Stephanson, Anders. *Manifest Destiny: American Expansion and the Empire of Right*. New York: Hill & Wang, 1995.

Still, Bayrd. *The West*. New York: Capricorn Books, 1961.

Susser, Bernard. *Existence and Utopia: The Social and Political Thought of Martin Buber*. London and Toronto: Associated University Presses, 1981.

*Tabenkin, Eva. "From the Diary of a Mother." *Working Women's Words (Anthology)*. Tel Aviv: Working Women's Union, 1930. 70–3.

*Tabenkin, Yitzchak. "On the Place of the Kibbutz in the Movement." *Mibifnim* (April 1933): 5–10.
*—— "Education to the Image of a Human Being and a Worker: Ten Years of Klosova." *Mibifnim* (April 1934): 6–14.
Talmon-Garber, Yonina L. *Family and Community in the Kibbutz*. Cambridge, Mass.: Harvard University Press, 1972.
**Tanhum*: *Memorial volume to T. Tanpilov*. [no editor cited]. Degania Aleph, 1969.
*Tanpilov, Tanhum. "With Joseph Bussel." *Ba'Avoda Uvahayim* (Journal of Degania Aleph) 17 June 1939.
Tiger, L. and Shepher, J. *Women in the Kibbutz*. New York: Harcourt Brace Jovanovich, 1976.
Troen, I. "The Transformation of Zionist Planning Policy: From Rural Settlements to an Urban Network." *Planning Perspectives* 3.1 (January 1988): 1–33.
Trotsky, Leon. *Literature and Revolution*. New York: Russell and Russell, 1957.
*Tsirkin (Tsafrir), David. "On the Tribulations of One *Kvutza*." *Mibifnim* 12 (1947): 360–70.
*Tsur, Muki (ed.). *Kehiliateinu*. Publ. by Hashomer Hatza'ir group on the Haifa-Jedda road [1922]. New edn Jerusalem: Yad Ben Zvi, 1988.
*—— *Doing It the Hard Way*. Tel Aviv: Am Oved, 1976.
*—— et al. *The Beginning of the Kibbutz*. Tel Aviv: Hakibbutz Hame'uhad & Sifriat Hapoalim, 1981.
Turner, Frederick Jackson. *The Frontier in American History*. New York: H. Holt and Company, 1920.
Weinberg, Albert. K. *Manifest Destiny: A Study of Nationalist Expansion*. Baltimore: Johns Hopkins University Press, 1935.
Whitman, Walt. *Leaves of Grass*. New York: Chapin, 1867.
*Widler, Y. "Problems of the Economy and Increased Production." *Niv Hakvutza* 1.2 (March 1952): 19.
Winks, Robin W. *The Myth of the American Frontier: Its Relevance to America, Canada, and Australia*. Leicester: Leicester University Press, 1971.
Wolins, L. and Gottesman, M. (eds). *Group Care: An Israeli Approach*. New York: Gordon and Breach, 1971.
**Working Women's Anthology*. Tel Aviv: Moetzet Hapo'alot, 1930.
*Wurm, Shalom (ed.). *The Book of Bussel*. Tel Aviv: Am Oved, 1961.
*Ya'ari, M. "On the Way to Equality." *Hedim* 2 (1936): 2–3.
*—— "Letters After Three Years." *On a Long Way*. Tel Aviv: Sifriat Hapo'alim, 1947. 21.
*"Yagur". [from the local news-sheet of kibbutz Yagur]. Repr. in *Mibifnim* (March, 1929). 8.

*Yassour, A. *Martin Buber's Social Philosophy*. Tel Aviv: Aleph, 1981.
Yearbook of the Kibbutz Movement. Tel Aviv: Kibbutz Movement, 2008.
Zablocki, Benjamin D. *Alienation and Charisma*. New York: Free Press, 1980.
Zborowski, M. and Herzog, E. *Life Is with People*. New York: International Universities Press, 1952.
Zicklin, Robert. *Countercultural Communes: A Sociological Perspective*. Westport, Conn.: Greenwood Press, 1983.
*Zilbertal, M. "Let Us Grip the Vital Link." *Hedim* 1 (June 1950): 9–13.

Index of Concepts and Places

adolescence, 28, 171
   extended, 187, 191
agrarian ethos, Chapter 6; 147, 148
alligator-horse, 149, 152
avantgarde, 123, 126, 127

Book of Acts, 17–18, 20
Boy Scouts, 170, 176, 177, 184
Bruderhof, 17, 221
Buddhism, 62, 81
Burma, 62

the Centre, Chapter 3; 45, 47, 48
Christians and Christianity, Chapter 2;
   159, 161, 165
cognitive dissonance, Chapter 5; 87, 90,
   101, 109
collective experience, Chapters 1, 2; 41,
   42, 64, 65
collectivism, 34, 36, 44, 48, 156
communal sleeping, 193
communes, 91, 100, 104, 106–8, 188, 197,
   220–1
Communion, 5, 18, 41–8, 56–7
community, 46, 49, 50–1, 57, 71, 93–4,
   100, 107–8, 116, 118, 119–21,
   156–60
Consider Your Call, 15
constructive Marxism, 199, 201
constructive socialism, 165–6
conversion, 11
"cosmic cooperation", 65
creativity, 38–40, 71, 127

Degania, 85, 88–9, 101, 105, 150, 153
democracy, democrats, xvi, 19, 25, 30, 45,
   48–50, 56–7, 92, 96, 100, 104,
   106, 111, 128, 141, 156–9, 167, 177,
   179, 184, 219
dialogue, 34–5, 45–6, 48–50
dung, metaphor of, 51–2, 54, 114
dystopia, 80, 93–4, 164

economic crisis, 103
education, Chapter 10; 11, 12, 18–19, 38–9,
   46, 84–5, 105, 146, 167, 211, 213,
   216–17, 221
   self-education, 85, 93, 97, 145
equality, Chapter 4; 32, 76, 93, 117–18
   Buber on, 50, 52
   gender equality, Chapter 7
   "organic" and "mechanical" equality,
      63–4, 65

fairness, 64
Feast of Weeks, 105
frontier, Chapter 9; 141, 144, 164, 168
   frontiersman, 148, 154–5, 156
   frontier theory, 167

garden archetype, 153–4
Gedud Ha'avodah, 94, 124, 198, 200, 201
Gemeinschaft, 5, 20, 21–4, 31
geographical displacement, 94
God, 9–10, 20, 23–5, 27–8, 47–8
Gordonia, 73, 180
Gush Emunim, 125, 162–3, 216

halutz, halutziut, Chapters 8, 9; 204, 208–12, 219–20
Hashomer Hatza'ir, 4, 41, 53, 72, 81, 173, 180
Hasidim, Hassidism, 6
Hechalutz (movement), 123, 125, 145, 152, 157, 171, 181
Hechalutz (journal), 122
Hever Hakvutzot, 205
Hinduism, 61
Histadrut, 124, 202
Hitler Youth, 29
Holy Communion, 26
Hutterites, 26–8, 221

I-Thou, Chapter 3; 31–43
ideal relationships, 33, 36
industry, Chapter 6
   and pioneering, 129, 148

Jeffersonian Republicanism, 159
Jewish Agency, 61, 157
juventism, Chapter 10; 188–9, 221
   counter-culture, 91
   democratic, 193
   frontier, 142
   Jewish, 110, 144, 183, 185

kibbutz, 105, 110. 116
   political, 122, 141, 167
   workers', 52, 152
   youth, 116
kibbutz education, Chapter 10; 12, 46, 105–6, 188–92
kibbutz holism, prophetic and commendatory, Chapter 11
kibbutz Marxism, 99–100, 115
kibbutz movements:
   and *halutziut*, 135–7

Kibbutz Me'uhad, 38, 135, 147–8, 190, 192, 198, 202, 215
Kibbutz Artzi, 180, 199, 205, 209, 215, 221

Labour Alignment, 209, 211
Land of Cockaigne, 154
latency period, 187
leadership, 123, 125, 135, 208–12, 216

Manifest Destiny, 161–4
Mapam, 61, 131, 132, 135–6
meshek shitufi, 205
micro- and macro-utopia, 70, 74, 93, 99, 100
model
   conceptual, 70–1
   halutz as, 163–4
   I-Thou relationship as, 19
   kibbutz as, Chapter 5; 31, 37, 82, 89, 101, 205, 206
   Lavi's, 84, 91
   monastery as, 18, 19
   post-Soviet, 93–4
   prototype and model, 205, 207
   utopian, 91, 92, 98
monasteries, monasticism, Chapter 2
mutual responsibility, 35–7
mutuality, 32–5, 39, 45
mysticism, Chapter 1; 41–2

Nachal, 212
nationalism, 177–8
New Age, 17
non-failure, 50–2, 206

partition of Palestine, 144
partnership, Chapter 4
perfectibility of man, 92, 213

Index of Concepts and Places 235

pioneering, pioneers, Chapters 8 & 9;
    40, 51
    Pioneer woman, 110, 115
    pioneering youth movements,
        Chapter 10; 216
post-catastrophic theory, 204, 215
post-classical pioneering, 161–5, 182–4
post-Soviet model, 93–8
Post-utopianism, post-utopian society,
    Chapter 5; 220
    post-utopian women, Chapter 7
prayer, 23, 24, 26, 159
pre-classical periods, 160–1
prototype, 205, 207, 215, 216
Psalms, 18

radiation of values, 205, 207, 211, 215
rationalism, triumph of, 49
redemption, 26
    of Land of Israel, 51, 54, 147, 154
    by labour, 165
reference group, 204–8, 215–16
Religion of Solidarity, 4, 13
revolt of youth, 179, 187, 190, 194, 216
revolution, revolutionary, 200, 203–4,
    209, 216
Rule of St. Benedict, 21, 22

salvation, 25–6, 75, 126, 159, 162
Scouts, scouting, 74, 170, 176, 177–80,
    192
scouts and settlers, 149–53, 155, 156,
    165
self-realization, 51, 53–5, 57, 190, 216
semantic, semantics, Chapter 8; 46, 54,
    63–4, 70, 91, 143–5, 148
service
    halutziut as, 109–10, 208–12,
        219

    military, 106, 187–8, 190, 212
    service branches, 112–13, 115
    to mankind, 54
    to the nation, 125–8, 184, 210, 212,
        216
serving elite, 173, 210, 220
social change, Chapter 11; 220
solidarity, Chapter 1; 43–5, 46, 48, 49, 57,
    159, 178
strategic settlement, 150
Sufi, 17

the Table, 48–9
theory of stages, 199–200
toughness and roughness, 151–5
transcendentalism, 5, 17

United Kibbutz Movement, 107, 211
United Nations, 61
utopia, utopianism, Chapters 5, 6, 7; and
    see post-utopianism
    Paths in Utopia (Buber), Chapter 3;
        69, 106n.

Wandervogel, 170, 177, 178
women in the Kibbutz, 115, 116
work, 37–40, 75, 92, 106–7
    agricultural, 145–8
    conquest of, 145
    women's, 110–16

Yom Kippur, 16, 159
Youth Aliyah, 195, 212
youth group, 174, 176
youth movements, Chapter 10; 221
    A.D. Gordon and, 146
    communal experience in, 4, 7, 12, 28,
        41
    educational methods, 29

history, 28, 157, 172–3
  kibbutzim and, 28–9, 216
  self-realization in, 54–5
  utopian thought in, 72–4, 114
  and see Gordonia, Hashomer
    Hatza'ir, Hechalutz
youth society, 180, 188, 190

Zionism, Zionist, Chapter 8; 51
  agrarian ethos in , 145–8, 166
  aims of, 147
  ideology, 154, 165–6
  movement, 157, 163, 165, 173
  propaganda, 147
  settlement, 147, 149–51, 153, 160–1

Index of Names

Aelred of Rievaulx, Saint, 18
Amalrik, Andrei, 95
Arnold, Heini, 27

Baldwin of Ford, 18
Bar Yehuda, Israel, 203
Baratz, Joseph, 81, 150, 25
Baratz, Miriam, 42, 82, 110
Bassevitz, Lilia, 114–16
Basil of Caesarea, Saint, 19
Bebel, August, 110
Bellamy, Edward, 4 5, 12–13, 98
Ben Gurion, David, Chapters 4, 8; 138, 209
Buber, Martin, Chapter 3; 6, 13–14 n., 28, 70, 206
Bussel, Joseph, 36–7, 60, 75, 85, 110
Bussel, Hayuta, 82

Cooper, James Fenimore, 149

Dar, Yehezke'el, 187
Davis, J.C., 92
de Waal, Esther, 24

Ehrenpreis, Andreas, 26–8

Festinger, Leon, 77–80

Ginsburg, Evgenia, 97
Gordon, Aharon David, 39, 40, 40n., 146, 147n.

Haffner, Sebastian, 29
Hillery, George A., 24

James, William, 7–8

Kateb, George, 70, 71
Katz-Oz, Avraham, 207–8
Katznelson, Berl, 123, 124, 152, 156
Keniston, Kenneth, 171
Khrushchev, Nikita, 96
Kimmerling, Baruch, 142
Krook, Dorothea, 49

Lamar, Howard and Thompson, Leonard, 141
Landauer, Gustav, 6, 13, 13n., 36
Lasky, Melvin, 96
Lavi, Shlomo, 37–8, 83–4, 91, 93, 102
Lavon (Lubianiker), Pinhas, 61, 180
Levi, Peter, 23

Mavrodes, George, 9–10
Merton, Thomas, 24
Moore, Arthur K., 153–4
More, Thomas, 70, 86, 90

Netanyahu, Benjamin, 162, 164

pseudo-Macarius, 19

Sartre, Jean-Paul, 96
Schatzker, Haim, 178

Schmalenbach, Herman, 5, 41
Shafir, Gershon, 141
Shatz, Zvi, 32–5, 33n.
Smetterling (Gil'ad), David, 75, 78, 82, 84–6
Solzhenitzyn, Alexander, 97

Tabenkin, Yitzhak, 52, 83, 125, 130, 193, 202
Talmon-Garber, Yonina, 5

Teresa of Avila, Saint, 9–10
Trumpeldor, Joseph, 71, 76
Tsur, Muki, 88
Turner, Frederick Jackson, Chapter 9

U Nu, 62

Whitman, Walt, 148, 164

Ya'ari, Meir, 81, 111, 204

Ralahine Utopian Studies

Ralahine Utopian Studies is the publishing project of the Ralahine Centre for Utopian Studies, University of Limerick, and the Department of Intercultural Studies in Translation, Languages and Culture, University of Bologna at Forlì.

The series editors aim to publish scholarship that addresses the theory and practice of utopianism (including Anglophone, continental European, and indigenous and postcolonial traditions, and contemporary and historical periods). Publications (in English and other European languages) will include original monographs and essay collections (including theoretical, textual, and ethnographic/institutional research), English language translations of utopian scholarship in other national languages, reprints of classic scholarly works that are out of print, and annotated editions of original utopian literary and other texts (including translations).

While the editors seek work that engages with the current scholarship and debates in the field of utopian studies, they will not privilege any particular critical or theoretical orientation. They welcome submissions by established or emerging scholars working within or outside the academy. Given the multi-lingual and inter-disciplinary remit of the University of Limerick and the University of Bologna at Forlì, they especially welcome comparative studies in any disciplinary or trans-disciplinary framework.

Those interested in contributing to the series are invited to submit a detailed project outline to Professor Raffaella Baccolini at Department of Intercultural Studies in Translation, Languages and Culture, University of Bologna at Forlì, Forlì, Italy or to Professor Tom Moylan, Dr Michael J. Griffin or Dr Joachim Fischer at the Department of Languages and Cultural Studies, University of Limerick, Republic of Ireland.

E-mail queries can be sent to ireland@peterlang.com.

Series editors:
Raffaella Baccolini (University of Bologna, at Forlì)
Joachim Fischer (University of Limerick)
Michael J. Griffin (University of Limerick)
Tom Moylan (University of Limerick)

Ralahine Centre for Utopian Studies, University of Limerick
http://www.ul.ie/ralahinecentre/

Volume 1 Tom Moylan and Raffaella Baccolini (eds):
Utopia Method Vision. The Use Value of Social Dreaming.
343 pages. 2007. ISBN 978-3-03910-912-8

Volume 2   Michael J. Griffin and Tom Moylan (eds):
            Exploring the Utopian Impulse. Essays on Utopian Thought
            and Practice.
            434 pages. 2007. ISBN 978-3-03910-913-5

Volume 3   Ruth Levitas:
            The Concept of Utopia. (Ralahine Classic)
            280 pages. 2010. ISBN 978-3-03911-366-8

Volume 4   Vincent Geoghegan:
            Utopianism and Marxism. (Ralahine Classic)
            189 pages. 2008. ISBN 978-3-03910-137-5

Volume 5   Barbara Goodwin and Keith Taylor:
            The Politics of Utopia. A Study in Theory and Practice.
            (Ralahine Classic)
            341 pages. 2009. ISBN 978-3-03911-080-3

Volume 6   Darko Suvin:
            Defined by a Hollow. Essays on Utopia, Science Fiction and Political
            Epistemology. (Ralahine Reader)
            616 pages. 2010. ISBN 978-3-03911-403-0

Volume 7   Andrew Milner (ed.):
            Tenses of Imagination: Raymond Williams on Science Fiction, Utopia
            and Dystopia. (Ralahine Reader)
            253 pages. 2010. ISBN 978-3-03911-826-7

Volume 8   Nathaniel Coleman (ed.):
            Imagining and Making the World: Reconsidering Architecture
            and Utopia.
            Forthcoming. ISBN 978-3-0343-0120-6

Volume 9   Henry Near:
            Where Community Happens: The Kibbutz and the Philosophy
            of Communalism.
            256 pages. 2011. ISBN 978-3-0343-0133-6

Utopian Studies

Nicole Pohl, editor

Utopian Studies is a peer-reviewed publication of the Society for Utopian Studies, publishing scholarly articles on a wide range of subjects related to utopias, utopianism, utopian literature, utopian theory, and intentional communities. Contributing authors come from a diverse range of fields, including American studies, architecture, the arts, classics, cultural studies, economics, engineering, environmental studies, gender studies, history, languages and literatures, philosophy, political science, psychology, sociology and urban planning. Each issue also includes dozens of reviews of recent books.

Founded in 1975, the Society for Utopian Studies is an international, interdisciplinary association devoted to the study of utopianism in all its forms. For information on becoming a member of the society, please contact Alex MacDonald. Membership of the Society includes a year's subscription of the journal and a newsletter, *Utopus Discovered*, and details on publications in the field.

"Utopian Studies . . . is a scholarly production whose particular interest lies in its interdisciplinary approach to social and political issues. . . . [It] offers scholarly commentary on utopias old and new, and a forum for all those who are fascinated by alternative futures."
-Barbara Goodwin, *TLS Review*

Alex MacDonald
Secretary/Treasurer
Society for Utopian Studies
c/o Campion College, University of Regina
3737 Wascana Parkway
Regina, SK S4S 0A2
Canada
alex.macdonald@uregina.ca

Institutions should contact the Johns Hopkins University Press for Print Subscription information.
Phone: 1-800-548-1784
Outside USA and Canada: 410-516-6987
Email: jrnlcirc@press.jhu.edu

ISSN: 1045-911X | E-ISSN: 2154-9648
Semi Annual Publication

penn state press

820 N. University Drive, USB 1, Suite C | University Park, PA 16802 | info@psupress.org
www.psupress.org | 1-800-326-9180